AFFECT IN FOREIGN LANGUAGE

— AND —

SECOND LANGUAGE LEARNING

A PRACTICAL GUIDE
TO
CREATING A LOW-ANXIETY CLASSROOM ATMOSPHERE

D1571601

The McGraw-Hill Second Language Professional Series

(FORMERLY "THE MCGRAW-HILL FOREIGN LANGUAGE PROFESSIONAL SERIES")

General Editors: James F. Lee and Bill VanPatten

Directions in Second Language Learning

(FORMERLY "DIRECTIONS FOR LANGUAGE LEARNING AND TEACHING")

Primarily for students of second language acquisition and teaching, curriculum developers, and teacher educators, *Directions in Second Language Learning* explores how languages are learned and used and how knowledge about language acquisition and use informs language teaching. The books in this strand emphasize principled approaches to language classroom instruction and management as well as to the education of foreign and second language teachers.

Affect in Foreign Language and Second Language Learning: A Practical Guide to Creating a Low-Anxiety Classroom Atmosphere
Edited by Dolly Jesusita Young (The University of Tennessee)
Order number: 0-07-038900-4

Communicative Competence: Theory and Classroom Practice, Second Edition
by Sandra J. Savignon (The Pennsylvania State University)
Order number: 0-07-083736-8

Beyond Methods: Components of Second Language Teacher Education
Edited by Kathleen Bardovi-Harlig and Beverly Hartford (both of Indiana University)
Order number: 0-07-006106-8

Making Communicative Language Teaching Happen
by James F. Lee and Bill VanPatten (both of University of Illinois, Urbana-Champaign)
Order number: 0-07-037693-X

Workbook to accompany *Making Communicative Language Teaching Happen*
by James F. Lee and Bill VanPatten
Order number: 0-07-037694-8

Perspectives on Theory and Research

Primarily for scholars and researchers of second language acquisition and teaching, *Perspectives on Theory and Research* seeks to advance knowledge about the nature of language learning in and out of the classroom by offering current research on language learning and teaching from diverse perspectives and frameworks.

Breaking Tradition: An Exploration of the Historical Relationship between Theory and Practice in Second Language Teaching
by Diane Musumeci (University of Illinois, Urbana-Champaign)
Order number: 0-07-044394-7

AFFECT IN FOREIGN LANGUAGE

— AND —

SECOND LANGUAGE LEARNING

A PRACTICAL GUIDE TO CREATING A LOW-ANXIETY CLASSROOM ATMOSPHERE

Dolly Jesusita Young, Editor

The University of Tennessee

McGraw-Hill College

Boston   Burr Ridge, IL   Dubuque, IA   Madison, WI   New York   San Francisco   St. Louis
Bangkok   Bogotá   Caracas   Lisbon   London   Madrid   Mexico City
Milan   New Delhi   Seoul   Singapore   Sydney   Taipei   Toronto

McGraw-Hill College

A Division of The McGraw-Hill Companies

This is an  book.

AFFECT IN FOREIGN LANGUAGE AND SECOND LANGUAGE LEARNING:
A Practical Guide To Creating a Low-Anxiety Classroom Atmosphere

Copyright © 1999 by The McGraw-Hill Companies, Inc. All rights reserved. Printed in the United States of America. Except as permitted under the United States Copyright Act of 1976, no part of this publication may be reproduced or distributed in any form or by any means, or stored in a database or retrieval system, without the prior written permission of the publisher.

This book is printed on acid-free paper.

3 4 5 6 7 8 9 0 QSR/QSR 0 9 8 7 6 5 4 3

ISBN 0-07-038900-4

Editor-in-Chief: Thalia Dorwick
Sr. Sponsoring editor: William R. Glass
Developmental editor: Becka McGuire
Sr. Marketing manager: Michael Alread
Project manager: Terri Edwards
Production supervisor: Rich DeVitto
Designer: Suzanne Montazer
Cover designer: Carol Barr
Editorial assistant: Beatrice Wikander
Compositor: The Clarinda Company
Typeface: Palatino
Printer and binder: Quebecor Printing/Fairfield, Inc.

Library of Congress Cataloging-in-Publication Data

Affect in foreign language and second language learning : a practical
   guide to creating a low-anxiety classroom atmosphere / Dolly
   Jesusita Young, editor.
      p.   cm.
   Includes index.
   ISBN 0-07-038900-4
   1. Language and languages—Study and teaching—Psychological
aspects.   2. Anxiety.   I. Young, Dolly J., 1956–   .
P53.7.A36   1998
418'.007—dc21
                                                98-44296
                                                CIP

http://www.mhhe.com

DEDICATION

*This book is dedicated with love
to the memory of
my friendship with
the late Darlene F. Wolf.*

CONTENTS

FOREWORD

Stephen Krashen's influential works on language learning and teaching helped bring widespread attention to the potential impact learners' emotional states have on successful language acquisition. Krashen maintained that two conditions were necessary for acquisition to take place. First, learners needed access to comprehensible input containing structures a bit beyond their current level of competence. Second, they needed a low or weak affective filter to allow the input into their second-language system (Krashen 1982, p. 33). The affective variables he discusses are motivation, self-confidence, and language anxiety. The latter is the focus of this collection of essays edited by Dolly J. Young.

Professor Young has long been associated with research on language anxiety. In this volume she strikes the balance between research, theory, and classroom implications and applications. The book includes readings that provide overviews of the research on language anxiety and that serve not only to introduce or review the topic, but also to give perspective on the work that has been done. The second section of the book, which is the heart of the volume, applies the research to classroom settings and situations. Most work on language anxiety, both theoretical and classroom-oriented, refers to anxiety related to oral language production. Young departs from this tradition to bring together works relating anxiety to reading, writing, grammar, and listening, as well as speaking. In the final section, Young includes empirical works on language anxiety.

This volume of essays on language anxiety offers a broader perspective on possible sources of language anxiety than has heretofore been available, as well as ways to address language anxiety in classroom learners. Bringing together theory, research, and practice, this book is a welcome addition to the McGraw-Hill Second Language Professional Series.

J. F. L.
B. V.P.

PREFACE

It has been over ten years since the publication of "Foreign Language Classroom Anxiety" in the *Modern Language Journal*. In the time since Michael Horwitz, Jo Ann Cope Powell, and I articulated an image of the construct, long suspected by foreign language learners and teachers, a great number of studies have been published and much practical advice has been given on the topic. From these efforts we have come to know a great deal about the nature and effects of foreign language anxiety. Perhaps more important, teachers and researchers have come to recognize anxiety as an integral variable in foreign language learning—a variable that must be respected in teaching and accounted for in research.

I am often asked why foreign language learning has such a great potential to evoke anxiety in otherwise well-functioning individuals. This is a question fundamental to both the understanding of the nature of foreign language anxiety and to the development of classroom procedures to alleviate anxiety. Teachers generally want to know which classroom practices "cause" language anxiety in order to eliminate these activities from the curriculum or at least adjust them to be less stressful. First of all, we must recognize, as the work of Sparks and Ganschow points out, that some anxiety reactions are not true anxiety reactions but rather a reasonable response to learning difficulties rooted in native language learning skills. Those learners who have greater than average difficulties in language learning owing to individual cognitive processing differences might continue to experience anxiety even if classroom practices were modified. In contrast, true foreign language anxiety reactions are based on an unrealistic reaction to one's ability in the target language; anxious learners feel uncomfortable using the foreign language even when their objective abilities are good.

Second, although some teaching and testing approaches have been found to be less anxiety-producing for many students, some students perceive these same activities as anxiety-inducing. Koch and Terrell (1991), for example, found that even within classes using the Natural Approach—a language teaching method specifically designed to reduce learners' anxiety—learners were more comfortable participating in some activities, such as pair-work and personalized discussions, than others. However, they also found great variability in learner reactions to the activities. In almost all cases, any task that was judged "comfortable" by some language learners was also judged "stressful" by others. I do not mean to argue, based on the variability of student responses, that teachers should not do their best to reduce the number and intensity of stressful classroom activities. Quite to the contrary, I am impressed by the scope and sensitivity of the chapters in this volume in addressing the anxiety-producing potential of all aspects of the language curriculum. I believe strongly that wherever the possibility exists of reducing foreign language anxiety, language teachers must do so. I also recognize, however, that some amount of anxiety is intrinsic to language learning; therefore, some people will experience anxiety no matter how language classrooms are organized.

Why, then, do some people with normal language and learning abilities find learning and using a second language so uncomfortable? This is the question we must answer to truly address the issue of foreign language anxiety. I believe that the answer to this question lies in the uniquely vulnerable and somewhat disingenuous position in which language learners necessarily find themselves. The essence of foreign language learning is the communication of personally meaningful and conversationally appropriate messages through unfamiliar and unmastered phonological, syntactic, semantic, and sociolinguistic systems. Thus, the learner is put in the position of communicating something that is meaningful to him or her without having sufficient command of the language to do so. In this way, "adult language learners' self-perceptions of genuineness in presenting themselves to others may be threatened by the limited range of meaning and affect that can be deliberately communicated" (Horwitz, Horwitz, & Cope 1986). Thus, self-aware language learners are confronted with the probability that the "world" will perceive them differently from the way they perceive themselves.

I sometimes think of the difficulties imposed by communication in a second language as similar to the discomfort we experience when wearing unflattering clothing. We know that the particular clothing does not represent us well, but the people we meet do not. Clothing can be easily changed; our ability to communicate in a second language cannot.

This book addresses the part of foreign language anxiety we can control: the anxiety that emanates from specific classroom practices. Young has done an admirable job assembling this collection of articles that deal with anxiety and the entire spectrum of the foreign language curriculum. Until recently, foreign language anxiety has been almost entirely associated with the oral aspects of language use—listening and speaking—and most discussions of foreign language anxiety have centered on the difficulties caused by anxiety with respect to oral performance in the foreign language classroom. However, as Lee and Leki point out in this volume, some students find reading and writing in the foreign language to be very anxiety-provoking. This volume takes the study of foreign language anxiety into its second decade by analyzing the role of anxiety in all aspects of language learning and offering realistic and thoughtful advice for its alleviation.

I see this past decade's concern with foreign language anxiety as part of a larger trend to place the learner at the center of the language learning process.

Attention to language learning strategies, motivation, cooperative learning, and learner autonomy all reflect the realization that language learning is ultimately controlled by the learner and that curricula must reflect this underlying reality. I have just one suggestion to add to the excellent advice offered by Young and her colleagues. I would make the sincere discussion of learners' feelings about language learning—their goals and their successes, as well as their fears—a fundamental part of the foreign language classroom experience.

Elaine K. Horwitz
The University of Texas at Austin

REFERENCES

Horwitz, E. K., Horwitz, M. B., & Cope, J. (1986). Foreign language classroom anxiety. *The Modern Language Journal, 70,* 125–132.
Koch, A., & Terrell, T. D. (1991). Affective reactions of foreign language students to Natural Approach activities and teaching techniques. In E. K. Horwitz and D. J. Young (Eds.), *Language Anxiety: From Theory and Research to Classroom Implications.* Upper Saddle River, NJ: Prentice Hall.

ACKNOWLEDGMENTS

I would like to recognize the various individuals who helped make this book possible. Many thanks to Gary Albrightson, who read and formatted most of the articles in this book according to the American Psychological Association stylesheet. His hard work allowed me the energy and time to focus on other aspects of the volume. My heartfelt thanks to James Lee and Bill VanPatten, the series editors, who had the wisdom to appreciate a pedagogically oriented book based on the idea of creating a comfortable atmosphere in the foreign language and second language class. James Lee also had the persistence to ensure that this volume was completed. I especially want to thank the contributors, whose hard work and creativity can be seen in the quality of the articles. I owe them the experience of an endeavor made pleasant because of their cooperation and collaborative spirits. I also would like to acknowledge St. Martin's Press, New York, for permission to reprint some pages from Ilona Leki's book *Academic Writing* (1995) and Patrick Brady, editor of *Synthesis,* for permission to reprint an expanded version of the article that constitutes the first chapter in this book.

Finally, special thanks go to Tim Woods for creating the drawing that opens Part One. The anxious expression on the face of the young man scaling the mountain is no doubt reminiscent of the faces of many of your language students. In their language-learning journey they are confronted with various obstacles, symbolized in the drawing by falling rocks. Although the acquisition of a second language can be a challenging experience, it is also a rewarding experience. Armed with the practical classroom suggestions from this volume, instructors can help reduce students' anxiety and thus facilitate their journey.

D. J. Young
The University of Tennessee

PART I

Introduction

ANXIETY

Affect in Foreign Language and Second Language Learning: A Practical Guide to Creating a Low-Anxiety Classroom Atmosphere

Dolly J. Young
The University of Tennessee

In the last thirty years we have seen an increase in the research on affective variables in foreign language (FL) and second language (SL) learning. In recent years, in particular, the concept of *language anxiety* has gained pronounced visibility. Researchers have provided anecdotal and empirical evidence that defines, describes, and sets a framework for understanding language anxiety. While journals continue to publish studies about anxiety as it relates to language learning, there are few other sources that disseminate in concrete terms what the research and theory may mean for language instructors. This book attempts to connect research and theory to classroom practices by exploring dimensions of language anxiety within empirically and/or theoretically based frameworks and relating those pedagogically to the language class. The first volume on language anxiety (Horwitz & Young 1991) introduced a conceptual framework for language anxiety and reported the latest research on it up to the beginning of the 1990s. In contrast, this book's purpose is to apply many of the previous research findings and suggestions to the FL/SL language classroom and to offer prospective and current language instructors concrete examples of language teaching approaches, practices, and materials that may help reduce the frustration and discomfort of learners in the process of learning an FL/SL.

THE SIGNIFICANCE OF REDUCING LEARNERS' LANGUAGE ANXIETY

Most high schools, colleges, and universities across the United States currently have some type of foreign language requirement. High school foreign language classes in the first and second year are robust and even crowded, particularly Spanish classes. At the college and university level, enrollments in first- and second-year language programs are also strong. Inevitably, however, the enrollments decrease significantly after the language requirement is met. For learners to communicate with native speakers of the FL or SL somewhat effectively, they must continue to engage in the language-learning process. If our goal is to produce language learners who are fluent, proficient, and competent in the SL or FL, we now know that the two-year requirement is not enough, especially at those institutions that hold language classes only three days a week, versus five days a week. We must, therefore, search for ways to engage language learners to the extent that they will choose to continue the language-learning process. It is clear that we must work harder in the class and out of it to meet the challenge of retaining more language learners after language requirements are met, both at the secondary and postsecondary levels.

Our first step in meeting this challenge is to recognize that one reason (obviously not the only one) many students drop out of the language program as soon as their requirement is met is that they find language learning to be an *unnecessarily* unpleasant experience. For example, a team of author-investigators, assembled by editor Trisha Dvorak to conduct ethnographic research for the 1995 Northeast Conference (NEC) Report, found common perceptions about FL learning in the interviews their authors conducted. The purpose of the volume was

> to gather information to help foreign language professionals understand more fully the impact and significance that foreign languages have in the lives of those who study them, as well as [to hear] the perceptions that people hold regarding the place and value of foreign language study in American education today (Dvorak 1995, p. 229).

The author-investigator team interviewed foreign language learners from a broad spectrum of constituencies: traditional classroom learners; nontraditional learners (e.g., study abroad programs, immersion programs, dual-language schools, summer language camps); native speakers who had studied in a traditional classroom environment; teachers of disciplines other than foreign languages; language learners who found employment in government, private industry, journalism, and the arts; and, finally, highly respected and well-known foreign language professionals, most of them retired.

A number of consistent themes echoed throughout the interviews. One of them involved aspects of the foreign language classroom environment. More specifically, participants spoke about "the important role that the teacher . . . played in creating or hindering one's excitement and ability to learn" and "the impact that classroom activities and resources . . . had on their developing and maintaining an interest in the language" (Dvorak 1995, p. 9). The following quote echoes the kind of experiences language learners associated with language learning. The quote is from an ex-language student, and it highlights the significant role the instructor plays in the language learning process.

> The professor . . . the way he comes across is very bad. And he would make you feel like you were so stupid to the point that you're almost

ready to leave his class, and one day a girl left in tears because he made her read something and she had a problem with stuttering when she got nervous. And he made her finish ten lines of something that he should have let her stop on one line and he saw what was happening and he didn't care (Kelly Hall & Davis 1995, p. 10).

5

CHAPTER 1
Affect in Foreign
Language and Second
Language Learning:
A Practical Guide to
Creating a Low-
Anxiety Classroom
Atmosphere

Wilga Rivers, in the chapter in *Voices from the Field* dedicated to interviews with several "venerable voices," spoke about the importance of considering affect in language learning. She offers the following insight:

I've had experience with other subjects, and learning a language is very different from the other subjects because you are putting people in a very vulnerable situation, you are asking them to reveal themselves in a way which is very threatening because when they don't know the language very well and they don't have the means to express themselves, they are unsure of what kind of expression they are giving and they feel threatened. They feel they're making a fool of themselves and they probably are. They feel, people, peers might laugh at them. . . . The classroom atmosphere must be an atmosphere of acceptance and mutual respect, where students know how to appreciate other students, teachers appreciate students, and students appreciate the teacher. When you've got that kind of relaxed atmosphere, then students can try to reveal themselves through another language in a genuine kind of way (Young & Kimball 1995, pp. 199–200).

In the same "venerable voices" chapter, Earl Stevick talks about why language learning, unlike other courses, can be an uncomfortable process.

One's speech is part of one's self. One's ability to interpret or remember history or to do mathematical gymnastics and so forth is a skill, but it's not part of one's self. This is particularly true with pronunciation. I think there's a strong social element to skill or lack of skill in pronunciation, although I certainly wouldn't claim that that's all there is to it (Young & Kimball 1995, p. 199).

We know that the instructor of an FL or SL class can greatly influence the atmosphere in class, both positively and negatively. What is more difficult to recognize is the broad spectrum of interpersonal interactions, activities, and materials that can also lead to unnecessarily unpleasant, frustrating, and uncomfortable experiences for the language learner. The following quotes are, once again, from language learners interviewed for the NEC volume *Voices from the Field*. Many classroom FL learners described the activities in the foreign language class as "boring," "hideous," and "awful" (Kelly Hall & Davis 1995, p. 11). The following Spanish major explains why he felt the first two years of Spanish were generally dreadful.

They spend 45 minutes discussing, you know, two phrases and you have people talk about it for two minutes and then you go the next day and no one remembers any of it. It's just a nightmare . . . she would speak in Spanish for about ten minutes out of the whole class . . .

I mean, pretty much if you're, if you have a pulse, you're not going to be challenged in those [classes] (Kelly Hall & Davis 1995, p. 11).

A high school student echoes these sentiments but offers suggestions for making activities more engaging.

I think we need more fun activities, things that involve us more with French . . . like when she tells us to speak French we really don't consider that a fun activity. . . . When she's like "have a conversation in the foreign language," no one has a conversation in French in the class. I mean everyone's talking in English and she knows it and we all know it. But I think there needs to be more, I guess what they would consider enrichment activities (Kelly Hall & Davis 1995, p. 12).

These quotes show by example that learners' frustrations and anxieties can stem from instructor/student interactions, but they can also be rooted in unengaging language activities, ineffective instruction, and weak FL materials. My hope is that this volume will offer current and future language teachers a clearer sense of sources of language anxiety and, at the same time, offer them practical illustrations of ways to make the language-learning experience more engaging and effective and less unnecessarily stressful—and, consequently, a more valuable experience.

ORGANIZATION OF THE BOOK

This book is organized into three parts: (1) Language Anxiety Theory and Research, (2) Attending to Affect While Developing Language Skills, and (3) Language Anxiety and Individual Differences. The purpose of the first part is to offer an historical perspective of foreign language instruction and to report the theoretical and empirical research that frames what we currently know about language anxiety. The second part focuses on the relationship between language anxiety and specific language skills. Little empirical data has been collected to date on this relationship, with the exception of speaking. The articles that constitute this section, therefore, are primarily essays based on research in areas such as cognitive psychology, psycholinguistics, applied linguistics, and Second Language Acquisition (SLA). They should serve to generate inquiries that will be researched in the future. The final part consists of some of the most current research on language anxiety. The purpose of this last section is to offer instructors insight into individual differences in language learners and to explain how these differences relate to language anxiety.

Each chapter in the second and third parts provides pre-reading and post-reading tasks, including a *Personal Reflections* segment that encourages the reader to reflect on the topic of the reading before engaging in the reading process. The questions that make up this pedagogical segment often activate personal experiences that the reader will bring to the chapter topic. The Personal Reflections segment is followed by *Fundamental Concepts*, which lists basic concepts the reader should understand after reading the chapter. *Portfolio Assignments* and *Action Research* constitute the post-reading tasks. The Portfolio Assignments were designed to provide readers the opportunity to

7

CHAPTER 1
Affect in Foreign
Language and Second
Language Learning:
A Practical Guide to
Creating a Low-
Anxiety Classroom
Atmosphere

develop concrete materials that apply to or test what they learned in the chapter. The Action Research tasks are designed for readers interested in researching ideas or recommendations from the chapter. Since the Portfolio Assignments and the Action Research tasks may be time-consuming, the reader may want to select only one Portfolio Assignment to develop and/or one Action Research task to complete.

Language Anxiety Theory and Research

Chapters by Young and MacIntyre form this first part. The first chapter in this section offers a perspective of FL/SL instruction since the mid-twentieth century. In this article, Young illustrates the significance of emotions (affect) in language learning by documenting how the profession has traditionally explained language learning in terms of behavior and cognition. Only recently has the role of emotions in the process of language learning been recognized.

In the second chapter, MacIntyre writes a review of the research on language anxiety for teachers and prospective teachers. In essence, he summarizes the research that has led to the conceptualization of language anxiety. By placing language anxiety within a global theoretical framework and then explaining how it is different from other forms of anxiety, he leads the teacher to a clearer understanding of what language anxiety is. He achieves this by first discussing general anxiety research, such as audience anxiety, math anxiety, interpersonal anxiety, and so on, then by discussing the research that comprises investigations into "language anxiety." In his discussion of investigations into anxiety, MacIntyre highlights the cognitive, affective, social, and personal effects of language anxiety. His chapter serves to explain the theoretical and practical foundations on which many of the other chapters in this volume were built.

Attending to Affect While Developing Language Skills

This part is the heart of the volume. Its chapters were conceived to help teachers create a low-anxiety atmosphere in the language class by using challenging classroom materials and effective pedagogical approaches to develop learners' language skills. Lee introduces this section with his article on myths about FL/SL reading and ineffective reading practices. He suggests that learners' anxiety and frustration in reading can be due to misconceptions they hold about the reading process. He highlights the ineffective reading practices in reading and reading instruction that are rooted in these misconceptions. He approaches FL/SL reading from a cognitive perspective. By connecting language and cognition to affect, he offers readers a thorough understanding of FL/SL reading. Moreover, his suggestions for dispelling myths about reading will lead to more effective reading instruction, which in turn should lead to less frustration and anxiety for the FL/SL reader.

Leki's article describes several pedagogical techniques for SL writing that could prove less stressful than the traditional in-class composition assignment. While her techniques have been written for ESL classes, they can be applied to FL classes as well. Leki's chapter underscores the need for pedagogical approaches to writing that focus on processes useful in developing writing skills. Her techniques for writing instruction enable the learner to become more successful in writing. Effective writing leads to a decrease in frustration with writing tasks, less anxiety, and, consequently, more confidence in writing skills. In this chapter we see how, once again, pedagogical practices relate to affect in language learning.

VanPatten and Glass wrote the next article on the relationship between grammar instruction and anxiety. Their article is an insightful discussion about sources of language anxiety that stem from traditional grammar instruction. This chapter stresses the importance of effective grammar instruction, without which learners can experience frustration and anxiety and have unrealistic expectations. They illustrate by example how cognition, linguistics, and affect work in concert in language learning. Teachers will find their suggestions for increasing the effectiveness of FL/SL grammar instruction useful in decreasing students' feelings of "overwhelmedness" owing to the sheer volume of grammar they are expected to learn.

Vogely writes about learners' frustrations and anxieties with listening comprehension tasks in the FL class. She describes the most common sources of listening comprehension anxiety and suggests ways it can be reduced. The sources and suggestions she provides are based on her own research, as well as on general research in listening comprehension.

Much of the language anxiety research reports a strong positive correlation between speaking in the FL/SL and language anxiety. Several studies indicate that "spotlighting" students to speak in the FL/SL may be one of the biggest sources of language anxiety. Philips' article offers teachers practical in-class oral activities that emphasize building a sense of community in the FL class and that take into account sources of learners' anxieties toward speaking in the FL/SL.

The final chapter in this part, by Beauvois, addresses the anxiety learners report experiencing when speaking in the FL/SL class. She offers an alternative to oral discussions in the FL/SL class through computer-mediated-communication (CMC). She presents interview data from language learners who have experienced CMC to suggest that it could be one way of building language skills that students find enjoyable and challenging at the same time. In this chapter, we hear through learner voices the advantages of building a supportive social environment ("community building") in the language class. For those teachers interested in CMC, she offers sample lessons, pedagogical suggestions, and information about obtaining the software (the Daedalus system) on which she based her classroom computer discussions.

Language Anxiety and Individual Differences

This part comprises three chapters. Each focuses on language learners' individual differences as they relate to language anxiety. Sparks and Ganschow wrote the first chapter in this part. In it they introduce the teacher to a heretofore rarely acknowledged source of language anxiety, the learners' native language skills. Their chapter suggests a strong relationship among native language skills, foreign language aptitude, and language anxiety. Many of their

9

CHAPTER 1
Affect in Foreign
Language and Second
Language Learning:
A Practical Guide to
Creating a Low-
Anxiety Classroom
Atmosphere

previous studies suggest that for some language learners poor native language skills can lead to poor FL/SL development, which in turn can be a primary source of language anxiety. Sparks and Ganschow sensitize the language teaching profession to the significance of native language competence and its effects in FL/SL learning, and they suggest ways instructors can identify weak language learners. Their research will influence how language anxiety is conceptualized in the future by broadening its field of interpretation and by suggesting areas for future inquiry.

The second chapter, by Campbell, summarizes her research on gender-based differences in language anxiety. Her findings will be of interest to both teachers and language learners and should serve to fuel ideas for others interested in gender-based research. Teachers will delight in her no-nonsense approach to dealing with language anxiety as it relates to male and female language learners.

The final chapter in this part, by Oxford, examines learning style clashes between the teacher and the learners. Oxford offers descriptions of various types of teacher and learner style clashes and the resulting feelings associated with such clashes. Style clashes can influence the interpersonal relationships between teachers and learners and greatly influence the classroom environment for individual learners. This is another fertile area of investigation for future research.

The chapters in this section attempt to broaden our view of language anxiety by taking into account recent research on the role of individual differences in language learners as these relate to language anxiety. Furthermore, these chapters offer prospective language anxiety researchers directions for future research.

REFERENCES

Dvorak, T. (Ed.). (1995). *Voices from the field: Experiences and beliefs of our constituents.* Lincolnwood, IL: National Textbook Company.

Horwitz, E. K., & Young, D. J. (1991). *Language anxiety: From theory and research to classroom implications.* Upper Saddle River, NJ: Prentice Hall.

Kelly Hall, J., & Davis, J. (1995). Voices from the traditional classroom: Learner reflections. In T. Dvorak (Ed.), *Voices from the field: Experience and beliefs of our constituents.* Lincolnwood, IL: National Textbook Company, pp. 1–32.

Young, D. J., & Kimball, M. (1995). Venerable voices. In T. Dvorak (Ed.), *Voices from the field: Experience and beliefs of our constituents.* Lincolnwood, IL: National Textbook Company, pp. 194–228.

PART II

Language Anxiety Theory and Research

CHAPTER 2

A Perspective on Foreign Language Learning: From Body to Mind to Emotions

Dolly J. Young
The University of Tennessee

Collectively, we can be more insightful, more intelligent than we can possibly be individually.
    —PETER SENGE, *The Fifth Discipline* 1990[1]

The changes we have recently seen in the foreign language classroom, as well as those we will see in the teaching of language and literature in the twenty-first century, stem from breakthroughs in such general disciplines as linguistics, psychology, anthropology, and science, to name only a few. These findings have led to the evolution of new paradigms within these general disciplines, such as sociolinguistics, psycholinguistics, neurolinguistics, discourse analysis, pragmatics, anthropological linguistics, and cognitive psychology (see Swaffar, Arens, & Byrnes 1991). The research in these subdisciplines has contributed to the formation of the field of Second Language Acquisition. The field of Second Language Acquisition, or "how people learn foreign or second languages," is in its infancy compared to traditional disciplines such as literature, history, or mathematics. Nevertheless, the voluminous inquiries of the past four decades have established sizeable multidisciplinary research bases that serve to inform foreign language pedagogy.

What we do in the foreign language classroom today is rooted in discoveries from various disciplines and subdisciplines that have joined and thus help explain the process of language learning. A variety of disciplines contribute to our knowledge about language learning; indeed, what is language learning but the symbiosis between the study of language and the study of all that constitutes humankind? To study how we learn a new language is to study how the body, mind, and emotions fuse to create self-expression.

This volume explores the relationship between pedagogical factors in language learning and language anxiety. This chapter attempts to offer an historical perspective of language instruction to contextualize the study of emotion or affect, specifically language anxiety, in the language-learning process. Its primary purpose is to highlight how discoveries in various disciplines have evolved in the second half of the twentieth century to inform language learning pedagogy and to discuss—in order to explain how people learn foreign languages—how the data of second language acquisition research can be characterized as moving from a focus on the body (figuratively speaking), in behaviorism; to a focus on the mind (literally speaking), in cognitive science; to a focus on affect (emotions), such as motivation, anxiety, and attitude.

THE BODY: SURFACE STRUCTURE AND BEHAVIORISM

We are as much as we see.
—HENRY DAVID THOREAU, *Journal*, April 10, 1841[2]

Research in two disciplines, psychology and linguistics, greatly contributed to the foreign language teaching pedagogy of the mid-twentieth century. Both advocated a form of instruction rooted in visible, or surface-level, manifestations of language learning. For example, the linguists of the 1950s and early 1960s, known as structural or descriptive linguists, emphasized "what" questions in their research endeavors: What are the differences and similarities across languages? Language learning, in the context of both materials and classroom practices, focused on contrasting the native language and the foreign language being studied. Leading scholars in contrastive analysis—such as Bull 1965, 1972; Lado 1964, 1971; Politzer and Stauback 1965; Stockwell and Bowen 1965; and Stockwell, Bowen, and Martin 1975—became household names in courses designed for teacher preparation.

At the same time, behavioral psychologists, such as Pavlov, Skinner, and Watson (1913) searched for the most effective approaches to learning. In his book *Verbal Behavior* (1957), Skinner described language learning as "the controlled practice of verbal operants under carefully designed schedules of reinforcement" (in Brown 1987, p. 65). Skinner believed human learning could be predicted and controlled, the observable scientifically examined and validated.[3] The Audiolingual Method (ALM) that dominated language teaching in the 50s, 60s, and 70s reflected both a Skinnerian view of language learning and a descriptive and contrastive analysis approach to languages. The ALM emphasized oral practice in the form of heavy pronunciation practice, pattern drills, and mimicry drills based on habit formation models. Structural patterns were taught using repetitive drills, and structures were sequenced based on contrastive analysis (Brown, p. 96). Language learners were usually not permitted to freely express an idea but only to repeat a pattern, for fear they would commit an error that would then become a bad habit. Shrum and Glisan (1994) characterize the ALM in the following way.

> The Audiolingual Method, which brought a new emphasis to listening and speaking, advocated teaching the oral skills by means of stimulus-response learning: repetition, dialogue memorization, and manipulation of grammatical pattern drills. Speaking in the ALM mode usually meant repeating after the teacher, reciting a memorized dialogue, or responding to a mechanical drill (p. 140).

During these decades, visible human acts were the foci of study in linguistics and psychology. For linguists, research into the meaning of language beyond the surface level, and for psychologists, the study of nonobservable behaviors and the organization of information, did not become legitimate domains of inquiry until the publication of works of linguists, such as Noam Chomsky (1968, 1975), and cognitive psychologists, such as David Ausubel (1968).

THE MIND: THE COGNITIVE MOVEMENT

Think, think, think.

—WINNIE THE POOH[4]

While Skinner continued to focus on the outward manifestations of language or language performance, Noam Chomsky (1959) introduced the notion that language was more than a question of observable stimuli and responses and more than a description of language structures, which in his view treated language only at superficial levels. For Chomsky, cataloguing the grammatical structures of a language certainly did not explain how the language was acquired. Furthermore, habit formation and mimicry did not explain the novel utterances that humans generated in learning a language. Instead, Chomsky posited that all humans possess a language organ in the mind (figuratively speaking)—that is, a Language Acquisition Device (LAD), a built-in mental ability to acquire languages. He argued that the mind was not a *tabula rasa* whereby language resulted from association–imitation–reinforcement practice but that language learning was a *process* that developed from the way humans are constituted and from their place in specific environments (Richard-Amato 1988, p. 14). To explore how people learn languages, Chomsky (1971) maintained that

> we must investigate specific domains of human knowledge or systems of belief, determine their character, and study their relation to the belief and personal experience on which they are erected. A system of knowledge and beliefs results from the interplay of innate mechanisms, genetically determined maturational processes, and interaction with the social and physical environment. The problem is to account for the system constructed by the mind in the course of this *interaction* (p. 21) [emphasis added].

Chomsky's challenge to Skinnerian theory and its behaviorism-based application to language learning is one of his greatest contributions to human thought. While generative and transformational linguistics, based on Chomskian linguistic theories, never contributed substantively to language learning pedagogy, nor did Chomsky intend it to, his work served as a catalyst for redirecting the course of research in linguistics and thus ultimately contributing significantly to the body of second language acquisition research.

While Chomsky was challenging behavioral theories as applied to language learning, psychologists and scholars, such as Wilga Rivers (1964) in her book *The Psychologist and the Foreign-Language Teacher*, began to challenge them for neglecting mentalistic domains of inquiry into human learning. Cognitive psychologists argued that meaning, understanding, and knowing (cognition) played roles in language learning and in explaining human behaviors. Cognitive psychologists, similar to generative linguists, began to explore motivations of human behavior and deeper structures of languages, thus moving scholars from exclusively building descriptive knowledge (the body) to offering explanatory knowledge (the mind). Thus, legitimate domains of inquiry became "how" and no longer exclusively "what," such as in "How do learners learn a second language?" Table 2.1 summarizes the parallels in linguistics and psychology that were prevalent during the latter half of the twentieth century.

The seeds of what is today popularly referred to as *Schema Theory* were also planted in these decades. Schema Theory, in essence, is a theory that attempts to explain how knowledge is organized in the mind (see Bransford 1979). This theory introduced the notion that the mind organizes thought and imposes structures on knowledge by the use of cognitive devices such as advanced organizers (see Ausubel 1968). An advanced organizer serves to prepare the learner to acquire information that would be hard to acquire otherwise. It attempts to bridge the gap between information a learner is about to acquire and the learner's current knowledge. For example, titles (such as book titles, article titles, newspaper column titles) serve to activate a reader's

TABLE 2.1. Linguistic-Psychological Parallels

Schools of Psychology	Schools of Linguistics	Characteristics
Behaviorist	Structural	Repetition and reinforcement Learning, conditioning Stimulus-response
	Descriptive	Publicly observable responses Empiricism Scientific method Performance Surface structure Description—"what"
Cognitive	Generative	Analysis and insight Acquisition, innateness States of consciousness Rationalism Process
	Transformational	Mentalism, intuition Competence Deep structure Explanation—"why"

Source: Adapted from Brown 1987, p. 11.

knowledge about a given topic and to prepare the reader to acquire new information on the topic.

Many Schema theorists were experts in computer science, and the concepts used to explain the theory parallel how we describe computer functions, processes, and programs. According to this theory, knowledge consists of basic units of memory, or *schemata* (also called *scripts* or *frames*), that are related to one another and often embedded in one another. Existing knowledge is used to give meaning to new knowledge and vice versa. Schema theorists contend that to understand what we hear, read, and see, we make many assumptions based on our preexisting schemata (frames or scripts). Bransford (1979) uses the following story to illustrate this point.

> Jim went to the restaurant and asked to be seated in the gallery. He was told that there would be a one-half hour wait. Forty minutes later, the applause for his song indicated that he could proceed with the preparation. Twenty guests had ordered his favorite, a cheese soufflé.
>
> Jim enjoyed the customers in the main dining room. After 2 hours, he ordered the house specialty—roast pheasant under glass. It was incredible to enjoy such exquisite cuisine and yet still have 15 dollars. He would surely come back soon (p. 184).

Even though the story may be in the readers' native language, English, it is difficult to process; something is wrong. The story violates our preexisting knowledge about going to a restaurant, such as knowledge about the typical cast of characters in a restaurant and the sequence of events. A "restaurant" script might include customers, waiters, chefs, and cashiers. The events might involve entering the restaurant, ordering from the menu, preparing the food, eating, paying, and exiting (Bransford 1979). The point here is to illustrate one way we use our preexisting or background knowledge to comprehend information. Within a Schema Theory framework, language learning becomes an interactive process that emerges when the learner's preexisting knowledge (such as linguistic, sociolinguistic, and cultural knowledge) and life experiences join with new knowledge (the foreign language and all that the study of that language encompasses).

The cognitive movement significantly influenced language-learning research, which in turn served to inform language-learning pedagogy. Since the 1970s, the language teaching profession has moved, however slowly, to recognize language learning as a process in which one exploits resources the learners bring to the foreign language class, such as their varied experiences and preexisting knowledge. Practice in the development of language skills or the use of the foreign language for negotiation of meaning and the acquisition of information emphasizes a mentalistic, process-approach to learning. The most current instructional models—from task-oriented language instruction[5] to cooperative learning[6] to content-based language instruction[7]—incorporate the principles discovered by researchers in linguistics and cognitive psychology who, in the second half of the twentieth century, focused on how the mind works in the acquisition of a foreign language.

Ahab never thinks, he just feels, feels, feels.
—HERMAN MELVILLE, *Moby Dick*[8]

By the 1980s, cognition research was the dominant theory that framed research in linguistics, psychology, brain science, and ultimately language learning pedagogy. In the 80s, however, brain scientists began to recognize that cognition research explains only a part of how the mind works, only that part related to reasoning and thinking; they had neglected emotions. As we know now, and as Joseph LeDoux, author of *The Emotional Brain* (1996), states, "Minds without emotions are not really minds at all. They are souls on ice-cold, lifeless creatures devoid of any desires, fears, sorrows, pain or pleasure" (p. 25).

The emotional part of learning was virtually ignored for so long for various reasons. First, the separation between thinking and feeling, cognition and emotion, had been a comfortable one. For centuries philosophers and, later, psychologists had made this distinction. Then, with the invention of the computer and the development of the popular metaphor of the mind as a computer, as a system of logical, reasoning processes, the "illogical" emotions were still not seen as significant. Second, emotions had a history of being treated as subjective states of consciousness and viewed as the unconscious product of information processing (cognition) (LeDoux, p. 37).

In studying emotions, brain scientists made a significant discovery, one that ultimately influenced and validated research in second language acquisition. In 1984, Robert Zajonc's research showed that affect, in other words, emotion, has primacy over cognition. Brain scientists found that emotions could exist before cognition and could also be independent of cognition. Emotions were no longer seen as the end result of cognition. They became the threads that were seen to hold mental life together but that were generated, most of the time, unconsciously. Thus, the unconscious, not merely the conscious, became part of brain research.

Brain science began to suggest that emotions were much more complex and that they involved more brain systems than had been previously realized. In fact, most of the later brain research indicated that "the emotional unconscious is where much of the emotional action is in the brain" (LeDoux, p. 64). For example, when a condition arises that is significant, perhaps life threatening, the brain channels much of its resources to address the situation. Brain activities focus on one thing, the problem at hand. Cognitive processing capacity is short-circuited by emotions, which trigger a complete synchronization of the brain's resources. In other words, emotions can monopolize the brain's system, or circuitry, to the extent that it can override conscious brain activity, or cognition.

Both Calvin (1996) and Goleman (1996) underscore the preeminence of emotion in the mind when they discuss the evolution of the human psyche; for example, they both note that the existence of emotions in people preceded the existence of language. Today, in the field of brain research, emotion has gained parity with cognition, and rightly so. Calvin, in his book, *How Brains Think*, juxtaposes two images to underscore this point (see Table 2.2).

For language-learning researchers, brain research on emotions had profound implications for studying how the mind works during the acquisition of a foreign language. Emotion, or affective variables, such as motivation, anxiety, and attitudes, which had been examined to some extent before the 80s, was scientifically validated as a legitimate domain of inquiry. Thus, research questions moved from "what?" even more into the realm of "why?" or "how?" Why are there differences in language learners in terms of their difficulty or success in learning a second language? How do we explain the differences in language learning among individuals? Research in affective variables in language learning helped explain why some learners had more difficulty than others in learning a foreign language. For example, in the late 1970s linguists and cognitive psychologists had begun to research sociopsychological factors that seemed to influence the process of language acquisition. In the late 70s, Schumann (1978a, 1978b) had posited his acculturation model and social distance hypothesis. These hypotheses suggested that the degree of social separation one language group experiences toward another affected the extent to which a foreign language would be learned and the degree to which acculturation would occur. In this case, the unconscious, emotionally based social distance felt by the learner would override, or at least interfere with, the cognitive processing of the foreign language necessary for language acquisition. In other words, the greater the degree of social distance, the less successful the learner would be in learning the foreign language. Thus, affect (the feelings associated

TABLE 2.2. Juxtaposition of Cognition and Emotion at Work in the Mind

Cognition at work in the mind	Emotions at work in the mind
[Language comprehension] involves many components of intelligence: recognition of words, decoding them into meanings, segmenting word sequences into grammatical constituents, combining meanings into statements, inferring connections among statements, holding in short-term memory earlier concepts while processing later discourse, inferring the writer's or speaker's intention, schematization of the gist of a passage, and memory retrieval in answering questions about the passage. . . . [The reader] constructs a mental representation of the situation and actions being described. . . . Readers tend to remember the mental model they constructed from a text rather than the text itself.	I often find that a novel, even a well-written and compelling novel, can become a blur to me soon after I've finished it. I recollect perfectly the feeling of reading it, the mood I occupied, but I am less sure about the narrative details. It is almost as if the book were . . . a ladder to be climbed and then discarded after it had served its purpose. —Sven Birkerts, 1994 in Calvin, W. H. (1996). *How Brains Think*. New York: Basic Books, p. 61.

Source: Adapted from Gordon H. Bower and Daniel G. Morrow, 1990. In Calvin, W. H., 1996. *How Brains Think*, p. 61.

with not belonging to a particular language group) could short-circuit cognition (the learning process) for certain learners.

Schumann and Schumann (1977) also researched learners' negative attitudes toward the learning environment and found that when the teacher's agenda was different from the learners', learners developed negative attitudes toward the learning situation that short-circuited language learning. Learners sometimes abandoned altogether learning the language (see Larsen-Freeman & Long 1991 for a thorough survey of research on individual variables in language learning).

Since the 1960s, Canadian psychologist Robert Gardner has studied the role of affective variables in language learning. His studies, as well as those of others, such as Guiora and associates (1972) and Lambert (1967), first introduced the notion that affect (as in anxiety, motivation, empathy, and attitude) could significantly influence the language-learning process. Their research, however, remained on the fringe of mainstream language-learning research until the early 80s, when Stephen Krashen (1982) posited his theory of second language acquisition. Krashen's theory of how people learn foreign or second languages was based, in essence, on a synthesis of research in first language acquisition (greatly influenced by Chomsky) and research in linguistics and psychology. He employed Dulay and Burt's (1977) metaphor of an affective filter to explain the role of emotions in language acquisition. In this particular metaphor, emotions act as a filter that controls whether language is allowed to flow into the language-learning system in the brain. For example, if anxiety is high, the filter is up and information does not enter the brain's processing system. However, if the filter is down, the brain's operating systems can focus on processing the foreign language input. Krashen's Affective Filter Hypothesis was instrumental in explaining the theory behind several foreign language teaching methods that developed in the 80s, such as Suggestopedia,[9] Community Language Learning,[10] and the Natural Approach.[11] These methods, or approaches, emphasized the need to create a positive, relaxed, foreign language classroom environment.

LANGUAGE LEARNING: INTERFACING THE BODY AND THE MIND (COGNITION AND EMOTIONS)

> *Declare the past, diagnose the present,
> foretell the future.*
> —HIPPOCRATES OF COS (460–377 B.C.E.)[12]

In offering a succinct explanation and history of how research from various disciplines is combined to offer insight into and influence language learning pedagogy, we may have given the impression that research and events happen at a specific point in time and space or that mental activities, such as feeling, thinking, and acting, can be categorized and separated and are mutually exclusive. In fact, most of the research framed by one theory or approach almost inevitably overlaps with the next one, just as the brain involves numerous spatiotemporal patterns of cellular activity spread out in time and space. It is a human tendency to try to understand how the brain works by compartmentalizing brain activities and talking about them as though they occur in one place and in one instant (Calvin 1996, p. 43). What we currently know, however, is that minds comprise thoughts *and* emotions, and they do not function independently of the body. Most emotions, for example, involve bodily responses. Emotions can also result from the cognitive appraisal or interpretation of a situation. In short, were we to study the brain or how it works to acquire language by focusing on only one part of it, we would never be fully satisfied with our results.

Similarly to explaining how the mind works, explaining how learners acquire a foreign language is a huge undertaking not easily simplified. For the moment, we know that behaviorism, cognition, and affect collectively offer researchers in second language acquisition significant insights into how the brain works to acquire new knowledge, to develop different language skills, and to learn foreign languages, in general. The constellation of disciplines involved in the study of humankind will continue to contribute to our understanding of the language acquisition process and how the brain works in that process. No doubt research from multiple disciplines, including brain research, will continue to advance our understanding of the language acquisition process and how the body, the emotional mind, and the cognitive mind work together to generate self-expression in the foreign language.

NOTES

1. From Peter Senge (1990). *The Fifth Discipline: The Art and Practice of the Learning Organization.* New York: Doubleday, p. 43.
2. From Bartlett, J. (1994). *Bartlett's Familiar Quotations.* New York: Little Brown and Co.
3. Much of the Skinnerian view of language and language learning was rooted in operant conditioning, as opposed to Pavlov's classical conditioning. In classical conditioning, learned behavior was the result of associations between stimuli and reflexive responses. Skinner's operant conditioning, in contrast, attempted to de-emphasize the importance of the stimuli. Instead, behavior operated on the environment. For Skinner "the events or stimuli—the reinforcers—that follow a response and that tend to strengthen behavior or increase the probability of a recurrence of that response constitute a powerful force in the control of human behavior" (Brown 1987, p. 63).
4. From A. A. Milne (1994). *The Complete Tales of Winnie the Pooh.* New York: Dutton.
5. *Task-oriented language instruction* refers to an approach to language learning whereby learners use the foreign language for a specific purpose, such as conducting a survey, interviewing classmates, filling out a diagram, or completing a chart. The emphasis is on the negotiation of meaning, the exchange of information, the acquisition of new information, and the sharing of information necessary to complete the given task. The foreign language, in this context, becomes a means (using the foreign language) to an end (the task), instead of vice versa (see Lee 2000).
6. *Cooperative learning* addresses social and emotional, as well as intellectual, components of acquiring new knowledge. One of several principles of cooperative learning includes instructional use of small groups so that learners can maximize their own learning and contribute to the collective learning of the group. Learners do this by sharing how they arrive at their responses. In doing this, they teach one an-

other the cognitive processes that lead to a particular response. The traditional competitive classroom is, therefore, replaced by a social community wherein learners work together to accomplish shared tasks (see Johnson, Johnson, & Johnson-Holubec 1990).

7. *Content-based instruction,* also known as *discipline-based instruction,* attempts to broaden the spectrum of traditional language courses. The argument made by proponents of content-based instruction is that "if students can study a foreign language through literary texts and literature in a foreign language, can they not also study other subjects through a foreign language and foreign language through other subjects?" (Krueger & Ryan 1993, p. 4). For this approach to language instruction, specific pedagogical objectives and tasks are suggested, such as step-by-step sequences whereby teachers guide learners through the cognitive processing of texts. These texts are the medium through which content (history, sociology, psychology) is conveyed.

8. From H. Melville (1988). *Moby Dick.* Notre Dame, IL: Cram-Cassettes.

9. *Suggestopedia* was one of the first methods to be based on unconscious and conscious functions of the language learner and on learners working in a relaxed, harmonious environment. The tension-free atmosphere of the foreign language classroom is created, in part, by the "concert" session of this method whereby, on the fourth day of the lesson, the learners listen to the teacher read the unit's dialogue while at the same time listening to soothing music (Oller & Richard-Amato 1983, p. 117).

10. *Community Language Learning* is based on a counseling-learning approach to instruction whereby learners function as clients and teachers as counselors. Charles Curran developed this approach to language learning to challenge the intellectual and competitive methods of language teaching. His intention was to consider the learner's emotional involvement and the need for a community experience in language learning (Oller & Richard-Amato 1983, pp. 146–147).

11. The late Tracy D. Terrell developed the *Natural Approach,* an approach to language instruction founded on Krashen's theory of second language acquisition. Terrell claimed that "the purpose of the Natural Approach was to focus on the meaning of genuine communication . . . and to bring anxiety down to a minimum" (Oller & Richard-Amato 1983, p. 267).

12. From J. Bartlett (1994). *Bartlett's Familiar Quotations.* NY: Little Brown and Co., p. 71.

REFERENCES

Ausubel, David (1968). *Educational psychology: A cognitive view.* New York: Holt, Rinehart, and Winston.

Bartlett, J. (1994). *Bartlett's familiar quotations.* New York: Little Brown and Co.

Bransford, John D. (1979). *Human cognition: Learning, understanding and remembering.* Belmont, CA: Wadsworth.

Brown, Douglas H. (1987). *Principles of language learning and teaching.* Upper Saddle River, NJ: Prentice Hall.

Bull, W. E. (1965). *Spanish for teachers: Applied linguistics.* New York: The Ronald Press.

Bull, W. E. (1972). *Spanish for communication.* Boston: Houghton-Mifflin.

Calvin, William H. (1996). *How brains think.* New York: Basic Books.

Chomsky, Noam (1959). A review of B. F. Skinner's *Verbal behavior. Language, 35,* 26–58.

Chomsky, Noam (1968). *Language and mind.* New York: Harcourt Brace and Jovanovich.

Chomsky, Noam (1971). *Problems of knowledge and freedom.* New York: Pantheon.

Chomsky, Noam (1975). *Reflections on language.* New York: Pantheon.

Dulay, H., & Burt, M. (1977). Remarks on creativity in language acquisition. *Viewpoints on English as a second language.* M. Burt, H. Dulay, & M. Finocchiaro (Eds.). New York: Regents, pp. 95–126.

Goleman, Daniel (1996). *Emotional intelligence.* New York: Bantam Books.

Guiora, A., Beit-Hallahmi, B., Brannor, R., Dull, C., & Scovel, T. (1972). The effects of experimentally induced changes in ego states on pronunciation ability in a second language: An exploratory study. *Comprehensive Psychology, 13,* 421–428.

Johnson, David W., Johnson, Robert T., & Johnson-Holubec, Edythe (1990). *Circles of learning: Cooperation in the classroom.* Edina, MN: Interaction Book Company.

Krashen, Stephen (1982). *Principles and practice in second language acquisition.* New York: Pergamon.

Krueger, Merle, & Ryan, Frank (1993). *Language and content.* Lexington, MA: D.C. Heath.

Lado, Robert (1964). *Language teaching: A scientific approach.* New York: McGraw-Hill.

Lado, Robert (1971). *Linguistics across cultures.* Ann Arbor: The University of Michigan Press.

Lambert, Wallace (1967). The social psychology of bilingualism. *Journal of Social Issues, 23,* 91–109.

Larsen-Freeman, Diane, & Long, Michael H. (1991). *An introduction to second language acquisition research.* New York: Longman.

LeDoux, Joseph (1996). *The emotional brain.* New York: Simon and Schuster.

Lee, James F. (2000). *An introduction to task-based instruction.* New York: McGraw-Hill.

Milne, A. A. (1994). *The complete tales of Winnie the Pooh.* New York: Dutton.

Melville, Herman (1988). *Moby Dick.* Notre Dame, IL: Cram-Cassettes.

Oller, John W., & Richard-Amato, Patricia (1983). *Methods that work.* Rowley, MA: Newbury House.

Politzer, Robert L., & Stauback, Charles N. (1965). *Teaching Spanish: A linguistic orientation.* London: Blaisdell Publishing Co.

Richard-Amato, Patricia A. (1988). *Making it happen.* New York: Longman.

Rivers, Wilga (1964). *The psychologist and the foreign-language teacher.* Chicago: The University of Chicago Press.

Schumann, F., & Schumann, J. (1977). Diary of a language learner: An introspective study of second language learning. *On TESOL '77.* H. Brown, C. Yorio, & R. Crymes (Eds.). Washington, DC: TESOL, pp. 241–249.

Schumann, John (1978a). The acculturation model for second language acquisition. *Second language acquisition and foreign language teaching.* R. Gingras (Ed.). Arlington, VA: Center for Applied Linguistics, pp. 27–50.

Schumann, John (1978b). Social and psychological factors in second language acquisition. *Understanding second and foreign language learning.* J. Richards (Ed.). Rowley, MA: Newbury House, pp. 163–178.

Senge, Peter (1990). *The fifth discipline: The art and practice of the learning organization.* New York: Doubleday.

Shrum, Judith L., & Glisan, Eileen W. (1994). *Teacher's handbook.* Boston: Heinle and Heinle.

Skinner, B. F. (1957). *Verbal behavior.* New York: Appleton-Century-Crofts.

Stockwell, R. P., & Bowen, J. D. (1965). *The sounds of English and Spanish.* Chicago: University of Chicago Press.

Stockwell, R. P., Bowen, J. D., & Martin, J. W. *The grammatical structures of English and Spanish.* Chicago: University of Chicago Press.

Swaffar, J., Arens, K., & Byrnes, H. (1991). *Reading for meaning.* Upper Saddle River, NJ: Prentice Hall.

Watson, John B. (1913). Psychology as the behaviorist views it. *Psychology Review, 20,* 158–177.

Zajonc, R. B. (1984). On the primacy of affect. *American Psychologist, 39,* 117–123.

CHAPTER 3

Language Anxiety: A Review of the Research for Language Teachers

Peter D. MacIntyre
University College of Cape Breton

The 1990s have seen a virtual explosion of research into the topic of language anxiety. A number of articles have been published that demonstrate the pervasive effects that anxiety has on the language-learning process. The purpose of this chapter[1] is to review that body of work with the language teacher and student in mind.

Anxiety is one of those topics on which significant differences of opinion can be found. Some people believe that anxiety is a minor inconvenience for a language student, perhaps an excuse for not participating in class or a guise to hide a lack of study. Others seem to feel that anxiety may be the linchpin of the entire affective reaction to language learning and that, as soon as students are made to feel relaxed, immediate positive results will be forthcoming. Noteworthy is that language learning is not alone in stimulating this sort of debate about the importance of anxiety; over the years similar discussions have occurred in the research literature on communication apprehension (Daly & McCroskey 1984) and test anxiety (Sarason 1980, 1986).

The opposing views on the importance of language anxiety have also been expressed in the research literature. Campbell and Ortiz (1991) state that the level of anxiety in language classrooms is "alarming"; Horwitz and Young (1991b) estimate that half of the students enrolled in language courses experience debilitating levels of language anxiety. However, a contrasting view is expressed by researchers such as Sparks and Ganschow (1991, 1993a, 1993b), who argue that studying anxiety does not add much to our understanding of the language achievement. For them, language anxiety is an unfortunate byproduct of difficulties rooted in native-language coding.

The following review of the literature shows that anxiety can influence both language learning and communication processes. It should be noted, however, that other factors, such as learning strategies, aptitude, attitudes, and motivation, also play a role in successful language learning. However, the focus here will be on the role of language anxiety.

Several issues will be addressed in order to capture the state of the art in language anxiety research. The first issue is conceptual; it is important to clearly define what *language anxiety* means. Second, the development of language anxiety will be considered. This issue can be tied to the conceptualization of anxiety and some interesting findings reported in the literature. Finally, we will examine the effects of language anxiety in four main areas: academic, cognitive, social, and personal. One issue that will be left for other contributors to this volume is methods for the remediation of language anxiety; some interesting instructional approaches have been proposed, and readers may find it useful to apply and evaluate the pedagogical suggestions offered for their potential effectiveness in different programs.

UNDERSTANDING LANGUAGE ANXIETY
CONCEPTUALIZATION AND RESEARCH

To understand the conceptualization of language anxiety and the research from which most theoretical frameworks in anxiety are based, an explanation of correlational research may be useful. Since anxiety is an abstract psychological phenomenon, most of the research in this field—and summarized in this chapter—relies on data from questionnaires, self-reports, and interviews. Most analyses of this data, with the exception of interview data, consist of correlations between and/or among variables. For example, to ascertain the relationship between language anxiety and test anxiety, researchers use correlational analysis whereby they measure how similar and different learners' responses are to questionnaire or self-report items designed to measure language anxiety and test anxiety. One statistical technique that can be used to measure the amount of relationship between two distributions of scores is called the *Pearson Product Moment Correlation*, or the *Pearson r*. A Pearson r of .90 indicates a very strong relationship between two variables.[2] If we square the correlation, it means that only 19% of the variance shared between the two variables is due to chance, whereas 81% is due to some type of relationship between the two variables. A correlation of .40 may still be considered worthwhile because it indicates that although much of the relationship is unexplained, 16% of the variance indicates some relationship between the variables. The lower the correlation, which runs from 0 to 1, the weaker the relationship between the variables; the higher the correlation, the stronger the relationship.

Correlational research does not indicate cause and effect. It merely indicates the strength and direction of a relationship among two or more variables. A positive relationship between two variables indicates that as the amount of one variable goes up, the other variable also goes up. The relationship of the variables moves in the same direction. For example, a positive correlation between language anxiety and test anxiety would mean that as language anxiety increases, so does test anxiety, and vice versa. A negative relationship means that as the amount of one variable goes up, the other variable goes down. In this case, the relationship of the variables moves in opposite directions. For example, a negative relationship between language anxiety and language performance indicates that as language anxiety increases, language performance decreases, and vice versa. No correlation between two variables indicates that the variables appear to be unrelated in that sample.

Correlational analysis helps researchers understand differences and similarities among constructs, which in turn can inform researchers about psychological constructs.

CONCEPTUALIZATION

Horwitz, Horwitz, and Cope (1986), in the introduction to their seminal article on language anxiety, note that "research has neither adequately defined foreign language anxiety nor described its specific effects on foreign language learning" (p. 125). At the time, the term *foreign language anxiety,* or more simply *language anxiety,* was just beginning to be used in the literature. This allowed for a more focused conceptual basis from which later research has flourished.

Horwitz and Young (1991b, p. 1) note that there are two general approaches to identifying language anxiety: (1) language anxiety is simply a transfer of anxiety from another domain (for example, test anxiety) or (2) something about language learning makes language anxiety a unique experience. These two approaches are not necessarily opposing positions but represent different perspectives from which to define language anxiety.

Theorists who adopt the first perspective view language anxiety as the transfer of other forms of anxiety, such as test anxiety or communication apprehension, into the second language domain. The advantage of this approach is that knowledge gained from research into those other types of anxiety can be assumed to apply to language anxiety as well. For example, Kleinmann (1977) considered the effect that forms of test anxiety might have on the use of difficult linguistic structures in the second language. Daly (1991) discussed the manner in which communication apprehension may operate in a second language context, and Mejías, Applbaum, Applbaum, and Trotter (1991) studied the communication apprehension of American and Hispanic-American students. Early studies conducted on anxiety and language learning used the "anxiety transfer" approach (see Scovel 1978) and found mixed and confusing results. Perhaps the best example was a study by Chastain (1975), which reported positive, negative, and near zero correlations between anxiety and second language learning in three languages: French, German, and Spanish. While the correlations between anxiety and language learning were tested for all three languages, the directions of the correlations were not consistent. For example, for one, language anxiety was positively related to language performance: the higher the anxiety, the higher the performance. For another language, Chastain found negative correlations between anxiety and language learning: the higher the anxiety, the lower the language performance. In this same study, results also indicated no relationship between anxiety and performance. The implications of Chastain's results are difficult to interpret because the same study indicates that anxiety facilitates second language performance, that anxiety hinders performance, and that there is no relationship between anxiety and performance. The other studies reported in Scovel's (1978) review of the literature showed similar contradictory results, both within and across studies. A summary compiled by Young (1991) listed sixteen studies of anxiety and language learning (see pp. 438–439). Several of the investigations showed some relation between anxiety and language learning, but, overall, the results were fairly inconsistent.

One of the problems associated with the research on the relationship between anxiety and language learning, as summarized by Scovel (1978) and Young (1991), is that the anxiety being studied was not what we would now consider to be language anxiety (MacIntyre & Gardner 1991a). For example, among the sixteen described by Young (1991), only three used a specific language anxiety scale. As Young indicates, this produced "scattered and inconclusive" results. For example, the study by Chastain (1975), mentioned previously, used scales of test anxiety and trait anxiety. Recent research has shown that these types of anxiety are not consistently related to second language learning (MacIntyre & Gardner 1989). The body of research reviewed by Scovel (1978) was consistent in assuming that anxiety from one domain could influence language learning. The results, however, did not support this assumption.

The second approach to identifying language anxiety proposes that language learning produces a unique type of anxiety. From this perspective, we can define language anxiety as the worry and negative emotional reaction aroused when learning or using a second language. MacIntyre and Gardner (1989, 1991b) found that language anxiety was distinct from more general types of anxiety and that performance in the second language was negatively correlated with language anxiety but not with more general types of anxiety. In other words, the higher the language anxiety score, the lower the language performance score. However, this pattern was not maintained for other types of anxiety measures. Since the mid-1980s, research has supported Gardner's (1985) hypothesis that "a construct of anxiety which is not general but instead is specific to the language acquisition context is related to second language achievement" (p. 34).

Whereas some of the early studies focused on language anxiety yielded conflicting conclusions (Scovel 1978), several studies by Gardner, Clément, and associates were able to show a consistent, negative relation between anxiety and language performance (Clément, Gardner, & Smythe 1977, 1980; Gardner, Smythe, Clément, & Gliksman 1976; Gardner, Smythe, & Lalonde 1984). These studies demonstrated that high levels of language anxiety were associated with low levels of achievement in the second language. Because the preceding studies were conducted in the broader context of research on attitudes and motivation for second language learning, and not exclusively on language anxiety, their contribution to the literature on language anxiety is sometimes overlooked. Nevertheless, these studies employed measures of anxiety experienced when using the second language, and the results were highly consistent in demonstrating a negative correlation between anxiety and indices of language achievement.

Bridging the two perspectives identified at the beginning of this section, Horwitz and associates (1986) argue that language anxiety stems from three primary sources: communication apprehension, fear of negative evaluation by others, and test anxiety. Some support has been obtained for each of these sources (Horwitz 1986; MacIntyre & Gardner 1989, 1991a, 1991b, 1991c). However, Horwitz and associates (1986) do not view language anxiety as the simple transfer of these three anxieties to the language classroom; they regard language anxiety as "a distinct complex of self-perceptions, beliefs, feelings, and behaviors related to classroom language learning arising from the uniqueness of the language-learning process." It is now clear that when discussing the effects of anxiety on language learning, one must specifically consider the anxiety aroused in second language contexts.

Even if one views language anxiety as being a unique form of anxiety, specific to second language contexts, it is still instructive to explore the links between it and the rest of the anxiety literature. It is hoped that this will lead to a clearer understanding of what language anxiety means. To place language anxiety in the broader context of research on anxiety (see Endler 1980; Levitt 1980), it is useful to distinguish between three broad perspectives on the nature of anxiety. These perspectives can be identified as trait, situation-specific, and state anxiety (see Cattell & Schier 1963; MacIntyre & Gardner 1989, 1991a; Speilberger 1966). An explanation of these types of anxieties will help clarify some of the issues involved in the discussion of the research to follow.

Trait anxiety refers to a stable predisposition to become nervous in a wide range of situations (Speilberger 1983). People with high levels of trait anxiety are generally nervous people; they lack emotional stability (Goldberg 1993). Someone with low trait anxiety is emotionally stable, usually a calm and relaxed person. Trait anxiety is, by definition, a feature of an individual's personality and therefore is both stable over time and applicable to a wide range of situations. Speilberger (1983) defines trait anxiety as a probability of becoming anxious in any situation.

The second level at which to conceptualize anxiety can be referred to as situation-specific. This is like trait anxiety, except applied to a single context or situation only. Thus it is stable over time but not necessarily consistent across situations. Examples of situation-specific anxieties are stage fright, test anxiety, math anxiety, and language anxiety because each of these refers to a specific type of context: giving a speech, taking a test, doing math, or using a second language. Each situation is different; a person may be nervous in one and not in the others. If one adopts Speilberger's conceptualization, situation-specific anxieties represent the probability of becoming anxious in a particular type of situation.

The term *state anxiety* is used in a somewhat different manner. State anxiety refers to the moment-to-moment experience of anxiety; it is the transient emotional state of feeling nervous that can fluctuate over time and vary in intensity. It is important to stress that state anxiety is essentially the same experience whether it is caused by test taking, public speaking, meeting the fiancé's parents, or trying to communicate in a second language. Both trait anxiety and situation-specific anxieties refer to the likelihood of becoming nervous in a certain type of situation. They do not refer to the experience of anxiety itself, which is best labelled *state anxiety*. State anxiety has an effect on emotions, cognition, and behavior. Its effect on emotions results in heightened levels of arousal and a more sensitive automatic nervous system; individuals with state anxiety feel energized or "keyed-up," but anything above a minimal level of anxiety is perceived as unpleasant arousal. In terms of its effect on cognition, when people experience state anxiety they are more sensitive to what other people are thinking of them (Carver & Scheier 1986). With regard to behavior, people with state anxiety evaluate their behavior, ruminate over real and imagined failures, and often try to plan ways to escape from the situation. The behavioral effects include physical manifestations of anxiety (wringing hands, sweaty palms, faster heartbeat) and attempts to physically withdraw from the situation.

The usefulness of discussing trait and situation-specific anxieties is to predict who will most likely experience state anxiety, which allows the prediction of the negative consequences of anxiety arousal (unpleasant emotions, worry, and physical symptoms). Applied to language learning, we can see that a person with a high level of language anxiety will experience state anxiety frequently; a person with a low level of language anxiety will not experience state anxiety very often in the *second language context.*

From a theoretical perspective, language anxiety is a form of situation-specific anxiety; therefore, research on language anxiety should employ measures of anxiety experienced in second language contexts. There are various questionnaire-type scales available that ask students to indicate how anxious they feel in the language classroom (Gardner 1985; Horwitz et al. 1986) (see Appendices A and B at the end of this volume) when using the new language (MacIntyre & Gardner 1988) (see Appendix C) and when learning the language (MacIntyre & Gardner 1994b) (see Appendix D). MacIntyre and Gardner (1988) and Young (1995) have compiled an extensive list of scales measuring language-related and other types of anxiety (see Appendix E). It is research on the relation between language anxiety and other types of anxiety that has clarified the conceptualization of the construct. Let us now consider those studies in more detail.

RELATION OF LANGUAGE ANXIETY TO OTHER ANXIETIES

Before discussing the results of the studies, a brief description of the statistical method called *factor analysis* is needed. Factor analysis is a technique for analyzing the relationships within a set of variables. Factor analysis uses the correlations among variables to identify those variables that occur in clusters. Each cluster of variables is separate from other clusters of variables. By examining the variables that cluster, patterns of relationships and influences common to several variables can be identified. These common, underlying influences are called *factors.* It is possible for any variable to be influenced by only one factor or by several different factors. One of the purposes of factor analysis is to take a large set of variables and summarize them by identifying a smaller number of factors (Tabachnick & Fidell 1989).

Following up on a similar study done in 1989, MacIntyre and Gardner (1991b) employed factor analysis to investigate the relations among various anxiety scales. They assembled a total of 23 scales representing trait anxiety, state anxiety, audience anxiety, communication apprehension, interpersonal anxiety, novelty anxiety, math anxiety, two measures of French test anxiety, French use anxiety, and French classroom anxiety. Results of a factor analysis showed that, among this large set of anxiety variables, there were three clusters of anxieties. The first factor was found to include most of the anxiety scales (including measures of trait anxiety, communication apprehension, interpersonal anxiety, and others) and was labelled *General anxiety*. The second factor was found to be *State anxiety*. The third factor, separate from the other two, was composed of *French use anxiety, French classroom anxiety*, and two measures of *French test anxiety*. This factor was labelled *Language anxiety*. The procedure used for this factor analysis specified that there could be no correlation among the anxiety factors. Thus, it is possible to separate language anxiety from other forms of anxiety.

The practical implications of this in the language classroom are interesting. Because the types of anxiety are relatively separate, it may be difficult to predict who will experience language anxiety. On the positive side, those who experience considerable anxiety in other courses may not feel at all nervous about learning a second language. Unfortunately, in some cases, students who have never experienced anxiety about any other subject may develop language anxiety. Even highly intelligent, capable students could experience debilitating levels of language anxiety. Teachers may find that these students are especially troubled about their perceived inability to learn languages. If a capable student is experiencing trouble in a language course, it is possible that language anxiety is at fault. Proper diagnosis of the nature of the problem and, if anxiety is an issue, steps taken to relieve the apprehension may prove especially successful with these students.

In summary, language anxiety is a situation-specific form of anxiety that does not appear to bear a strong relation to other forms of anxiety. This means that it is difficult to predict those students likely to experience this type of anxiety. Teachers may want to pay special attention to those students for whom anxiety about learning is a relatively new experience; they may be the ones for whom the negative effects of anxiety can most easily be reversed. To see how the effects of language anxiety may be ameliorated, let us consider the manner in which it may have developed.

DEVELOPMENT OF LANGUAGE ANXIETY

Unfortunately, there is not much empirical research on the origins of language anxiety. Several authors have identified the potential sources of language anxiety based on their experience, theoretical sophistication, and discussions with anxious language learners (Bailey 1983; Horwitz et al. 1986; Lucas 1984; Young 1992). In addition, a model has been proposed that is consistent with research in other areas of psychology and communication.

Based on the work of Horwitz and associates (1986) and others (e.g., Lucas 1984; Young 1986), MacIntyre and Gardner (1989) described the way in which language anxiety is likely to develop. At the earliest stages of language learning, a student will encounter many difficulties in learning, comprehension, grammar, and other areas. If that student becomes anxious about these experiences, if he/she feels uncomfortable making mistakes, then state anxiety occurs. After experiencing repeated occurrences of state anxiety, the student comes to associate anxiety arousal with the second language. When this happens, the student *expects* to be anxious in second language contexts; this is the genesis of language anxiety. Note that this is consistent with the preceding discussion of the difference between state and situation-specific anxiety.

This model is also consistent with psychological theories of the development of anxiety and other emotions, such as communication apprehension (McCroskey & Beatty 1984). Beatty and Andriate (1985) have proposed that a similar process underlies the development of a similar situation-specific anxiety: public speaking anxiety. Beatty and Andriate found support for the model just described when tested at the beginning and end of a communication course in which students were required to give public speeches. Initially, state anxiety experiences did not correlate significantly with scores on a public speaking anxiety scale, but after some experience with giving speeches, the two measures were significantly correlated.

This model also describes how language anxiety can come to be separate from other types of anxiety. Language anxiety occurs when a student reliably associates anxiety with the second language. Students doing well in other courses may find language-learning to be very different, possibly because of personality, specific problems with language acquisition, or specific reactions to a language learning context. As noted by Skehan (1991) and others, a shy, introverted personality will usually do well in most school subjects. However, the extrovert is more likely to enjoy the communication associated with language learning; thus the introvert may find language learning to be a very different experience. With respect to language acquisition deficits, Sparks and Ganschow (1991) suggest that students doing well in other courses may experience language anxiety because they have specific language-encoding difficulty. Such students may develop strategies to compensate for the problem in the native language but not in the second language (MacIntyre 1995). Finally, it is also possible that a specific teacher, set of classmates, or intercultural setting provokes an intense anxiety reaction (Bailey 1983; Clément 1980; Clément, Dörnyei, & Noels 1994), possibly because self-esteem, self-presentation, identity, and the ability to communicate are so intimately tied (Brown 1991; Cohen & Norst 1989). For these reasons, language learning may provoke reactions that are quite different from those instilled in other learning situations.

Several authors have examined the potential origins of language anxiety. Price (1991) summarized several sources of language anxiety in the classroom. She noted that students seemed to be most concerned about speaking in front of their peers. Fear of being laughed at, embarrassed, and making a fool of oneself are major concerns of anxious language students. The more technical aspects of language learning also cause problems among students. Price's interviews show that students were very concerned about making errors in pronunciation and that they in particular wished to develop an accent that approximated that of a native speaker. Students were also worried about not communicating effectively. These fears about communicating and social evaluation are likely based on a students' relationships with their teacher and peers, although Clément, Dörnyei, and Noels (1994) did not find ratings of group cohesion to be correlated with language anxiety.

Young (1991) offered a more extensive list of the potential sources of language anxiety, stemming from the learner, the teacher, and instructional practice. A learner's personal problems, such as low self-esteem, and interpersonal problems, like competitiveness and fear of losing one's sense of identity, can be the seeds for anxiety. Unrealistic learner beliefs, such as beliefs about how quickly the language can be learned or that speakers need excellent accent and pronunciation, add to the apprehension. Further, some instructors believe that they must become drill sergeants and/or intimidate their students into learning; these behaviors can cause anxiety. The method of error correction may sour the relationship between teacher and student and lead to nervous students, especially if harsh, embarrassing error correction is done in front of other students. Finally, methods of testing may arouse anxiety, though oral testing is not always the most disturbing (see Madsen, Brown, & Jones 1991).

In cases where language learning occurs in a multicultural setting, Clément (1980) notes that the frequency and quality of contact with native speakers will have an important influence on anxiety levels. Ultimately, motivation for language learning will be based on a tension created between the desire to learn a new language/culture and the opposing fear of losing one's own language and ethnic identity. Within this framework, Clément (1980, 1986) considers language anxiety to be part of a larger construct called *self-confidence*, which also includes the perception of proficiency in the second language. Low levels of anxiety, a positive self-perception of proficiency, and high levels of self-confidence are seen as a second motivational process for language learning.

MacIntyre and Noels (1994) found evidence that students' self-perceptions of their proficiency may be affected by language anxiety. On one hand, students with high levels of language anxiety tend to underestimate their ability to speak, comprehend, and write the second language. On the other hand, the more relaxed students tended to overestimate their ability in these areas. Having expectations of failure may be an important manner in which anxious learners maintain their high levels of anxiety. By underestimating their ability, anxious students may avoid those learning and communication activities that would both validate their current level of ability and facilitate language learning. Language anxiety affects not only the way in which learners perform but also the way in which they perceive their performance, which can serve to maintain high levels of anxiety.

The personality of the learner seems to predispose him or her to developing language anxiety. Based on work by Lalonde and Gardner (1984), who found that personality traits may indirectly influence language learning, MacIntyre and Charos (1995) investigated the role of personality in the development of language-related attitudes, motivation, and language anxiety among beginning language students. The results show that language anxiety is more closely related to introversion than it is to a personality trait of nervousness. This is consistent with the previous research showing that general anxiety does not necessarily dispose a student to language anxiety (MacIntyre & Gardner 1989, 1991b). The data supports the suggestion that people who are shy and introverted are likely to develop language anxiety, possibly because they are less willing to engage in the communication necessary for language-learning success (for a practical discussion see Brown 1991). The results further show that language anxiety influences a student's desire to affiliate with members of the second language community, which has been shown to affect motivation for language learning (e.g., Clément, Dörnyei, & Noels 1994; Gardner & Tremblay, this volume).

Overall, the single most important source of language anxiety seems to be the fear of speaking in front of other people using a language with which one has limited proficiency. For this reason, language learning has more potential for students to embarrass themselves, to frustrate their self-expression, and to challenge their self-esteem and sense of identity than almost any other learning activity. Cohen and Norst (1989) describe the concern well when they say, "there is something fundamentally different about learning a language, compared to learning another skill or gaining other knowledge, namely, that language and self are so closely bound, if not identical, that an attack on one is an attack on the other" (p. 61).

In summary, it would appear that the development of language anxiety is partly based in the personality of the individual student. Those who are shy appear to be more likely to develop language anxiety. However, those who tend to be nervous individuals do not appear to be disposed toward language anxiety. Further, the results reported in the literature are consistent with the notion that negative experiences, both inside and outside the second language classroom, contribute to the development of a situational-type anxiety, language anxiety (Aida 1994; Young 1991; but see Clément, Dörnyei, & Noels 1994). It appears likely that one of the reasons language anxiety persists is its negative effect on a students' self-perception of proficiency.

The results reported above represent only the first steps in understanding the sources of language anxiety; further research into its development would likely be productive. Once the origins of language anxiety are more completely understood, we may be in an even better position to explain its effects on language achievement.

EFFECTS OF LANGUAGE ANXIETY

Interest in language anxiety may be most strongly related to its effects. One of the major reasons for concern, particularly among educators and administrators, is its potential negative effect on academic achievement, including course grades and standardized proficiency tests (Cope-Powell 1991; Young 1986). Students also may spend a considerable amount of time and effort simply compensating for the effects of debilitating levels of language anxiety, because anxiety arousal has a number of specific cognitive effects (MacIntyre & Gardner 1994a, 1994b; Price 1991). In addition, the importance of language learning in the global economy may make language anxiety a barrier to a successful career (Daly 1991) and to successful intergroup relations (Clément 1980; 1986). In addition, the unpleasant personal experience of a severe anxiety reaction makes its effect on the person a major concern as well. Each of these effects, academic, cognitive, social, and personal, will be examined below.

Academic Effects

Several studies have investigated the relation between language anxiety and language course grades. For example, Aida (1994), Horwitz (1986), MacIntyre and Gardner (1994b), and Young (1986) have all shown significant, negative correlations between language anxiety and grades in a variety of language courses. These correlations range up to a high of $r = -.65$ (MacIntyre & Gardner 1994b), which indicates the potential for a substantial relationship between anxiety and academic achievement in language courses.

In an extensive study reported in an article by Gardner, Smythe, Clément, and Gliksman (1976) and subsequently in a detailed monograph by Gardner, Smythe, and Lalonde (1984), the relation between attitudes, motivation, and anxiety was investigated in seven locations across Canada. The results pertaining to language anxiety indicated that it was among the strongest predictors of second language achievement and that the correlation between anxiety and course grades was strongest among students in higher grades, particularly in grade 11 (Gardner, Smythe, Clément, & Gliksman 1976). Further, considering the nature of the different regions of the country and the various grade levels of the students, the results are remarkably consistent in showing that language anxiety was associated with both the perception of second language competence and measures of actual second language competence (Gardner, Smythe, & Lalonde 1984). Clearly, low course grades and impaired performance on tests is one of the effects of language anxiety.

An additional academic effect of language anxiety can be identified as "overstudying" (Horwitz et al. 1986). It has been reported that students who experience anxiety feel the need to compensate for the negative effects of anxiety arousal by increased effort at learning (Price 1991), and experimental data shows this effect (MacIntyre & Gardner 1994b). This is a common response when an individual notices that he or she is not performing well because of anxiety arousal (Eysenck 1979; Schwarzer 1986). In an academic setting, this often leaves students with lower levels of achievement than would be expected based on the work and time that they invest in language study. This complaint was noted prominently by Price (1991) in a series of interviews with nervous language learners.

It seems clear that high levels of language anxiety are associated with low levels of academic achievement in second or foreign language courses. To examine the origins of these effects, studies have been conducted to investigate specific cognitive processes required for language learning and the manner in which anxiety can interfere with cognition.

Cognitive Effects

In a series of experiments to examine the effects of language anxiety on cognitive processing, MacIntyre and Gardner have shown that such effects may be quite pervasive. At the core of these studies is a model of the effects of anxiety arousal on learning from instruction, as in a language classroom (Tobias 1979, 1980, 1986). A variation on the Tobias model is shown in Figure 3.1. The model shows three stages—Input, Processing, and Output—and is generic enough to be applied to many types of situation-specific anxiety. The arousal of anxiety may interfere with cognitive performance at any or all of these stages. Briefly, anxiety arousal is associated with self-related cognition: thoughts of failure, worry over how one is performing in the situation, and self-deprecating thoughts. These types of thoughts compete for cognitive resources with normal cognitive demands (for example, in communicating one must encode the words, comprehend the meaning of phrases and the structure of a message, and plan what one is about to say next). Because the capacity to process information is limited, anxiety-related cognition usually hinders performance (Eysenck 1979). Further, if anxiety disrupts the cognitive work at one stage, then information is not passed along to the next stage.

At the input stage, anxiety acts like a filter preventing some information from getting into the cognitive processing system. This is analogous to Krashen's well-known concept of the "affective filter." For example, in language class, anxious students may not be able to take in spoken dialogue fast enough because anxiety interferes with their ability to process information. Relaxed students would be better able to gather information because they do not experience this type of interference. Naturally, if words or phrases do not enter the system, they cannot be processed or used later. Wheeless (1975) has identified this as the problem of "receiver apprehension," which has been shown to have a number of negative effects on communication (Preiss, Wheeless, & Allen 1991).

During the processing stage, anxiety can influence both the speed and accuracy of learning. Because anxiety acts as a distraction, students may not be able to learn new words, phrases, grammar, and so on when they are worried. This worry may take the form of preoccupation with future communication or more simply the fear of misunderstanding something. Students who process

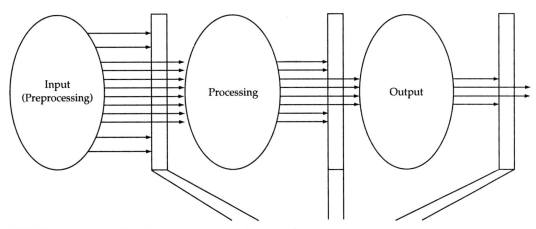

FIGURE 3.1. Model of the effects of anxiety on learning from instruction

information more deeply, who integrate it with existing knowledge, who attempt to understand both what they hear and its structure, create a better understanding of the language and its use. Research in the area of language-learning strategies shows that deeper processing of language input facilitates learning (Cohen 1990; Oxford & Nyikos 1989).

Anxiety arousal at the output stage can influence the quality of second language communication. Many people have had the experience of "freezing-up" on an important test; they know the correct answer but it will not come to mind. This happens because the presence of anxiety acts as a disruption to the retrieval of information. Similar effects can be observed when speaking or writing in the second language; the correct word may be on the "tip of the tongue," but no amount of effort will bring it forward. If a student becomes embarrassed by this gaffe, anxiety may increase, making further communication even more difficult.

Several laboratory studies, informed by this three-stage model, have been conducted. The initial study (MacIntyre & Gardner 1991b) examined the effects of language anxiety on the input and output stages. To examine the input stage, a task was used that did not require learning, only taking in second language stimuli. For this task, native English speakers were read a series of numbers spoken in English and another series spoken in French. The test required the listeners to write down the numbers on a sheet of paper in the same order in which the digits were presented. This kept interpretation and production of the second language to a minimum. To measure performance at the output stage, participants were asked to recall vocabulary items fitting a particular category, again in both English and French. Results showed that high levels of language anxiety were associated with low scores at both the input and output stages, but only for the second language tasks.

A later study expanded on these results by employing at least three measures of performance at each of the three stages: input, processing, and output (MacIntyre & Gardner 1994b). Several of the tasks were constructed to show that language anxiety may affect one stage but not another, such as when increased effort at processing compensates for information missed during the input stage. Further, some of the tasks were administered in both native and second languages to again examine the degree to which language anxiety affects only second language processing.

Results show that performance at all three stages may be hindered by language anxiety but that the strongest correlations were observed for the processing and output stages. Significant correlations were obtained with time required to recognize words, ability to hold words in short-term memory, memory for grammar rules, ability to translate a paragraph, length of time studying new vocabulary items, memory for new vocabulary items, time required to complete a test of vocabulary, retrieval of vocabulary from long-term memory, ability to repeat items in native language (L1) and second language (L2), ability to speak with an L2 accent, complexity of sentences spoken, and fluency of speech. Further, it was shown that language anxiety is negatively correlated with second language tasks but not with native language tasks. Finally, the results clearly indicate that the effects of language anxiety on a particular task may be observed at one stage and not the others. Results on some tasks show that anxious students may require more time to intake information, but this extra effort can reduce the effects of language anxiety at later stages (in essence, the extra effort pays off, and performance at later stages is not affected by anxiety). Other tasks show that when giving extra effort is not an option (e.g., because of a time limit), language anxiety may hinder performance at the processing and output stages. MacIntyre and Gardner (1994b) conclude that "the potential effects of language anxiety on cognitive processing in the second language appear pervasive and may be quite subtle" (p. 301).

Two other studies were conducted that attempted to arouse anxiety during vocabulary learning to determine its effects on cognitive processing in a controlled environment. In both studies, a video camera was used to increase the anxiety of one group of learners. The first of these studies (Gardner, Day, & MacIntyre 1992) examined both language anxiety and Gardner's concept of integrative motivation (Tremblay & Gardner 1995). English-speaking students were required to complete an attitude and motivation test battery and then to learn French vocabulary items using a computer. Half of the subjects performed this task in the presence of a video camera. Results showed that students who were integratively motivated, that is motivated to learn French in order to meet and communicate with Francophones, learned the vocabulary at a faster pace. The video camera, however, did not appear to affect the rate of learning, possibly because it did not create the expected elevation in anxiety.

A more extensive follow-up study (MacIntyre & Gardner 1994a) also tried using a video camera to arouse anxiety. To examine the effects of anxiety arousal on the three stages of learning, four groups were created by introducing the video camera immediately before the input, processing, or output stages; a control group never saw the video camera. All learners were told that they were learning the new vocabulary in order to use the items later in the study. Analysis of learners' reactions showed that this emphasis on communication may have made the video camera more effective in arousing anxiety because each group showed the expected elevation in anxiety just after the camera was introduced. Further, as the anxiety dissipated, the effects on learning diminished, and formerly anxious students were partially able to compensate for deficits created by anxiety. However, the results showed that the anxious students were not fully able to make up the deficit within the time span of the experiment. Thus, the effects of anxiety are strongest immediately after it is aroused, dissipate with time, and can be overcome if sufficient time and effort are given.

The effects of anxiety observed in this study were considered to be analogous to the effect of anxiety on a language student. When anxiety is aroused, students may need more time to achieve the same results as their relaxed counterparts. Anxious students may also take more time to write tests, and the quality of their written or spoken output may be diminished. In any event, a nervous student risks performing more poorly than a relaxed one.

It should be made clear that the effects of anxiety on cognitive processes are a consequence of state anxiety arousal. As defined previously, language anxiety can be defined as the tendency to experience a state anxiety reaction during language learning or communication. This accounts for the correlation observed between language anxiety scales and measures of L2 performance. It also may account for some of the difficulties in communication that anxious learners experience in social settings.

Social Effects

There are many ways in which the social context can influence language anxiety. A competitive classroom atmosphere, difficult interactions with teachers, risks of embarrassment, opportunity for contact with members of the target language group, and tension among ethnic groups may all influence language anxiety.

Studies conducted by Clément, Gardner, and Smythe (1977, 1980) show the important role that social context plays in second language learning. Clément (1980) notes that in situations where minority group members are learning the language of a majority group, there is a tension between the desire to learn the new language/culture and the fear of losing one's native language/culture. In addition to its influence on motivation for language learning, this tension influences linguistic self-confidence, which is defined by a lack of anxiety and the self-perception of competence with the second language. Self-confidence is considered to be a motivating influence, directing the language learner toward contact with the second language community (Clément 1980, 1986). In contact situations, a self-confident learner will be more highly motivated to communicate with speakers of the target language.

In one example of a study in which language groups are in contact, Mejías and associates (1991) investigated the communication apprehension of bilingual Mexican-American students in Texas. The students were native speakers of Spanish but predominately used English in their daily lives. They found that both high school and college students felt less anxious when speaking in their second language (English) than when speaking in their native Spanish. The authors concluded that the frequency of language use may be more influential than the distinction between native and second languages in determining the communication anxiety reaction. The results also show that a considerable number of Mexican-American high school students experienced high communication apprehension in both Spanish and English. Comparison groups of Anglophone students were very anxious speaking Spanish but much more relaxed speaking English. As Clément (1980, 1986) suggests, the majority and minority groups experience different effects of intergroup contact. One effect appears to be that the Anglophone students experience high communication apprehension in Spanish (their second language) but the Mexican-American students are relatively more comfortable with their second language (English). The apparent "downside" is that Mexican-American students appear to experience higher apprehension in their native language, Spanish, than otherwise would be expected.

Perhaps the most recurring finding in the literature on language anxiety, and one of its most important social effects, is that anxious learners do not communicate as often as more relaxed learners (MacIntyre & Gardner 1991a, 1991c). The prospect of communicating in a second language appears to be the major source of language anxiety. Although there has not been much research on the interpersonal effects of avoiding second language communication, it is clear that avoiding communication in the native language generates a number of negative assumptions about a reticent speaker (Daly & McCroskey 1984). How anxious second language communicators are perceived by others in the classroom and in interactions outside the classroom would be interesting topics of future research. Skehan (1991) has stated that successful language learners possess a willingness to "talk in order to learn." Evidence from a preliminary study (MacIntrye & Charos 1995) indicates that anxious learners are less willing to communicate and, when given the opportunity to communicate in a natural setting, do so less frequently.

Personal Effects

Among the most troublesome effects of language anxiety is the severe anxiety reaction for an individual language learner. Although extreme anxiety is a rare occurrence, language learning should not be a traumatic experience. Unfortunately, for some students, it is just that. Although the intention of this chapter is to concentrate on quantitative research, the personal side of the language-learning process should not be ignored.

Some interesting, well-stated opinions from language students have appeared in the literature. Perhaps the most strongly worded one was offered by a language student participating in a series of interviews conducted by Price (1991): "I'd rather be in a prison camp than speak a foreign language" (p. 104). Such strong emotion can be interpreted in a number of ways. Anxious individuals often engage in self-deprecating cognition (Schwarzer 1986), and this is true of language students as well (Young 1991). "I just know that I have some kind of disability" (Horwitz et al. 1986, p. 125). "I feel so dumb in my German class," "Sometimes when I speak English in class, I am so afraid I feel like hiding behind my chair" (Horwitz & Young 1991b, p. xiii). Students worry that others would think that they are "stupid," "a total dingbat," or "a babbling baby" (Price 1991, p. 105) because they are having trouble using simple vocabulary and grammar structures. The anxiety response may also be physiological: "my heart starts pumping really fast, and the adrenaline running. Then I feel myself start to go red . . . and by the end of the ordeal—for it is— I am totally red, my hands shake, and my heart pounds . . . It's pure trauma for me . . . if I am ever asked to [answer a question in class again] I'll probably have a coronary." The same student described language learning as the "smashing of a well-developed positive self-concept" (Cohen & Norst 1989, pp. 68–69).

The literature contains numerous examples of this kind. Some readers might be tempted to dismiss these excerpts as exaggerations. Even if they are somewhat melodramatic, the statements express deep-seated feelings, and the underlying sentiment should not be ignored. Language learning provokes a traumatic reaction in some individuals. If we consider Young's (1991) findings that some teachers feel it necessary to induce anxiety in order to stimulate learning, then the stage is set for some potentially severe anxiety reactions. The frequency with which this occurs is an interesting avenue for future research.

CONCLUSION

This review has necessarily omitted several details of some studies. Interested readers are encouraged to consult the appropriate sources for more complete discussions of the issues. (See Table 3.1 for references to specific areas of language anxiety research.)

TABLE 3.1. Language Anxiety Research

General Theoretical Approaches to Anxiety

> Eysenck, 1979
> Leibert & Morris, 1957
> Priess, Wheeless, & Allen, 1991
> Schwarzer, 1986
> Tobias, 1979, 1980, 1986

Language Anxiety: Theoretical Approaches and Literature Reviews

> Horwitz, Horwitz, & Cope, 1986
> MacIntyre, 1995
> MacIntyre & Gardner, 1991a
> Scovel, 1978
> Sparks & Ganschow, 1993a, 1993b

The Relation of Language Anxiety to Other Concepts

> Clément, 1980
> Gardner, Day, & MacIntyre, 1992
> MacIntyre & Gardner, 1989, 1991b
> Sparks & Ganschow, 1991

Causes of Language Anxiety

Qualitative studies
> Cohen & Norst, 1989
> Price, 1991

Quantitative studies
> MacIntyre & Charos, 1995
> Mejías et al., 1991

Effects of Language Anxiety

Academic
> Aida, 1994
> Gardner, Smythe, Clément, & Gliksman, 1976
> Gardner, Smythe, & Lalonde, 1984
> Horwitz, 1986
> Young, 1986

Social
> Clément, 1980, 1986
> Clément, Gardner, & Smythe, 1980
> MacIntyre & Gardner, 1991a, 1991c

Cognitive
> MacIntyre & Gardner, 1994a, 1994b

Research into language anxiety has reached a number of conclusions that may interest language teachers and students alike. There appears to be a discernible situation-specific construct of language anxiety that is separate from other types of anxiety. It would appear that this anxiety develops from negative experiences, particularly early in language learning. Language anxiety has consistently shown a negative correlation with second language achievement and with the perception of second language proficiency. The combination of high levels of anxiety and low self-rated proficiency creates students with low levels of linguistic self-confidence, which reduces motivation for study and communication in the second language. The beliefs of both language students and language teachers, and the classroom context, may contribute to anxiety arousal.

Several types of language anxiety effects have been reported. Compared to relaxed students, anxious learners achieve lower grades, spend more time studying, and have more trouble taking in information in the second language, processing that information, and displaying their L2 abilities. The cognitive disruption caused by anxiety arousal appears to be responsible for these negative effects. In addition, some students report that language learning evokes a severe anxiety reaction that approximates trauma.

The study of language anxiety has progressed a great deal in the past few years, and our understanding of the concept continues to grow. Research is no longer beset by the vague definitions, inconsistent measurement, and confusing results that plagued the area in the past. Despite this progress (or maybe because of it), much more work needs to be done. The stage is set for future work that more fully develops the concept, assesses its variety of obvious and subtle effects, estimates the degree to which language anxiety negatively affects language learning in general, and explains why these effects occur. Perhaps the most pressing need is to conduct research on strategies and programs that may ameliorate the negative effects of language anxiety. The other contributions to this volume provide many specific ways in which this literature may be expanded and continue to develop. As language pedagogy continues to move toward an emphasis on authentic communicative competence and a communication-oriented classroom, the need to assess the effects of language anxiety becomes more and more salient.

NOTES

1. Preparation of this manuscript was supported by a post-doctoral fellowship awarded by the Social Science and Humanities Research Council of Canada. Correspondence may be sent to Peter MacIntyre, Department of Psychology, University College of Cape Breton, PO Box 5300, Sydney, Nova Scotia, Canada B1P 6L2. E-mail may be sent to *pmacinty@sparc.uccb.ns.ca*

2. A correlation of .90 in and of itself is not significant without an indication of probability. The researcher sets the acceptable probability level for his or her study. Generally speaking, when a probability level is less than .05, this indicates that the findings are significant and not likely to be due to mere chance. Findings with a probability level .01, .001, or .0001 are even more highly reliable.

REFERENCES

Aida, Y. (1994). Examination of Horwitz, Horwitz, and Cope's construct of foreign language anxiety: The case of students of Japanese. *Modern Language Journal, 78,* 155–168.

Bailey, K. M. (1983). Competitiveness and anxiety in adult second language learning: Looking at and through the diary studies. In H. W. Seliger & M. H. Long (Eds.), *Classroom-oriented research in second language acquisition.* Rowley, MA: Newbury House, pp. 67–102.

Beatty, M. J., & Andriate, G. A. (1985). Communication apprehension and general trait anxiety in the prediction of public speaking anxiety. *Communication Quarterly, 33,* 174–184.

Brown, H. D. (1991). *Breaking the language barrier.* Yarmouth, ME: Intercultural Press.

Campbell, C. M., & Ortiz, J. (1991). Helping students overcome foreign language anxiety: A foreign language anxiety workshop. In E. K. Horwitz & D. J. Young (Eds.), *Language anxiety: From theory and research to classroom implications.* Upper Saddle River, NJ: Prentice Hall, pp. 153–168.

Carver, C. S., & Scheier, M. F. (1986). Functional and dysfunctional responses to anxiety: The interaction between expectancies and self-focused attention. In R. Schwarzer (Ed.), *Self-related cognition in anxiety and motivation.* Hillsdale, NJ: Erlbaum, pp. 111–142.

Cattell, R. B., & Scheier, I. H. (1963). *Handbook for the IPAT anxiety scale* (2nd ed.). Champaign, IL: Institute for Personality and Ability Testing.

Chastain, K. (1975). Affective and ability factors in second language acquisition. *Language Learning, 25,* 153–161.

Clément, R. (1980). Ethnicity, contact, and communicative competence in a second language. In H. Giles, W. P. Robinson, & P. M. Smith (Eds.), *Language: Social psychological perspectives.* Oxford: Pergamon Press, pp. 147–154.

Clément, R. (1986). Second language proficiency and acculturation: An investigation of the effects of language status and individual characteristics. *Journal of Language and Social Psychology, 5,* 271–290.

Clément, R., Dörnyei, Z., & Noels, K. (1994). Motivation, self-confidence, and group cohesion in the foreign language classroom. *Language Learning, 44,* 417–448.

Clément, R., Gardner, R. C., & Smythe, P. C. (1977). Motivational variables in second language acquisition: A study of Francophones learning English. *Canadian Journal of Behavioral Science, 9,* 123–133.

Clément, R., Gardner, R. C., & Smythe, P. C. (1980). Social and individual factors in second language acquisition. *Canadian Journal of Behavioral Science, 12,* 293–302.

Cohen, A. D. (1990). *Language learning: Insights for learners, teachers, and researchers.* Boston: Heinle & Heinle.

Cohen, Y., & Norst, M. J. (1989). Fear, dependence and loss of self-esteem: Affective barriers in second language learning among adults. *RELC Journal, 20,* 61–77.

Cope-Powell, J. (1991). Foreign language classroom anxiety: Institutional Responses. In E. K. Horwitz & D. J. Young (Eds.), *Language anxiety: From theory and research to classroom implications.* Upper Saddle River, NJ: Prentice Hall, pp. 169–176.

Daly, J. (1991). Understanding communication apprehension: An introduction for language educators. In E. K. Horwitz & D. J. Young (Eds.), *Language anxiety: From theory and research to classroom implications.* Upper Saddle River, NJ: Prentice Hall, pp. 3–14.

Daly, J., & McCroskey, J. C. (1984). *Avoiding communication: Shyness, reticence, and communication apprehension.* Beverly Hills, CA: Sage.

Desrochers, A. M. (1980). *Imagery elaboration and the acquisition of French vocabulary.* Unpublished doctoral dissertation, University of Western Ontario, London, Canada.

Ely, C. M. (1986). An analysis of discomfort, risktaking, sociability, and motivation in the L2 classroom. *Language Learning, 36,* 1–25.

Endler, N. S. (1980). Person-situation interaction and anxiety. In I. L. Kutash (Ed.), *Handbook on stress and anxiety.* San Francisco: Jossey-Bass, pp. 249–266.

Eysenck, M. W. (1979). Anxiety, learning and memory: A reconceptualization. *Journal of Research in Personality, 13,* 363–385.

Fischer, W. F. (1988). *Theories of anxiety* (2nd ed.). Lanham, MD: University Press.

Gardner, R. C. (1985). *Social psychology and second language learning: The role of attitudes and motivation.* London: Edward Arnold.

Gardner, R. C., Day, B., & MacIntyre, P. D. (1992). Integrative motivation, induced anxiety, and language learning in a controlled environment. *Studies in Second Language Acquisition, 14,* 197–214.

Gardner, R. C., Smythe, P. C., & Clément, R. (1979). Intensive second language study in a bicultural milieu: An investigation of attitudes, motivation, and language proficiency. *Language Learning, 29,* 305–320.

Gardner, R. C., Smythe, P. C., Clément, R., & Gliksman, L. (1976). Second language acquisition: A social psychological perspective. *Canadian Modern Language Review, 32,* 198–213.

Gardner, R. C., Smythe, P. C., & Lalonde, R. N. (1984). *The nature and replicability of factors in second language acquisition* (Research Bulletin No. 605). London, Canada: University of Western Ontario, Department of Psychology.

Goldberg, L. R. (1993). The structure of phenotypic personality traits. *American Psychologist, 48,* 26–34.

Horwitz, E. K. (1986). Preliminary evidence for the reliability and validity of a Foreign Language Anxiety Scale. *TESOL Quarterly, 20,* 559–562.

Horwitz, E. K., Horwitz, M. B., & Cope, J. (1986). Foreign language classroom anxiety. *Modern Language Journal, 70,* 125–132.

Horwitz, E. K., & Young, D. (1991a). Afterword. In E. K. Horwitz & D. J. Young (Eds.), *Language anxiety: From theory and research to classroom implications.* Upper Saddle River, NJ: Prentice Hall, pp. 177–178.

Horwitz, E. K., & Young, D. (1991b). *Language anxiety: From theory and research to classroom implications.* Upper Saddle River, NJ: Prentice Hall.

Kleinmann, H. H. (1977). Avoidance behaviour in adult second language acquisition. *Language Learning, 27,* 93–107.

Lalonde, R. N., & Gardner, R. C. (1984). Investigating a causal model of second language acquisition: Where does personality fit? *Canadian Journal of Behavioral Science, 15,* 224–237.

Levitt, E. E. (1980). *The psychology of anxiety.* Hillsdale, NJ: Lawrence Erlbaum Associates.

Liebert, R. M., & Morris, L. W. (1967). Cognitive and emotional components of test anxiety: A distinction and some initial data. *Psychological Reports, 20,* 975–978.

Lucas, J. (1984). Communication apprehension in the ESL classroom: Getting our students to talk. *Foreign Language Annals, 17,* 593–598.

MacIntyre, P. D. (1995). How does anxiety affect second language learning?: A reply to Sparks and Ganschow. *Modern Language Journal, 79,* 1–32.

MacIntyre, P. D., & Charos, C. (1995, June). *Personality, motivation and willingness to communicate as predictors of second language communication.* Paper presented at the annual conference of the Canadian Psychological Association, Charlottetown PEI.

MacIntyre, P. D., & Gardner, R. C. (1988). *The measurement of anxiety and applications to second language learning: An annotated bibliography* (Research Bulletin No. 672). London, Canada: The University of Western Ontario, Department of Psychology. (ERIC Clearinghouse on Languages and Linguistics # FL017649.)

MacIntyre, P. D., & Gardner, R. C. (1989). Anxiety and second-language learning: Toward a theoretical clarification. *Language Learning, 39,* 251–275.

MacIntyre, P. D., & Gardner, R. C. (1991a). Methods and results in the study of anxiety in language learning: A review of the literature. *Language Learning, 41,* 85–117.

MacIntyre, P. D., & Gardner, R. C. (1991b). Language anxiety: Its relation to other anxieties and to processing in native and second languages. *Language Learning, 41,* 513–534.

MacIntyre, P. D., & Gardner, R. C. (1991c). Investigating language class anxiety using the focused essay technique. *The Modern Language Journal, 75,* 296–304.

MacIntyre, P. D., & Gardner, R. C. (1994a). The effects of induced anxiety on cognitive processing in second language learning. *Studies in Second Language Acquisition, 16,* 1–17.

MacIntyre, P. D., & Gardner, R. C. (1994b). The subtle effects of language anxiety on cognitive processing in the second language. *Language Learning, 44,* 283–305.

MacIntyre, P. D., & Noels, K. A. (1994, June). *Communication apprehension, perceived competence, and actual competence in a second language.* Paper presented at the annual conference of the Canadian Psychological Association, Penticton, British Columbia.

Madsen, H. S., Brown, B. L., & Jones, R. L. (1991). Evaluating students' attitudes toward second-language tests. In E. K. Horwitz & D. J. Young (Eds.), *Language anxiety: From theory and research to classroom implications.* Upper Saddle River, NJ: Prentice Hall, pp. 65–86.

McCroskey, J. C., & Beatty, M. J. (1984). Communication apprehension and accumulated communication state anxiety experiences: A research note. *Communication Monographs, 57,* 79–84.

Mejías, H., Applbaum, R. L., Applbaum, S. J., & Trotter, R. T. (1991). Oral communication apprehension and Hispanics: An exploration of oral communication apprehension among Mexican American students in Texas. In E. K. Horwitz & D. J. Young (Eds.), *Language anxiety: From theory and research to classroom implications.* Upper Saddle River, NJ: Prentice Hall, pp. 87–97.

Oxford, R., & Nyikos, M. (1989). Variables affecting choice of language learning strategies by university students. *Modern Language Journal, 75,* 292–300.

Phillips, E. M. (1992). The effects of language anxiety on students' oral test performance and attitudes. *Modern Language Journal, 76,* 14–26.

Preiss, R. W., Wheeless, L. R., & Allen, M. (1991). Potential cognitive processes and consequences of receiver apprehension. In M. Booth-Butterfield (Ed.), *Communication, cognition, and anxiety.* Beverly Hills, CA: Sage, pp. 15–172.

Price, M. L. (1991). The subjective experience of foreign language anxiety: Interviews with highly anxious students. In E. K. Horwitz & D. J. Young (Eds.), *Language anxiety: From theory and research to classroom implications.* Upper Saddle River, NJ: Prentice Hall, pp. 101–108.

Sarason, I. G. (1980). *Test anxiety: Theory, research and applications.* Hillsdale, NJ: Erlbaum.

Sarason, I. G. (1986). Test anxiety, worry, and cognitive interference. In R. Schwarzer (Ed.), *Self-related cognition in anxiety and motivation.* Hillsdale, NJ: Erlbaum, pp. 19–34.

Schwarzer, R. (1986). Self-related cognition in anxiety and motivation: An introduction. In R. Schwarzer (Ed.), *Self-related cognition in anxiety and motivation.* Hillsdale, NJ: Erlbaum, pp. 1–17.

Scovel, T. (1978). The effect of affect on foreign language learning: A review of the anxiety research. *Language Learning, 28,* 129–142.

Skehan, P. (1991). Individual differences in second language learning. *Studies in Second Language Acquisition, 13,* 275–298.

Sparks, R. L., & Ganschow, L. (1991). Foreign language learning differences: Affective or native language aptitude differences? *Modern Language Journal, 75*, 3–16.

Sparks, R. L., & Ganschow, L. (1993a). The impact of native language learning problems on foreign language learning: Case study illustrations of the linguistic coding deficit hypothesis. *Modern Language Journal, 77*, 58–74.

Sparks, R. L., & Ganschow, L. (1993b). Searching for the cognitive locus of foreign language learning difficulties: Linking first and second language learning. *Modern Language Journal, 77*, 289–302.

Spielberger, C. (1966). *Anxiety and behavior.* New York: Academic Press.

Spielberger, C. D. (1983). *Manual for the state-trait anxiety inventory* (Form Y). Palo Alto, CA: Consulting Psychologists Press.

Tabachnick, B., & Fidell, L. S. (1989). *Using multivariate statistics* (2nd ed.). New York: Harper & Row.

Tremblay, P. F., & Gardner, R. C. (1995). Expanding the motivation construct in language learning. *Modern Language Journal, 79*, 505–518.

Tobias, S. (1979). Anxiety research in educational psychology. *Journal of Educational Psychology, 71*, 573–582.

Tobias, S. (1980). Anxiety and instruction. In I. G. Sarason (Ed.), *Test anxiety: Theory, research and applications.* Hillsdale, NJ: Erlbaum.

Tobias, S. (1986). Anxiety and cognitive processing of instruction. In R. Schwarzer (Ed.), *Self-related cognition in anxiety and motivation.* Hillsdale, NJ: Erlbaum, pp. 35–54.

Wheeless, L. R. (1975). An investigation of received apprehension and social context dimensions of communication apprehension. *The Speech Teacher, 24*, 261–268.

Young, D. (1986). The relationship between anxiety and foreign language oral proficiency ratings. *Foreign Language Annals, 19*, 439–445.

Young, D. J. (1991). Creating a low-anxiety classroom environment: What does the anxiety research suggest? *Modern Language Journal, 75*, 426–439.

Young, D. J. (1992). Language anxiety from the foreign language specialist's perspective: Interviews with Krashen, Omaggio Hadley, Terrell, and Rardin. *Foreign Language Annals, 25*, 157–172.

Young, D. J. (1995). New directions in language anxiety research. In C. Klee (Ed.), *Faces in a crowd: Individual learners in multisection programs.* Boston, MA: Heinle and Heinle.

PART III

Attending to Affect While Developing Language Skills

Clashes in L2 Reading: Research Versus Practice and Readers' Misconceptions

James F. Lee
Indiana University

Personal Reflections

a. Can you remember ever being overwhelmed by reading an article, short story, or novel in your L2?
b. Have you ever correctly answered all the comprehension questions that accompanied a reading passage but still did not understand what you read?
c. Do you read only in private? Have you ever read with someone else?
d. Do you understand everything you read in your L2? Do you need to?

Fundamental Concepts

Cognitive processing

Cognitive deficits

Limited capacity processors

Multiphase reading practices

Reading as a social versus private act

Nonlinear reading

The artichoke analogy for reading

Reading readiness

Reorienting readers' goals

Very little research examines the relationship between reading in a second language and language anxiety. We know that speaking and listening activities evoke higher levels of anxiety than reading or writing, but this finding may be due to a bias toward speaking and listening happening in the classroom and reading and writing happening outside the classroom, public versus private performances. For example, Swaffar (1991) and Young (1993) both noted the lack of reading material in introductory language textbooks. If learners are not provided sufficient opportunity to read, it becomes difficult to examine the relationship between reading and anxiety. Only recently have the benefits of second language reading on language development come to the forefront (Bernhardt 1991; Krashen 1993; Lee & VanPatten 1995; Swaffar, Arens, & Byrnes 1991), and only recently have language materials begun to reflect what Krashen calls the *power of reading*.

In this chapter, I will discuss the relationship between second language reading and language anxiety from two perspectives: cognitive and pedagogical. The discussion of cognition centers on the theory that language anxiety takes up processing capacity, thereby diminishing language learners' reading performance. The discussion of pedagogy centers on four misconceptions of the reading process: (1) that successful reading equals answering comprehension questions; (2) that reading is a private act; (3) that reading is a linear process; and (4) that comprehension is an absolute. In doing so, I hope to illustrate problems in second language reading instruction that surface from clashes between reading research and in-class practices and misconceptions about what it means to read in a second language. Such clashes most likely contribute to readers' language anxiety.

A COGNITIVE PERSPECTIVE ON ANXIETY

The working assumption underlying this chapter is that language anxiety can funnel off or otherwise take up processing capacity. An affective response to the task of reading can influence deriving meaning from text in several ways. First, heightened levels of anxiety may direct attentional capacity away from reading processes. Second, they may simply slow down and make effortful the application of reading processes such as letter and word recognition. Third, they may influence a reader's decision making processes, decisions about meaning, and strategy use. In other words, when less processing capacity is available, reading processes will not take place automatically and/or efficiently. When reading is slowed down, comprehension suffers in that readers will not be able to create coherent discourse models of what they read.

Empirical evidence supporting a relationship between language anxiety and second language reading is only beginning to emerge. Over the last two decades, research on reading has exposed the many complexities of the many processes involved in deriving meaning from printed text. MacIntyre and Gardner's research (1991, 1994a, 1994b) examines anxiety from a cognitive perspective and thus ties in with much of the reading research. They found that

51

CHAPTER 4
Clashes in L2
Reading: Research
Versus Practice
and Readers'
Misconceptions

high levels of anxiety significantly impede processing language input. Specifically, high levels of anxiety are associated with short digit spans, a finding that directly relates to reading processes. An anxious reader is taking in few digits (symbols or letters), thus making reading inefficient and laborious. To paraphrase MacIntyre and Gardner, anxiety creates cognitive deficits. Their cognitive perspective has served as a catalyst for new insights into the relationship between language anxiety and second language reading.

Cognitive researchers accept that human beings are limited-capacity processors. In other words, we have only so much attentional capacity to use during any processing task. VanPatten (1990) clearly demonstrated this phenomenon for second language learners. When given multiple listening tasks to perform simultaneously, their comprehension suffered. When reading in our native language, low-level processes such as letter and word recognition are automatic and require hardly any processing capacity to be taken up. Native language readers can experience effortful letter and word recognition when reading a bad photocopy or print that is very small. When someone's language system is underdeveloped or incomplete, such recognition processes take up processing capacity. The language learner must expend capacity on processes that are automatic for the native reader. As VanPatten's (1990) research demonstrated, comprehension suffers when capacity is allocated to competing tasks.

A PEDAGOGICAL PERSPECTIVE:
MISCONCEPTIONS ABOUT READING

In the remainder of this chapter I will examine four potential sources of anxiety for second language readers. In particular, I hypothesize that misconceptions about reading, both as a process and the pedagogical practices surrounding it, can lead to learner anxiety. Such anxiety creates cognitive deficits by taking up some of the already limited processing capacity. Funneling off capacity will negatively affect comprehension. I address each of these misconceptions in turn.

Misconception: Successful Reading Equals Answering Comprehension Questions

Traditionally, instructional practices surrounding reading can be summed up as follows. Readers are given a passage (usually no longer than four paragraphs) and fifteen comprehension questions to answer about the passage. They are told to go home and read and answer the questions, which they turn in the next day. This practice is problematic not only from the perspective of isolating the reader but also from the perspective of how readers tend to carry out the assignment. The typical reader uses the comprehension questions not to enhance their interaction with the text but to restrict it. For example, many a reader starts with the question and uses its wording to search for the answer in the text. The task is not reading the text but answering the questions; success is defined by getting answers to the questions. To permit second language readers to associate successful reading with answering questions about a short paragraph will eventually produce conflicts. For example, what happens when they are asked to read an article instead of a passage? or a short story? What happens when a reading assignment does not come accompanied by comprehension questions? Can these readers discuss content? A heightened level of anxiety is the most likely result because readers have been limited in their interactions with the text.

In response to this misconception many language educators have advocated structuring instructional practices differently. Swaffar, Arens, and Byrnes (1991) propose a six-stage approach to sequencing reading tasks. Phillips (1984) recommends adopting a three-phase approach to sequencing exercises that moves from skimming to scanning to comprehension checks. Lee and VanPatten (1995) propose that texts be read in three phases (i.e., preparation, guided interaction, and assimilation) with appropriate tasks and activities developed for each phase. I will present in subsequent pages preparation phase activities (Activities A and B), a consciousness-raising activity (Activity D), a confidence-building activity (Activity F), guided interaction activities (Activities E, G, and H), and an assimilation phase activity (Activity C). Lee and VanPatten (1995) recommend creating a string of such activities to support readers' interaction with each text. Certainly such a multiphase approach would be appropriate for structuring the interaction of the reading/discussion groups described below.

Misconception: Reading Is a Private Act

While some instructors are comfortable having students read in class, many others feel that reading, owing to time constraints, can and ought to take place outside class because of its "individualized" nature. Lee and VanPatten (1995) conceive of this difference as one of treating reading as a private versus social act and advocate that reading be recast as a social act. When reading is treated as a private act, readers are isolated from one another; they do not communicate. Readers who experience difficulty can certainly begin to feel more anxious about reading because they have no outlets. They may feel that they are the only ones who are having difficulties with the text because they have no reference point. They can internalize their fears rather than externalize them simply because they are alone.

To address the issue of reading as a private versus social act, reading needs to take place in class. I will present reading as a social act in Activities A–I (pp. 54–60) in that these activities always refer to working with classmates. Alternatively, reading can be assigned outside of class but still be constructed as a social act by forming reading/discussion/work groups. Such work groups are more common in the sciences than in language study, but they serve the same purpose. The instructor would first need to form work groups and incorporate such groups into the fabric of the class. The readings would then be assigned as a collaborative group project. The reading materials would have to be oriented toward group work, and, by incorporating synthesis activities (exemplified below) into the materials, the group would have a specific task toward which to work.

Misconception: Reading Is a Linear Process

53

CHAPTER 4
Clashes in L2
Reading: Research
Versus Practice
and Readers'
Misconceptions

Many second language readers misconceive of the reading process as a linear process. These readers want to approach the text by starting at the first word and proceeding through the text, word by word by word, until reaching the last word in the text. Their reading goal is to get through the text, to reach the bottom of the page, or to get to the end of the chapter. Following Lakoff and Johnson (1980), we live by linear metaphors such as "line our ducks up in a row," "toe the line," "follow the straight and narrow," "begin at the beginning," "you're on the right road (path)." Such metaphors reinforce the misconception that reading, too, is a linear construct.

Hosenfeld's classic research (1977) on reading strategies demonstrated that such readers do not reread what they do not understand; they simply move on. She also found that these readers tended to conceive of each word in the text as having equal importance, which caused them to try to look up every unknown word in a dictionary rather than skipping certain words or trying to use context to determine a word's meaning. Approaching a text linearly is not conducive to comprehension, and not comprehending may lead to anxiety. High levels of anxiety will decrease comprehension, and thus is born a cycle in which low comprehension and anxiety reinforce each other.

There are three ways to address the misconception that reading is a linear process. They are (a) to provide readers a different metaphor or analogy for the reading process; (b) to begin the process not at the first word of the text but with reading-readiness activities; and (c) to reorient the readers' goal from reaching the last word to organizing the information in the text. I will discuss each of these in turn.

Let's begin with an alternative analogy provided by Musumeci (1990) in the preface of her book on reading strategies, *Il carciofo* ("The Artichoke").

> Reading is somewhat analogous to eating an artichoke. The artichoke consists of many layers, the first of which are rather unceremoniously pulled away and eaten with the fingers, until the inedible "choke" is reached (which requires dexterity and a knife and fork!); finally conquering that, one arrives at the delectable "heart." A text can be approached in much the same way, from getting the "gist" at a very superficial layer to an in-depth reading to determine the author's point of view or the implications that may be drawn. Like eating an artichoke, reading takes time, especially if it is accompanied by discussion (p. xi).

Musumeci emphasizes the layers involved in comprehending a text, from superficial to deep. She also emphasizes that the process of discovery is analogous to peeling away layers and that each layer reveals something different than the other ones. Providing students this metaphor may help reconceive the reading process.

Research in both first and second language reading has demonstrated that the place to begin reading is not necessarily with the first word of the text. Schema-theoretic research carried out in the 1970s and 1980s revealed that individual readers contributed to the comprehension process, so that comprehension was then seen to result from the interaction of a reader's knowledge base and the textual characteristics and content. (Bransford [1979] provides a synthesis of this research.) Second language research demonstrated the effectiveness of intervening in the process before reading began (Hudson 1982; Lee 1986). Since Grellet's (1981) landmark work of suggested reading activities, all second language educators have advocated the use of prereading activities in order to activate the appropriate background knowledge in the readers (e.g., Lee & VanPatten 1995; Omaggio Hadley 1986; Phillips 1984; Swaffar, Arens, & Byrnes 1991). "To begin at the beginning" must take on new meaning. It must refer to beginning with the readers' knowledge rather than with the text.

Lee and VanPatten (1995, pp. 200–204) categorize reading-readiness activities into several types: brainstorming; use of titles, headings, and illustrations; applying world knowledge; scanning for specific information; and pretest/posttest formats. The following brainstorming activity demonstrates quite clearly that the process begins with what the readers already know about the topic. Note that while the first two steps of the activity focus on the readers, the last two steps focus on the text.

Activity A. Brainstorming

Step 1. Working with a partner or in groups of three, write five things you associate with Argentina [*or whatever the topic of the reading is*]. Try to come up with five very different things. You have 2 minutes.

    1.

    2.

    3.

    4.

    5.

Step 2. Write your list on the board and compare it to what the other groups came up with. Jot down any ideas that you did not already think of.

Step 3. Working individually, skim the text as quickly as possible to determine whether or not the ideas on the board are actually in the text. All you have to do is say whether or not the information is there; you do not have to know (not yet anyway!) what the author says about that information. You have 5 minutes.

Step 4. Share what you found with the class. As you do, erase from the board all those ideas that are *not* in the text. Do you all agree?

(Adapted from Lee & VanPatten, pp. 200–201.)

Whereas reading-readiness activities focus on what readers already know, it is important to always point readers toward the text. What readers know is a starting point but not an endpoint since, after all, the purpose of reading is to learn information.

The pretest/posttest format is an adaptation of a procedure used in psychological and educational experiments. By giving subjects the same test before and after an experimental procedure, researchers measure the effects of the procedure. In a reading situation, the test would measure how much a reader comprehended or learned from the material. Lee and VanPatten offer the following general direction lines for use with this type of reading-readiness activity.

55

CHAPTER 4
Clashes in L2
Reading: Research
Versus Practice
and Readers'
Misconceptions

Activity B. Test

Step 1. To the best of your ability, answer each of the following questions. Leave no question unanswered. If you are uncertain, then make as good a guess as you can. [*Test items can be true/false, multiple choice, or open-ended questions.*]

Step 2. Compare your answers with a partner [*or group or whole class*]. Did you have the same answers? Which answers are you sure of? Which ones are you unsure of?

Step 3. Now read through the passage looking for the answers to the test. How did you do?

(Adapted from Lee & VanPatten, p. 203.)

Working through the test items is analogous to peeling the outer layer of an artichoke. As readers do test items in Step 1 and discuss them in Step 2, they become aware of the topic of the passage and some of the content. They will have a set of expectations in place in their minds before they begin reading the passage.

The third way to address the misconception that reading is a linear process is to reorient the readers' goal from reaching the last word to organizing the information in the text. That is, readers could be given an activity that requires them to go back into a text in order to organize, synthesize, and assimilate the information. Whereas reading-readiness activities alter how readers approach a text, assimilation activities alter how readers respond to a text. Reaching the last word of the text is no longer a signal that the reader is through; carrying out the synthesis activity marks the end point. Again, the artichoke analogy is appropriate here in that the synthesis activity gets the readers to the heart of the text.

Many of the writing activities Leki presents in this volume (Chapter 5)—for example, looping, cubing, outlining, and mapping—are synthesis activities that could be used in conjunction with a reading passage. The following synthesis activity refers to an article that relates information on an isolated region of Ecuador where the inhabitants regularly live beyond 100 years. The article speculates why the inhabitants live so long and what effects "civilization" will have on the region's inhabitants.

Activity C. Synthesis

Step 1. Go back to each section of the reading and summarize the content of the section in one sentence.

    A. Introduction

_____

_____

B. Vilcabamba is a paradise almost isolated from the world!

C. An attitude toward life, a decisive factor in longevity!

D. The arrival of civilization, has it affected the population?

E. Conclusion . . .

Step 2. Using the sentences you have written for Step 1, write a paragraph in response to the question posed in the subtitle of the article; are civilization and longevity compatible? Note: A paragraph is more than just a series of unconnected sentences; you have to link your ideas together in order to have a cohesive paragraph. To do so, you can use words and phrases like *therefore, on the other hand, in general, nevertheless.*

(Adapted from Lee, Binkowski, & VanPatten 1994, pp. 135–136.)

Synthesis activities provide the readers the mechanism by which to go back through what they have read. It is the means by which they can organize their thoughts. Whereas reading-readiness activities begin the process by focusing on the readers themselves, synthesis activities cap the process by focusing on the text.

To summarize, second language readers who view the reading process as linear may find themselves in a cycle of low comprehension and increased anxiety. To address both of these, readers could be given a new analogy for the reading process: peeling away the layers of an artichoke. Additionally, two types of instructional practices address the issues of comprehension and anxiety by reorienting the reading process. Reading-readiness activities that focus on the readers' knowledge clearly demonstrate that the process is not linear, that the process does not begin with the first word of the text. Synthesis activities that focus on integrating the information in a text clearly demonstrate that the act of reading is not completed by simply arriving at the last word of the text.

Misconception: Comprehension Is an Absolute

Another misconception that causes second language readers anxiety is that they conceive of comprehension as an absolute. That is, readers express frustration over not being able to comprehend every word and idea in a text. In the extreme, second language readers have been known to declare that they have understood nothing in a text when in fact they have understood some of the text. What these readers do is define successful reading as comprehending everything. Of course, repeated frustration may lead readers to be anxious about reading in general.

57

CHAPTER 4
Clashes in L2
Reading: Research
Versus Practice
and Readers'
Misconceptions

To address this problem, second language readers can be taught to view comprehension as consisting of shades of gray and to redefine what *success* means. The first requires a certain amount of consciousness raising, just as giving readers a new analogy did. The second can be addressed through instructional practices and techniques.

The following activity aims to raise readers' consciousness regarding comprehension. It has been designed for class discussion.

Activity D. Consciousness raising

Step 1. Work in groups of three or four. Use the following questions as the basis for interviewing each other.
  1. Do you read magazines while waiting in the grocery checkout line? Which ones?
  2. Do you read magazines in the dentist's or doctor's office? Why?
  3. Do you read in bed? When? Why?
  4. Do you read your history assignments before going to class or after? Why?
  5. Do you subscribe to any magazines? Which ones?
  6. Do you read novels for pleasure?

Step 2. Using the information you have gained from the interviews, write a profile of the group's reading behavior and present it to the rest of the class. How much does the class read and under what circumstances?

Step 3. As a class, comment on each of the questions listed in Step 1. In which contexts is comprehension going to be the greatest? the least? Are all reading contexts similar?

This activity should demonstrate to the readers that they do not read everything the same way or for the same purpose. Reading a magazine in the dentist's office is a distraction. Reading the *National Enquirer* at the checkout stand is a way to pass the time. The conclusion to which the discussion should lead is that we read differently according to the context in which we read. This conclusion helps set the stage for the next activity.

Activity E is designed to focus readers on performing one particular task for each text they are directed to read. The activity serves to heighten their awareness that they do not need to understand everything; they only need to do the task required of them. This activity begins to help readers redefine successful reading. The new definition of success they will be working toward is that success equals performing the task. Moreover, if they can perform the task, then they have comprehended enough!

Activity E. It's not the text, it's the task

Step 1. Following the title of each article is a question for you to answer.
  a. "The Marvelous Marine Life of the Caribbean"
     How many species of fish are mentioned in the section on coral reefs?

b. "The Trouble with Violence on TV"
How many reasons does the author give in favor of censoring TV networks?

c. "The Centenarians of Vilcabamba, Ecuador"
What are the names of the people living in Vilcabamba who are over the age of 100?

d. "Where the President Went Wrong and How He Can Get Back on Track"
What issues does the author say the President handled poorly?

Step 2. Verify your answers with two or three classmates. Then, describe how you went about finding the answer to each question.

Activity E is also a consciousness-raising activity. The instructor's role is to lead the discussion of what it means to comprehend enough. Eventually, as reading instruction moves into more complex levels of comprehension, synthesis activities can be used by readers as the measure of how much they have comprehended.

Unknown words are often a source of anxiety. Anxious readers may feel that these words will block their comprehension of the passage and may spend as much time looking words up as they do trying to comprehend the global meaning of the passage. The following activity addresses the issue of known versus unknown and allows the reader to exert some control over the unknown.

Activity F. Blue for the known, yellow for the unknown

Step 1. Using a yellow highlighting marker, go through the reading passage and mark the words you already know.

Step 2. Using a blue highlighting marker, go through the reading passage and mark the words you do not know.

Step 3. You may look up in the dictionary only five of the words you don't know. Which ones will they be?

Step 4. Now read the passage.

The highlighting markers physically demonstrate to the readers how much of the passage they already know. The activity should build readers' sense of confidence before they approach the text.

Anxiety that stems from viewing comprehension as an absolute, an all or nothing proposition, can also be addressed through strategy training. A fairly typical exchange between a reader and an instructor is the following:

READER: I didn't understand that text.
INSTRUCTOR: What didn't you understand?
READER: The whole thing.

It may be the case that the reader comprehended nothing, but it also may be that the reader simply did not comprehend bits and pieces of the text. The reading strategy that might best benefit this reader is metacognitive awareness. We can teach language learners to monitor their comprehension and identify when they do not comprehend. Once they identify what they do not comprehend, they would then need to employ other strategies to work through the passage, but at least the reader would not simply push along to the end of the text in a more or less mindless manner.

59

CHAPTER 4
Clashes in L2
Reading: Research
Versus Practice
and Readers'
Misconceptions

If readers approach comprehension as an absolute, they will not engage in efficient reading. Inefficiency will require attentional capacity to be allocated, and it may cause anxiety, which would also require some attentional capacity to be expended. To address the problems of limited attentional capacity and the misconception of comprehension as an absolute, instructors can divide readings into small, manageable units. Some texts naturally break up into small units through the use of headings and subtitles. Other texts might need to be broken up into thematic groupings, by the instructor or by the readers as part of the reading process. The following activity directs the readers to do that.

Activity G. Finding the thematic groupings

Step 1. After the brief introductory paragraph, this article examines three themes related to marine algae farms. This article, therefore, could be divided into three sections:
  I. The cultivation and processing of marine algae
  II. The nutritive and economic value of algae
  III. The commercial possibilities of algae
Read the article rapidly in order to find each of these themes. Then, look for where the author first begins to develop the theme and write the name of the section next to that paragraph.

Step 2. Verify your answers with the class.

(Adapted from Lee, Binkowski, & VanPatten 1994, p. 104.)

Alternatively, readers can be directed to read paragraph by paragraph. But as they do, they should be given a task to complete that indicates to them that they have comprehended enough. For example, readers could be asked to select three key words to help them remember the content or to write a one-sentence summary of the content. The following activity demonstrates this technique.

Activity H. After each paragraph

Step 1. Read the first paragraph of the article. Then, select up to three key words that will help you remember what the paragraph is about.

Step 2. Now, write a one-sentence summary of the paragraph incorporating the key words.

Step 3. Show your key words and sentence to two or three classmates. Did they choose the same words? Did they write similar sentences?

The following activity also accomplishes the goal of monitoring readers' comprehension. It focuses readers on various textual elements so that they use the pieces to build a picture of the whole.

Activity I. Building to the whole

Step 1. Read the first three paragraphs of the article. Find and underline the sentence that you think expresses the main idea of the article. Check your answer with several classmates.

Step 2. Continue working with your classmates. Which of the following is the best paraphrase of that sentence? Be sure to verify your selection with the rest of the class.
   a. Men live shorter lives, and the article will explain some things men can do to lengthen their life expectancy.
   b. Anyone can control their life expectancy, and the article will explain how.
   c. Women's life expectancies are higher than those of men, and the article will explain why that is and what men can do about it.

Step 3. We have purposefully left off the title of this article. Many times (although not always) the title helps us figure out the main idea of an article. Which of the following do you think is the original title of this article? Make your own selection, then see what the rest of the class chose.
   a. Women, men, and longevity
   b. Why do men live shorter lives than women?
   c. How can you live a longer life?
   d. Female superiority: Sociological, biological, and cultural factors

(Adapted from Young & Wolf 1994, pp. 202–203.)

CONCLUSION

In this chapter, I discussed the relationship between second language reading and language anxiety from two perspectives: cognitive and pedagogical. The discussion of cognition centered on the theory that language anxiety takes up processing capacity, a limited commodity. When anxiety funnels off some processing capacity, reading processes will not take place automatically and/or efficiently. Slow and inefficient reading would diminish comprehension, which in turn could create an even more heightened level of anxiety.

The discussion of pedagogy centered on four misconceptions of the reading process. First, I examined the misconception that successful reading equals answering comprehension questions. The traditional comprehension question invites readers to conceptualize reading as the task of answering the questions, not reading the text, thereby restricting the readers' interactions with the text. The remainder of the chapter presented alternative instructional practices.

Second, I examined the misconception that reading is a private act that takes place outside the classroom by an isolated reader. Such isolation invites frustration and anxiety, which take up processing capacity. The instructional practices presented in this chapter were all cast as social acts involving multiple readers who interact not only with the text but with each other.

Third, I examined the misconception that reading is a linear process that begins with the first word on the page and proceeds directly to the last word on a page. Second language readers who view the reading process as linear may find themselves in a cycle of low comprehension and increased anxiety. To address both of these, readers could be given a new analogy for the reading process: peeling away the layers of an artichoke. Two types of reading activities were recommended as a means to address this misconception: reading-readiness and synthesis activities. The former demonstrate that the process does not begin with the first word on the page, and the latter provide readers with a concrete goal different from the traditional approach of answering a series of comprehension questions.

Finally, I examined the misconception that comprehension is an absolute. Many readers believe incorrectly that they understand everything in their native language and should also understand everything in their second language. To address this, several types of instructional practices were recommended: consciousness-raising activities about comprehension; instructional practices that monitor ongoing comprehension; dividing readings into manageable units; and strategy training.

The preceding discussion attempted to illuminate certain aspects of the relationship between second language reading and reading anxiety, demonstrating ways in which readers' affective states affect reading processes. Certain problems in second language reading instruction surface from clashes between reading research and in-class practices and misconceptions about what it means to read in a second language. The activities presented in this chapter demonstrate a variety of ways in which instructional practices can work to lower anxiety.

61

CHAPTER 4
Clashes in L2
Reading: Research
Versus Practice
and Readers'
Misconceptions

PORTFOLIO ASSIGNMENTS

1. a. In this chapter, Lee introduces several activity types that, at the same time, help reduce reading anxiety and provide effective reading instruction. Find an authentic passage on a topic of interest to students and design one reading activity using one or a combination of the phases he suggests, such as a preparation phase, an interaction phase, or an assimilation phase.
   b. Share your activity with your classmates and have them guess which activity phase(s) you have applied.
2. a. Examine a first- or second-year FL language textbook for an activity that could be adapted to more effectively promote reading comprehension and reduce anxiety associated with reading in an SL or FL.
   b. Adapt the reading activity so that it also dispels readers' misconceptions about reading comprehension and reflects a more effective approach to reading instruction.
   c. Describe in writing (or orally in class) your activity, contrasting the original and adapted versions and illustrating precisely how your activity addresses learners' misconceptions about reading, which often lead to reading anxiety, and how the adapted version is a more effective reading activity.

ACTION RESEARCH

1. a. Administer the Reading Anxiety self-report questionnaire (Appendix F) to six beginning FL or SL learners characterized as strong, average, and weak language learners (two per category).
   b. Tally learners' responses to the twenty-one items and identify the top three items that indicated the highest levels of reading anxiety.
   c. Compare your findings with your class.
   d. Can any of the top three sources of reading anxiety be rooted in learner misconceptions? Which ones?

2. a. Interview one strong language learner and one weak one to determine whether they hold misconceptions about reading comprehension.

   You may use the following statements (or make up your own) to elicit students' perception. Students can agree or disagree with the statements. Each one reflects a misconception about FL reading. You may also make up your own statements. Remind students to apply these statements to reading in the FL, as opposed to the native language.

   - Reading is something you do alone.
   - If you can correctly answer the comprehension questions at the end of a reading passage, then you have successfully comprehended the passage.
   - Reading consists of starting with the first word in a text and proceeding through it word by word until the last word is read.
   - When you come across a word you don't know, you should look it up in the dictionary.
   - When you read a text, you either understand it or you don't.

   b. Share your findings with the class.
   c. What do the class findings as a whole suggest?

REFERENCES

Bransford, J. D. (1979). *Human cognition: Learning, understanding and remembering.* Belmont, CA: Wadsworth.

Bernhardt, E. B. (1991). *Reading development in a second language: Theoretical, empirical and classroom perspectives.* Norwood, NJ: Ablex.

Grellet, F. (1981). *Developing reading skills: A practical guide to reading comprehension exercises.* Cambridge: Cambridge University Press.

Hosenfeld, C. (1977). A preliminary investigation of the strategies of successful and non-successful readers. *System, 5,* 110–123.

Hudson, T. (1982). The effects of induced schemata on the "short-circuit" in L2 reading performance. *Language Learning, 32,* 1–30.

Krashen, S. (1993). *The power of reading: Insights from the research.* Englewood, CO: Libraries Unlimited.

Lakoff, G., & Johnson, M. (1980). *Metaphors we live by.* Chicago: University of Chicago Press.

63

CHAPTER 4
Clashes in L2
Reading: Research
Versus Practice
and Readers'
Misconceptions

Lee, J. F. (1986). Background knowledge and L2 reading. *Modern Language Journal, 70,* 350–354.

Lee, J. F. (1990). Constructive processes evidenced by early stage non-native readers of Spanish in comprehending an expository text. *Hispanic Linguistics, 4* (1), 129–148.

Lee, J. F., Binkowski, A., & VanPatten, B. (1994). *Ideas: Estrategias, lecturas, actividades y composiciones.* New York: McGraw-Hill.

Lee, J. F., & VanPatten, B. (1995). *Making communicative language teaching happen.* New York: McGraw-Hill.

Leki, I. (1997). Techniques for Reducing Second Language Writing Anxiety (in present volume).

MacIntyre, P. D., & Gardner. (1991). Language anxiety: Its relation to other anxieties and to processing in native and second languages. *Language Learning, 41,* 513–534.

MacIntyre, P. D., & Gardner, R. C. (1994a). The effects of induced anxiety on cognitive processing in second language learning. *Studies in Second Language Acquisition, 16,* 1–17.

MacIntyre, P. D., & Gardner, R. C. (1994b). The subtle effects of language anxiety on cognitive processing in the second language. *Language Learning, 44,* 283–305.

Musumeci, D. (1990). *Il carciofo: Strategie di lettura e proposte di attività.* New York: McGraw-Hill.

Phillips, J. K. (1984). Practical implications of recent research in reading. *Foreign Language Annals, 17,* 285–296.

Omaggio Hadley, A. C. (1986). *Teaching language in context: Proficiency oriented instruction.* Boston, MA: Heinle & Heinle.

Swaffar, J. K. (1991). Language learning is more than learning language: Rethinking reading and writing tasks in textbooks for beginning language study. In B. F. Freed (Ed.), *Foreign Language Acquisition Research and the Classroom.* Lexington, MA: D. C. Heath, pp. 221–251.

Swaffar, J. K., Arens, K. M., & Byrnes, H. (1991). *Reading for meaning: An integrated approach to language learning.* Upper Saddle River, NJ: Prentice Hall.

VanPatten, B. (1990). Attending to form and content in the input: An experiment in consciousness. *Studies in Second Language Acquisition, 12* (3), 287–301.

Young, D. J. (1993). Processing strategies of foreign language readers: Authentic and edited input. *Foreign Language Annals, 26,* 451–468.

Young, D. J., & Wolf, D. F. (1994). *Esquemas.* Fort Worth: Holt, Rinehart and Winston.

Techniques for Reducing Second Language Writing Anxiety

Ilona Leki
The University of Tennessee

Personal Reflections

a. What feelings do you associate with writing assignments? Be specific if those feelings are different depending on the course content, the writing assignment, or the length of the assignment. Look over the words you used to describe your feelings for signs of being an apprehensive writer.
b. Take Daly and Miller's Writing Apprehension Test (Appendix G) and compare your results with your response in **a.** Are you an apprehensive writer?
c. When you have to write or compose, what steps do you take to prepare for writing?
d. When you turned in a composition or paper in your FL classes, what type of criteria did your instructors use to evaluate your work? Did they focus primarily on accuracy, or did they also take into account content?

Fundamental Concepts

Writing apprehension	Looping
Branching/clustering	Peer responding
Cubing	Outlining
Drafting	Sequenced writing projects
Heuristics	

Why should writing create anxiety? In some ways it would seem that writing should be the least anxiety-producing of the language functions. Unlike when listening and reading, when writing one controls the language and the content of the message. Unlike speaking, writing allows time to think about the message, to find words and syntactic structures to communicate the message, and to change the content and the language after the first attempt is written down. Yet many people find writing difficult even in the native language (L1). (See Daly & Miller 1975a, 1975b for a description of an instrument to measure writing apprehension; see MacIntyre & Gardner 1994 for a contemporary discussion of the effects of anxiety on cognitive processing in the second language [L2]; see Pajares & Johnson 1994 for a discussion of writing apprehension in relation to performance outcomes.)

Early research on writing anxiety developed out of studies of communication apprehension (McCroskey 1970) and referred to the problem as *writing apprehension* (Daly & Miller 1975a). According to Raisman (1982), the effects of writing anxiety, or writing apprehension, can be significant. Students often cope with writing anxiety by choosing careers that do not require much writing, by avoiding writing situations altogether, and by completing writing assignments as swiftly as possible without giving much thought to them, so as to minimize the discomfort evoked by writing anxiety. Raisman contends that some students accept the notion that they are not good writers and knowingly turn in sloppy writing because by accepting careless writing, "they get the illusion that they are directing their actions and the anxiety is not" (p. 23).

Anecdotal accounts suggest that even professional writers experience a resistance to beginning the writing process. Writers engage in avoidance tactics such as waiting until the night before a deadline to get started, finding that the house simply cannot wait any longer to be vacuumed from top to bottom, preferring cleaning out closets to finally sitting down at the desk and writing. Many people also experience "writer's block," whereby even after the writer bites the bullet, puts away the vacuum cleaner, and sits down to write, no words come, or every word, phrase, or sentence written down seems completely unacceptable and is scratched out and thrown out.

The purpose of this chapter is to sensitize teachers to the phenomenon referred to as *writing anxiety* and to suggest approaches to writing instruction that may reduce anxiety in high-writing-apprehensive language learners. The activities suggested in this chapter are based on pedagogically sound approaches to writing instruction and are also appropriate for learners who do not experience writing anxiety.

REVIEW OF WRITING ANXIETY RESEARCH

Research on writing apprehension indicates that writing anxiety clearly negatively affects writing performance (see Pajares & Johnson 1994; Smith 1984). Dislike of writing stems from a variety of sources, most of which are, sadly, the probable results of educational experiences. The primary sources of writing anxiety stem from an individual's writing ability, the degree of preparation the writer has to do to successfully complete a writing task, the misconceptions learners have about writing, the fear of being evaluated and judged on the basis of writing tasks, and the mixed messages writers often receive in the predominant approach to writing instruction that exists in the native language, as well as the foreign language (Daly & Miller 1975a, 1975b; Fox 1980; Pajares & Johnson 1994; Raisman 1982; Smith 1984).

Students anxious about their writing often avoid writing and writing instruction, thus neglecting opportunities to develop their writing skills. They also approach writing differently from low-anxiety writers. They take fewer risks in their writing, write shorter compositions, are less straightforward and clear when they write, compose longer sentences, use more jargon and nominalizations, and are more prone to procrastinate (Smith 1984). It is possible that individuals who experience writing anxiety are not skillful writers and that their anxiety merely reflects this awareness. However, Daly (1979) believes that more research into this relationship needs to be done before we can conclude that poor writing skills cause writing anxiety. He posits, instead, a reciprocal interaction between skills and anxiety, since highly skilled writers can also experience high levels of writing anxitety.

Since poor writing skills may be a source of writing anxiety, one approach to reducing writing apprehension in language learners is to design writing instruction that helps learners develop their writing skills and maximizes successful writing at the same time. Fox (1980) developed a writing program designed to reduce writing apprehension by carefully preparing students for writing tasks. His program offers students activities that help them achieve the ultimate objectives of the writing assignment by breaking down the writing process into manageable pieces (also see Smith 1984).

Another source of writing anxiety, documented by Newkirk (1979), originates from perfectionism. Newkirk contends that students who strive for perfection often fail to realize that even the most proficient and eloquent writers create various drafts of their work. Common sense suggests that emphasis on a process approach to writing, as opposed to a product-oriented approach, would guide learners through various drafts of their writing and may help reduce writing anxiety.

As mentioned, a major source of writing anxiety comes from learners' fear of being evaluated and judged on the basis of their writing ability. Precisely because it is the writer who determines the content and form of the message, he or she may feel particularly exposed and vulnerable to an audience. Writers are judged by the sophistication of the ideas they express, by the cleverness of the arguments they develop, by the range of the vocabulary they use, by the aesthetic quality of their texts, and, most terrifying of all, by the *errors* they may make in mechanics, spelling, morphology, syntax, and/or word choice; a writer's intelligence, experience, education, meticulousness, and accuracy are all on the line. Furthermore, a great deal of the educational testing that students experience takes place through writing. Thus, not only do students feel threatened by evaluation of their written texts, but these texts also expose every misunderstanding in and every tiny detail missing from the material they were expected to cover (Raisman 1982).

Yet, in content courses, students can nevertheless expect professors to evaluate their written work by giving credit for correct information even if the writing shows flaws. It is in the courses devoted to language, such as composition courses and foreign language courses, where good content typically cannot save students and where papers are returned covered with red correction marks, little stab wounds marking every linguistic and print code transgression the writer has committed. To make matters worse, it is precisely in these "no-content" language courses that students are the most confused about "what the teacher wants" in the first place. Fox's program to reduce writing apprehension acknowledges the learners' fear of evaluation by using peer evaluations instead of teacher evaluations. He argues that peer evaluation can help alleviate much of the writing anxiety that originates from the fear of being evaluated and judged by the teacher.

Much of the frustration and anxiety learners experience may also be rooted in the mixed messages they receive from well-intentioned teachers. We tell students that we are interested in their ideas about a topic, that we want to hear what they think or have to say. But neither writing teachers nor students seem to really expect that a piece of student writing in a language class will be judged by the ideas expressed (Cohen 1987; Leki 1991; Zamel 1985). When papers are returned in writing or language classes, students find that most comments address grammar, mechanics, and/or organization of the paper. Students would probably consider evaluation on the basis of ideas expressed or opinions held something of an outrage (Radecki & Swales 1988). And yet, when teachers make such comments as "you haven't expressed your ideas clearly/well," "your paper is disorganized," or "your writing is a little vague," exactly what these comments mean is so unclear to students that they are often heard to complain that a low grade is the result of the teacher's not agreeing with the student's ideas. As writing teachers we may be subjected to racist, sexist, or politically insensitive or even repugnant ideas, and yet many writing teachers adhere to the belief that students have the right to express such ideas and that we are not in a position to give students' papers low marks because we may find the ideas distasteful or the logic spurious.

Thus, we create a problem for writers when we send a mixed message about how we evaluate a piece of writing, claiming that we value their ideas and yet showing we ignore their ideas in favor of how they express those ideas. In this uneasy balance between form and content, a special problem arises for adult second language writers. In addition to all the hardships that writing creates, these writers experience the frustration of having ideas but not being able to find the L2 forms for expressing them, of knowing what to say but not how to say it. Even relatively advanced L2 learners experience the realization that the sophistication, complexity, and subtlety of their thought are destroyed by their limited knowledge and capacity in their second language, suitable only to reflect simplistic, flat, bald understandings on the level of a child. Expression of thought is so constrained by this limited language capability that L2 writers may never experience the feeling that what they have written truly expresses their ideas. One of Silva's (1993) students complained, for example, "I have to give up some good ideas for I cannot find the available words." Another student struggles with vocabulary, not daring to use more than the most common words, although she knows that this makes her text "wordy and powerless." A third talks about being forced to write superficially, having to ignore "deeper meanings" that he cannot express in his L2.

Despite the note of frustration in these L2 writing students' comments about their inability to express their *ideas*, historically, writing in second language classrooms was seen (and in some L2 classes still is seen) primarily as a means of practicing grammar. But many language and writing teachers and Second Language Acquisition (SLA) researchers have come to believe that it is only by engaging in a language activity that learners become proficient in that activity. Thus, if writing is a means of expressing thought in language, facility with that skill can come about only by focusing on expressing thought in language and will not come about by focusing on correctness of language. (See, for example, low-level L2 textbooks such as those by Chan 1989; Reid 1987; Segal & Pavlik 1985; Shoemaker 1985; White & Arndt 1991.) Such notions are supported by L1 language acquisition researchers who maintain that we learn the rules of our first languages *because* we engage in conversation, not that we engage in conversation because we have acquired language. Using this reasoning, L2 writing teachers might say that writers do not learn to express ideas as a result of acquiring, learning, or practicing language, but rather they learn language as a result of attempting to express ideas.

An approach to teaching L2 writing that focuses on grammar, then, suffers from at least two essential flaws: (1) It is not primarily focused on ideas and therefore denies students practice with expressing ideas. Yet it is the very practice with expressing ideas that in the long run allows L2 learners to develop range and flexibility in their language use. (2) By definition, using writing primarily as a means of practicing grammar exposes students' still tentative grasp on the L2, potentially breeding excessive caution and creating maximal anxiety and fear of failure in L2 students.

The remainder of this paper, then, will focus on ways to reduce L2 writers' anxiety about writing by adopting a nonpunitive, nonjudgmental, non-mixed-message process approach to teaching L2 writing, one that regards writing as primarily a means of exploring and expressing ideas. The activities center on the use of techniques from process approaches to teaching writing and sequenced writing assignments.

L2 WRITING TECHNIQUES FOR REDUCING WRITING ANXIETY

One of the most useful insights process approaches to teaching writing have yielded is the realization that a piece of writing does not have to be done alone or at one sitting. Experienced writers break up the process and often seek responses to their work from other people. In the L2 classroom that views writing as a means of exploring and expressing ideas, students are encouraged to use heurisitcs to think up and through ideas, to accept the notion that a piece of writing may go through several intermediate, imperfect drafts, and to have colleagues read their papers while focusing on ideas. The following section, then, will cover:

1. a variety of heuristics or invention strategies to help intermediate and advanced FL/SL students prepare for writing and to develop their writing skills, thereby decreasing writing anxiety for some students;
2. drafting hints that teach writing as a process, as opposed to a one-time product;
3. suggestions for peer responses that empower the writer and emphasize peer response to writing, as opposed to instructor evaluation of writing;
4. the use of writing journals and sequenced writing assignments that focus the writer on content, as opposed to form exclusively.

Heuristics

The literature on composition details many techniques for generating ideas and supports the idea that such techniques lead to better and more easily produced writing (Elbow 1973; Gungle & Taylor 1989; Miller 1983; Raimes 1983, 1984; Rico 1986; Smith 1984; Spack 1984). L2 students may be familiar with some of the following techniques from their L1 writing classes. Examples of each of these techniques are included in the Appendix and are taken from I. Leki (1995), *Academic Writing: Exploring Processes and Strategies.* New York: St. Martin's Press. (All examples are from English L2 student writers.)

Brainstorming

In a group, writers quickly jot down any and all ideas associated with the topic they plan to write about. Being able to rely on the ideas of others to supplement their own ideas helps writers feel less alone and thus less anxious about what to say on a topic. Since this activity often produces an abundance of ideas, writers have the luxury of choosing those ideas that are particularly interesting to them. They work from abundance rather than from scarcity. The following is a student example of this technique.

Student Example: Brainstorming

SUNDAY NIGHT, MASSEY HALL LOBBY

Noisy: everybody returning from weekends

Crowded

Parents, boyfriends

Floor wet and white, snow

Coke machine noisy

R.A. at front desk bored, answers phone

Two guys playing Pac-Man

Others waiting

One guy on the phone for a long time

Two others waiting to call

Couples sitting in lobby, laugh, talk, forbidden to go upstairs in this dorm

Employees from pizza places delivering Sunday dinner

Snowball thrown in from outside, becoming a water hole

Someone playing piano, several voices singing a carol

Change machine broken, I have been asked for change twice

Girls come down for Coke, laundry tickets, sweets

Suitcases everywhere

Elevator broken

Cold as a bus station

R.A.'s pictures on the walls

On the opposite wall, announcements for parties, movies, free coupons, videos

Big blackboard in front of the doors, announcing that *Purple Rain* is playing

Poster saying "Happy Birthday, Linda. We love you." I know her.

Garfield muppet on the table—forgotten by someone

From the window see white smoke from the heater system outside

The following is what the student eventually wrote based on the preceding brainstorming session.

On Sunday afternoon, Massey Hall lobby looks as busy as a bus station. The place is really crowded because the students are coming back from their weekends away. Parents or boyfriends are carrying suitcases and standing around speaking with female residents. At one end of the lobby, two boys are playing a video game, "Pac Man," while some others are waiting for their girlfriends. Other girls come down into the lobby very often to buy a Coke or laundry tickets. Every ten minutes, employees from Domino's Pizza or Mr. Gatti's deliver pizzas for Sunday dinner. As in every public place, the lobby is very noisy. Couples sitting on the blue sofas behind the front desk are laughing and speaking animatedly. The Coke machine next to them is terribly noisy, and it's difficult to hear the piano in the small room close to the lobby. The telephone keeps on ringing in the lobby office, and the R.A. has to answer it every minute. Everybody seems too busy to notice details in the lobby. Nobody is interested in the poster announcing Linda's birthday nor in the announcements for parties and movies on the wall opposite the front desk. The blackboard in front of the doors, announcing the movie *Purple Rain* for Monday night, seems useless too. And people constantly open the doors to come in or go out, so it's cold. Just like in a bus station.

Anne Gouraud (France)

Freewriting

71

*CHAPTER 5
Techniques for
Reducing Second
Language Writing
Anxiety*

The writer sets aside 10 or 15 minutes and, in effect, "dumps memory" on the topic in focus. Many writers have trouble beginning a writing project because they feel they must begin at the beginning and at the outset find the right ideas and the right words to express what they want to say, an attitude unfortunately fostered by timed writing exams. Freewriting for 10–15 minutes, like brainstorming, produces a large amount of material quickly and frees the writer from the concern that the writing must be good or ready to read after the first attempt to address the topic. Here is an example of one student's freewriting and a draft of her subsequent paper.

Student Example, Freewriting

> Indonesia is not as popular as other places such as Thailand, Philippines, etc.—don't know the reason why—maybe it's not publicized that much—especially in America, almost nobody knows what or where Indonesia is. Sort of aggravating experience—feel embarrassed. Lots of interesting sights—Australian people go to Indonesia very often but seldom see American tourists. Bali is often visited—most popular place, often called Paradise Island because of its beautifulness—many beaches—clean and refreshing. Java has many points of interest too. Yogya often called tourist city because of its many temples and again it has three beaches. Jakarta, capital city is metropolitan city—filthy side and beautiful side all together—island of Sumatra—mostly contains forests but North side, Lake Toba—beautiful scenery.

The following is a draft of the essay this student eventually wrote based on her freewriting.

> Although many people in America have never been to Indonesia, I think Indonesia is a place they must visit at least once in a lifetime. Part of the reason the Americans seldom visit Indonesia is because they do not know much about the place. Another reason is that they do not think there is anything worth going for. But they are wrong. In fact, there are many beautiful places in this country. For example, on the island of Bali there are two beautiful, white, and sunny beaches. Kuta is especially beautiful when the sun sets, and Janur has a spectacular view when the sun rises. Another example is on the island of Java, where there are two cities that are very popular for their beautiful sites; they are the cities of Yogya and Jakarta. In Yogya, there are many ancient temples, and in Jakarta there is a big playground similar to Disneyland. The last example of a tourist attraction is on the island of Sumatra; there is one most particular point of interest there and that is Lake Toba. When we see Late Toba from the mountains surrounding it, it creates a breathtaking view. These are just three of the many beautiful places in Indonesia, and I think it is a shame that more tourists don't know about them.

Prandanita Soepono (Indonesia)

Looping

This technique may be useful in helping writers discover more precisely what they might have to say about a subject. It consists of three sessions of 5-minute freewrites. At the end of the first session, the writers reread the text they have written looking for the text's center of gravity—that is, the most interesting or most important point they seem to have been moving toward. This idea is then summarized (or copied from the text) in one sentence that the writer is instructed to try to keep mentally in focus during the next session of freewriting. This is repeated for the next two sessions. On completion, the writers usually feel they have moved closer to what they want to say about their topic. To demonstrate how looping works, teachers might suggest a general topic, such as "Traditions." Given this topic, students write for 5 minutes, reread their writing, and then summarize the gist or note their most interesting idea in a single sentence, which then functions to guide the next 5-minute writing session.

Branching and Clustering

Like brainstorming, this technique calls for writers, in groups or alone, to make quick associations with the chosen topic, but it also aids writers by allowing graphic representation of associated terms and ideas. In branching and clustering, the topic under discussion is noted in the middle of the board or on a piece of paper and, as ideas associated with the topic are brainstormed, they are written down in related groupings around the central topic. This kind of preliminary organization often prompts the inclusion of

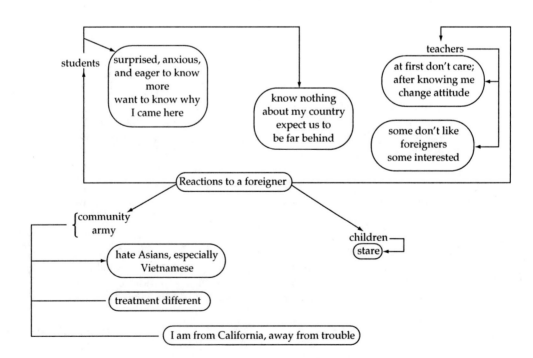

yet further associations. At the end of a branching exercise, writers have not only a number of ideas associated with the topic they will write about, but they also have ideas that are grouped together in clusters. Teachers might introduce branching by having the entire class work together to create a cluster on, for example, "Being 16 Years Old." One branch of the central topic might list associations with parents, another recollections of high school, another relations with the opposite sex, and so on. The following is the first draft of a student essay written on the basis of the branching-clustering example on page 72.

First Essay Draft

It is a great experience to be in a foreign country and trying to communicate with the local people even though sometimes it turns out to be a nightmare. First, the students, who are surprised to know where I am from and anxious to know more. That really is a good start, but soon I realize that they know nothing. They even expect people in Singapore to be staying in tree-houses. What a shame. Most of them expect my home country to be still very far behind in science and technology and still to have a lot of catching up to do. Therefore, when I explain to them what is really happening, they are surprised and say, "I don't believe it!" Second, the instructors who just don't care about where I am from when they first meet me. Anyway after some time when they start to know me well enough they start to get interested in me. They ask about what is going on in my home country, especially in the architectural field. They are surprised to find out how advanced we are. All these instructors are all very nice people, but there are a few instructors in the school don't like foreigners. If I signed up for their classes, I would be in a lot of trouble. I could expect myself to be deserted by the rest of the class and, of course, to get a low grade too.

Third, the community, which I consider to be the most interesting, because this is the group where I have all kinds of strange encounters. Generally, the retired army hate Asians, especially Vietnamese. Since all Asians look the same to them, I get in a lot of trouble when I try to communicate with them. As a result, when I meet a stranger and he or she asks me where I am from, I tell them I am from California. That really saves me a lot of trouble. Another interesting encounter I face is at a community gathering place like the Flea Market, where I am treated differently from all the others there. If an American could buy a used fan for ten dollars, I would have to pay fifteen dollars for it. Sometimes that really makes me frustrated because I am a human too.

Lastly, the children look at me in a very strange way. Maybe I'm special, unique, or even a rare species over here. From the way they look at me, I feel like they are trying to dig everything out of me just to satisfy their curiosity.

Even if some reactions are bad, I think this is a valuable experience for me because it helps me to be more mature in handling strangers and different types of people.

Tai Herng Kong (Singapore)

Outlining

Used as a heuristic, or means of discovering what a writer wants to say, outlining is no longer a strict method of organizing ideas according to rules about Roman numerals, capital and small letters, and indentations. Instead, writers are encouraged either to use outlining after an activity like brainstorming in order to begin organizing ideas or to initially think through how to divide up a single broad topic before generating more specific ideas about the topic. The next example illustrates one student's outline and her subsequent draft from the outline.

Student Example, Outlining

Beauty in the United States

> In general: artificial
>
> Face: makeup
>
> Hair: any color is okay
>
> Clothes: many colors, plaids, stripes

Beauty in Greece

> In general: natural
>
> Face: no makeup
>
> Hair: blond, blue eyes preferred
>
> Clothes: simple, European styles, single colors

Here is the draft of the paper the student wrote based on this informal outline.

One of the many differences between Americans and Greeks is what these two groups consider good-looking or stylish. Certain things that Americans seem to think look good would not be considered very attractive in Greece. In general the American look is somewhat artificial. Nearly all the women I see here wear makeup even very young high school girls who do not need it yet. And the makeup is not always very subtle either, for example, red lipstick in class and dark purple fingernails. Although Americans do not seem to care much what color their hair is, they seem obsessed with washing it, many people washing their hair every single day, both men and women. In fact, men even get permanents and use hair spray. But the strangest thing about American style is the clothes people wear, stripes, plaids, polka dots on their shirts and even on their pants. I have also noticed to my surprise that many of the men wear polyester pants in very bright colors, like green and red. These are called golf pants.

In Greece we admire natural beauty more. Not many women, except over the age of 40, wear makeup and even then it is usually for a special event, not to go to school. Most Greeks have thick black hair and even though blond hair and blue eyes are considered ideal good looks, no one would think of changing their hair color, not many people have permanents either. Most people just wear their hair long or short but simply, naturally. Greek clothing styles are very much like European styles, natural fabrics, cotton or wool, in subdued colors and in simple styles. I cannot imagine seeing someone in Greece (besides a tourist) wearing red, green, or polka-dotted pants. Perhaps when Americans look at Greek styles, they find them as strange as I find many American styles. I suppose I will become more used to seeing the American styles, too, and maybe next year I'll be the first in Greece to wear those pants.

Annabel Drousiotis (Cyprus)

Cubing

This heuristic is a systematic exploration of the writer's knowledge about a topic. It consists of answering six groups of questions about the topic in any way possible. Imaginative answers are to be encouraged.

1. Describe it. What is it (the topic) like physically? What does it look, feel, taste, or smell like?
2. Compare it. What is it similar to and different from?
3. Analyze it. What are its parts?
4. Associate it. What does it remind you of?
5. Apply it. What can it be used for?
6. Argue for or against it.

An appealing way to introduce this topic is to ask students to bring a candy bar to class and then to use the cube heuristic to analyze the candy bar from the six different angles above. Writers are often surprised at how much they have to say and how amusing, clever, and ingenious their ideas on such a pedestrian subject are when the candy bar is analyzed in this way.

The point in all these heuristic activities is to arm writers with ways to generate ideas on the topic they plan to write about. The activities increase writers' confidence and the likelihood of more effective writing. The more skilled their writing, the less anxiety they may experience. For some students, some of these techniques will be more appealing and useful than others. Different topics also lend themselves more or less easily to different heuristics. Thus, it makes sense to ensure that students are familiar with a number of these heuristics so that they can match their preferences with a given writing task. Having a large amount of preliminary material to select from and in some cases a preliminary organizational scheme in mind breaks up the writing process into manageable chunks and, more importantly, puts primary emphasis on ideas and idea generation.

When teachers look over invention writing of this kind they should never do so with an eye toward correctness. Rather a teacher's role at this stage might be to suggest additional ideas for the writer to explore or think about. However, since this type of writing is intended to be for the benefit of the writer, teachers need to be sensitive to writers' possible reluctance to expose themselves to any scrutiny at all at this stage.

The issue arises here of whether to use the L2 or the L1 in the generation of ideas from these heuristic techniques. Both research and anecdotal evidence exist to suggest that developing ideas in one language and writing in another language may create problems for some writers as they shift across language boundaries (Friedlander 1990). Use of the L1 in the idea-generating stage may negatively influence the writer's choice of phrasings in the L2 and result in the awkwardness that often comes from translation. However, other research

suggests that for some writers, tapping into L1 words with their rich association of meanings for the writer is more fruitful and generates more, and more
complex, ideas about a topic than does a strict adherence to only the L2 (Lay 1982;
Lee 1986). The approach least likely to produce tension or frustration for L2
students requires writing teachers to explain the pros and cons of each method
and to encourage students to make their own decisions about which language
to use, including a combination of both. It seems reasonable to expect that L2
writers will begin to use the L2 to generate ideas when they *can*—that is, when
they have enough L2 and enough confidence to benefit from using it. If using
the L2 to generate ideas stunts the ideas being generated, its use obviously becomes counterproductive. Requiring students to generate ideas in the L2 before they can comfortably do so means inappropriately subordinating ideas to
language. By placing the emphasis exclusively on language and not content,
we increase the likelihood of students experiencing writing anxiety.

Drafting

Once writers have a number of ideas to play with and feel they have considered
them sufficiently to be able to write, they may start their first draft, or parts of
it. Again, breaking down the process of creating text into manageable pieces
should help reduce the anxiety associated with writing. But beginning even a
sentence is often difficult, perhaps because of an unconscious conviction that
what is written must be perfect. In fact, some writers do need to get the first line
down first and may not be able to continue until they feel they have it right.
However, most writers seem to benefit from the reassurance that it makes no
difference where they begin in a first draft because they will have time to return
to the beginning. When the time comes to start a draft, their ideas for the conclusion or for a particular section may be ripe but their ideas for other sections
may not yet be ready to be put on paper. Encourage writers to begin at the end
or in the middle or wherever they can. Most writers seem comforted and stimulated by having at least some ideas already written down. This is accom-
plished initially through the use of heuristics and promoted through the development of a flexible attitude toward which ideas to expand first in a draft.

At times in writing a draft, writers become stuck or hit a dry spot. Any of
the heuristics used to initially develop ideas can be used at any point in the
writing process to further explore, develop, or expand ideas.

Activity for students: Once you have finished gathering your ideas for the topic
you will write on, you may be ready to begin your first draft. Remember that
your first draft does not have to be perfect, since you will have the opportunity
to revise it. To get ready to write, reread what you wrote using the heuristic
techniques we have covered, and circle everything you want to be sure to include
in your draft. Then number the sections you circled in the order in which you
want them to appear in your draft. Add any other ideas or comments that come to
mind as you read through your work. Now answer the following self-analysis
questions:

1. Who is your audience? What does your audience already know about
   this subject? What special terms or concepts might you use that you
   will have to explain to this audience?

Note: Remember that you may eventually change your mind about your audience.

2. What is your purpose in writing about this subject? What do you want to communicate to your audience? Why do you want to communicate this information to this audience?

Note: Your purpose may be to inform your classmates and/or teacher about a subject you think they do not know about but should; or you may want them to know about an experience you have had; or you may want to communicate what you have learned about the subject you are discussing. Your purpose may change eventually, but try to decide what you want to accomplish right now.

3. Read your first draft again. List what you think you will have to concentrate on to shape that invention writing into a good draft.

Note: Think in terms of which ideas you want to express, how much you want to say, and in what order you want to present your ideas. Don't worry about grammar, spelling, punctuation, or finding the exact word in English. You will have time to worry about all that later. For now, if you cannot find a word in English, write it in your own language or leave a blank. Think: To make this into what I think is a good draft,

    a. What must I be sure to mention about my subject?
    b. What should I discuss first, second, third, and so on to make this easy for my audience to understand?
    c. What background information may I have to give in order to help my audience understand what I am saying?
    d. What special terms may be unfamiliar to my audience that I will have to explain?
       What else will I have to keep in mind as I write?
       I'll have to _____
       I'll have to _____
       I'll have to _____
       Continue the list.

When you have finished, gather and reread everything you have written to get ready for this draft, including your answers to the self-analysis questions, and write your new draft.

Peer Responses

Many writing teachers who use process approaches to teaching writing feel that their role in the classroom has changed from evaluator to coach. That is, rather than only judging the merits of student writing, they now see their role as more collaborative. Such a change in role mirrors what language acquisition researchers call *scaffolding*, or working with an L1 or L2 language acquirer to create the message the acquirer wants to communicate but cannot because of language inadequacy. In language acquisition, scaffolding takes the form of supplying what the listener thinks the speaker is trying to say. In writing, the teacher (or possibly a more fluent peer) works together with the writer to help construct the writer's message in the L2 text. The teacher no longer needs to play the anxiety-producing role of judge of the student's abilities; instead, the teacher's new role as participant in the writing process makes the teacher into a promoter of those language abilities and places the student comfortably in the hands of a supportive collaborator.

However little text a writer may have produced, showing a draft to a sympathetic reader is an excellent way to regain momentum in a writing project. One of the mistakes of L2 writing classes has been to use peer responses as an opportunity for students to try to correct each other's grammatical and mechanical errors. This seems to be a misuse of the potential of peer interaction. In most L2 writing classes, fellow students are likely to be only slightly different from one another in their ability to locate and correct errors. Errors students are likely to catch on one another's papers, especially if those students share the same L1, are likely to be insignificant. What fellow students can offer one another, however, is adult responses to ideas, such as suggestions for expansion or clarification. Such activity is not only helpful to the writer in terms of the creation of a text; it is also satisfying for both the writer and the peer reader, since most people are more interested in dealing with ideas than with points of grammar. And it is likely to reduce a writer's anxiety since the text is understood to be only in its preliminary stages.

If students are to be expected to respond helpfully to their classmates' written ideas, they need to be encouraged and guided in that direction. Many teachers give out peer-response guide questions for students to answer for the author. Questions like the following direct students toward content:

What is the best part of this text?

What ideas are especially funny, ingenious, or insightful?

Can you think of any other ideas that might fit in this paper, or can you help the writer expand any of the ideas here?

Can you think of any objections to the author's ideas expressed here that he/she might think about addressing in the next draft?

Student writers appreciate peer responses that focus on ideas rather than only on error correction since students receive not only supportive responses to their own ideas but also have the opportunity to read what other students are writing and even to use ideas stimulated by that reading in their own writing. The sense of community such sharing fosters also works toward mitigating fear of writing. Far from feeling intimidated by allowing classmates to read their writing, some students consider peer-response day the most interesting and useful of all class sessions. A sense of community is also fostered by activities that allow the most appreciated papers to be publicly displayed or read aloud to the whole class. Often the selection of such papers is made by the peer responders themselves. For example, a group of four students may read one another's papers and agree on the one they like best. That paper may be read to the class by the author or by the teacher. The reading is then followed by the group's explanation of why they selected that paper as the best.

Finally, although peer response is intended to be supportive, the need to share one's ideas, not display one's proficiency in language, may also have the effect of creating facilitative anxiety—that is, just enough tension at the thought of a public display of ideas to enhance creativity and risk-taking.

Peer response activity for students: Students should bring to class one of the drafts they have written for this course. Form groups of three or four with classmates who have not already read one another's draft. Then do one of the following:

1. Take turns quickly (not more than about a minute or two) telling the group what each of you said in your draft. Then exchange papers and read and analyze one another's drafts.
2. Exchange papers without discussion. If you choose this option, proceed as follows:
   a. Read the title (if there is one), the first sentence, and the last sentence of the paper.
   b. Begin at the beginning, and read the whole paper quickly. Don't worry if there are parts you don't quite understand. In this reading you need to get only a general idea of the discussion.
   c. Begin at the beginning once again, and this time read carefully to the end.

Choose the methods your group feels comfortable with. Keep a pencil in hand as you are reading, and mark places you especially like and places you have trouble understanding. Don't hesitate to ask the author about words you cannot read, but don't spend time discussing or debating the paper. When you have finished reading, take a full-sized, clean sheet of paper, and prepare it as shown:

	Author's name
	Reader's name
	Date and name or subject of paper

You will now answer questions on your classmate's paper. Answer the questions as fully, honestly, and specifically as you can. If you do not understand something in the paper, say so. If you need or would like more information from the writer, say so. (Caution: The point of this procedure is to help, not to criticize, one another. Be honest but not harsh or unkind. Remember that you too are only an apprentice reader, not an expert critic.)

1. What was the best/most interesting part of this paper?
2. If your classmate described an object, device, or machine, did you understand what it looks like and/or how it functions? If your classmate described a process or concept, did you understand it?
3. Was there any part of this paper where you wanted more information because you were interested? What else did you want to know?
4. Was there any part of this paper where you needed more information just to understand? What else did you need to know?
5. Who is the intended audience for this paper? How can you tell?
6. What was your classmate's purpose in communicating these ideas? Did he or she want you to know something that you did not already know?
7. Did the draft follow the typical English three-part pattern?
8. If you had to reduce the length of this paper, what would you eliminate?
9. List everything you like about this draft.
10. Do you have any additional comments or suggestions?

When everyone in your group has read all the drafts, give your classmates the comments you wrote analyzing their papers. Read the comments you receive and respond to them. Note what you agree with, what you do not understand, and how you might change something a reader commented on, as well as any other reactions you have.

When you have finished reading the comments on your draft, ask your readers any questions you may have about their comments, especially if they make comments that contradict one another. Even contradictory comments can be useful.

Other techniques for writing instruction that may reduce writing anxiety include journal writing and sequenced writing projects. Both focus on process and content, as opposed to product and form exclusively.

Journals

The use of writing, reading, or working journals has spread from writing and reading courses through the curriculum so that it is now possible to find students in math classes being asked to keep math journals reflecting on their progress in those courses. Journals in an L2 writing class build fluency and have the great advantage for L2 writers of allowing them to experiment with L2 forms. The disadvantage the L2 students often point to is that students sometimes feel there is no purpose to this writing since no one corrects it and sometimes no one even reads it. However, if students use their journals almost as artist sketch pads in which they record ideas for possible use later in a more formal type of writing, the journal then operates as a no-risk storehouse of ideas from which students may draw at will.

The usual recommendations for using journals in writing classrooms suggest that students write three to five times a week for a minimum of 10–15 minutes without interruption, allowing ideas to flow freely, if possible. However, simply sending students off to write in journals may prove less useful than giving students specific subjects to write on in the L2 or even lists of questions pertaining to a subject to reflect on in their journals. If these journal entries are tied into other writing assignments, they can function as an invention technique or heuristic, since students could incorporate journal entries into their drafts of subsequent papers.

Activity for students: The following journal suggestions are meant to stimulate your thinking. You may want to answer some or all of the questions, but you do not have to. Write for more than 15 minutes if you feel inspired.

- Begin your journal with a time line of life. Write down the date of your birth, and then, in approximate chronological order, record as many events as you can remember of your life up to the present. These may include strong childhood memories, births of siblings, changes of residence, travels, political events that affected you, and so on. Try to remember what events you associate with each year. Include trivial events as well as major events you associate with each year. When you have finished, look over your time line. Did you remember anything you hadn't thought of for years?
- Begin your journal by spending at least 10 minutes listing the subjects you are most interested in and/or most knowledgeable about. After 10 minutes, choose one or two of the subjects and spend 10 more minutes or so writing about it/them.
- Think about what your parents were like before they had children. Do you know any stories about them from that time? Have you seen any pictures of them from that time? What do you know about their childhood years? How do you think they have changed?
- Think of something or someone that is popular right now that you dislike: a hairstyle or way of dressing, a singer or movie star, a place to visit, a way of looking at an issue, or anything else you think of that certain people like and approve of but you do not. Then make two lists. In the first, list the reasons for the popularity of this person, style, concept, or whatever. In the second, list your reasons for not liking him/her/it.
- Think of something that is unpopular right now among many people but that you like. Explain the reasons for this unpopularity and your own reasons for feeling differently.
- Look back to the essay you wrote in one of your previous writing assignments. Begin your journal by commenting on what you think about that first assignment. What are you most satisfied with in your essay? Is there anything you would change or add if you were going to write it again?
- Begin your journal by writing about anything you want to write about.

Suggestions for keeping a writing journal

1. Write your journal on looseleaf paper. By using this type of paper, you can add entries to your journal even when you do not have your notebook with you. Get a looseleaf binder in which to store all your entries.
2. Begin each entry on a new sheet of paper.
3. Date each entry. Also, write down at the top of the entry where you are as you are writing. Try to write in a place where you are not likely to be interrupted.
4. Before you begin to write anything, relax and let your mind empty itself. Sometimes it helps to concentrate only on your own breathing for 1 minute.
5. Once you begin to write, keep writing continuously for 15 minutes.
6. Write legibly and leave plenty of space in case you want to add comments later.
7. Use the suggestions for journal entries given throughout [this chapter] to stimulate your thoughts. However, allow your thoughts to take whatever direction they will. If you run out of things to say on the suggested topic, just keep writing on whatever topic is in your mind. If you can think of nothing to say, either repeat what you have been saying or describe what it feels like to find nothing to write about. You will most likely discover that the very act of writing itself stimulates your thinking.
8. After 15 minutes, go back and reread what you wrote. Add comments if you feel like doing so.
9. Do this three times each week, and keep all your journal entries—dated and numbered—in your journal binder. The binder should contain nothing except your journal entires.
10. Note that this writing journal is not the same as a diary. Your journal is meant to be a source of raw material from which you can draw ideas for your formal writing. It should include observations about life around you, about yourself, about other people. It should include descriptions of significant events, insights, memories, thoughts, and opinions. It will probably not include information such as what time you got up and what you had for breakfast. Include in your journal any ideas you think might eventually be useful to you in an essay.

Determine with your teacher whether these journals are to be private (no one reads what you write except you), semi-private (you occasionally read from your journal to your classmates), or public (your teacher or your classmates will read your entires).

Sequenced Writing Projects

A steady source of anxiety among writers doing school-sponsored writing is the fear that they will not have enough to say. This anxiety is quieted by writing assignments that call on students to write about what they already know well. While such assignments certainly have their place, it can be argued that they never serve to stretch the learner's knowledge through use of the L2. As a result of writing only about themselves, their more-or-less unsubstantiated opinions, and their personal histories, the range of L2 writers' competence is limited to those personal domains. Yet, in order to write, students need to know something about a topic, and in order to write intelligently about a topic, they must first build on that knowledge base.

In most writing classrooms, teachers make a certain number of assignments over the course of the term, but the topics students write about in these assignments may have no relationship to one another. As a result, whatever students may learn from doing one assignment is unlikely to be directly useful for the next assignments. Sequenced writing assignments function cognitively somewhat like Krashen's notion of narrow reading (Krashen 1988). Each assignment builds on the last as the writers develop knowledge of both the subject matter and the language structures with which to communicate that knowledge. Sequenced assignments may take several forms, but all share the characteristic of requiring students to gather information and write several texts about a single topic. One possible formulation of a sequenced writing project consists of five individual assignments.

1. Students select a topic they feel they have enough interest in to sustain them over all five assignments. They are also required to have some personal experience to draw on in writing on this topic. ESL students have chosen such topics as financial aid available to international students on a given campus, the issue of Puerto Rico becoming a state, and the means of developing American friends. The first assignment requires writers to explain their topic, its significance, their personal interest in it, and what they hope to learn about it through the data gathering they will do.

2. The second assignment requires students to find three pieces of published information on the topic they have selected. The information can be printed, such as articles or brochures, or it may be in documentary movies or radio broadcasts, for example. In this assignment students summarize the information they found.

3. In the third part of the sequenced writing project, students create and administer a survey on their topic that includes questions on subjects on which they want other people's opinions. The written assignment is to report on the survey and its results. In an FL environment students can poll their classmates or students in other classes in the target language.

4. The fourth assignment is a report on an interview the students conduct with someone deemed to be an expert on the topic the students are exploring. Students prepare interview questions beforehand, schedule an appointment for the interview, and either take notes on or tape record their session with the expert. This assignment is potentially difficult to accomplish in an FL setting with limited numbers of speakers of the target language. However, in a worst-case scenario in which there are no subject matter experts who speak the target language, students may interview teachers or other students who speak the target language. If these people have no particular expertise in the topic, the writers may use the interview to pursue in greater depth areas that proved to be interesting or puzzling in the survey data collected.

5. Finally, in the last assignment, writers pull together all the information they have been collecting over the course of the several weeks of the project and write up a final report. This report need not be longer than the other assignments; rather, students select the most interesting or informative portions of their previous work. In this assignment they may draw heavily on writing they have already completed.

Sequenced writing activity for students.

1. Select a topic you already know something about, have some experience with, and are interested in learning more about. (a) Write about your experience with the topic, (b) explain why you think it is important or interesting enough to warrant further exploration, and (c) discuss what you hope to learn about it.
2. Find three pieces of published information on your topic and summarize the information you found.
3. Develop and administer a survey on your topic, asking questions about topics you are interested in learning other people's opinions on. Then write a report on the survey and its results.
4. Interview someone you feel is an expert on the topic you have chosen. Prepare interview questions, schedule an appointment for the interview, and either take notes on or tape record the session with the expert. Then write a report on what you learned from the interview.
5. Gather all the information you have been collecting for this project and write a final report. Select and summarize the most interesting or informative material you have gathered.

Since all the assignments are linked, this project permits students to make use of what they have learned about both the content related to their topic and the language needed to discuss that content; both have been extensively explored and commented on by their peers and teacher over the course of the term. Typically, this project increases students' confidence in their ability to write in the L2 and expands students' linguistic ability and real-world knowledge base.

CONCLUSION

This chapter has suggested activites for writing instruction that may reduce writing apprehension and develop writing skills at the same time. More specifically, the activities in this chapter were designed to:

1. help students prepare for writing tasks, therefore increasing their chance of successful writing, through prewriting practices such as brainstorming, freewriting, looping, clustering and branching, outlining, and cubing;
2. help writers develop a process approach to writing whereby drafts are recognized as part of the writing process, thus showing writers how to break down writing into manageable steps;

3. promote peer responses to writing whereby the focus is on content first rather than word-for-word error correction; and
4. offer teachers new ideas for writing instruction, such as journal and sequenced writing, that could reduce writing anxiety.

The activities suggested in this chapter are rooted in sound pedagogical writing instruction and address known sources of writing anxiety. For example, writing in the L2 provokes anxiety when the text is regarded as a test in which students inevitably reveal their failings, even though we know that errors and awkwardness of expression in L2 are inevitable. Using writing activities to prove to L2 students that they do not yet fully control the target language makes little sense. If L2 students experience revelation of their failings as the reason for writing, it can hardly be surprising that they are reluctant to write and fearful of exposing themselves in the permanent kind of way that writing affords. Instead, when writing becomes a means of exploring ideas and language, it develops the students' sense of power over the L2, as they realize that language is a tool for human self-expression and communication.

PORTFOLIO ASSIGNMENTS

1. a. In this chapter, Leki introduces several prewriting techniques, such as cubing, drafting, looping, and outlining. Select two of these and apply them to two different writing topics. You will need to write out the complete activity with instructions.
   b. Present one of the prewriting techniques you developed above to the FL Method's class and discuss how it could alleviate writing anxiety.
   c. Was there one particular technique that was popular, or was there a mix of techniques your classmates applied?
2. a. If you already teach or are doing an internship, interview a writing specialist at your school or university for other sources of writing anxiety in a second language class (or even in the native language).
   b. Design a couple of activities that address the sources of writing apprehension in **2a** above. (For additional ideas on writing instruction, you may consult the following sources.)

   Lee, J., & VanPatten, B. (1995). *Making communicative language teaching happen*. San Francisco: McGraw-Hill.
   Leki, I. (1995). *Academic writing*. New York: St. Martin's Press.
   Omaggio Hadley, A. (1993). *Teaching language in context*. Boston: Heinle and Heinle.

   c. Share your activities with your classmates in search of three you would like to include in your portfolio.
3. In groups of three, design guidelines for peer responses to one of the writing activities generated in activity **1** or **2** above. These peer-response guidelines should promote a process approach to writing and take into account sources of writing anxiety as discussed in this chapter.

ACTION RESEARCH

1. a. Randomly select a first-year or second-year foreign language textbook and describe the writing tasks in three chapters in this book.
     - Does the textbook approach writing as a one-time product, or is there a process approach to writing tasks?
     - Are there idea-generating prewriting activities that help prepare students for the writing task?
     - How successful will students be at completing most of the writing tasks in this book?
     - Are there specific activities that you think may evoke writing anxiety in some students? Describe them.
     - Can you tell how the writing tasks will be evaluated? How would this be related to writing anxiety?

   (You may want to consult the following articles, which offer sample analyses of specific types of activities in textbooks.)

   Swaffar, J. K. (1991). Language learning is more than learning language: Rethinking reading and writing tasks in textbooks for beginning language study. In Barbara Freed (Ed.), *Foreign language acquisition research and the class.* Lexington, MA: D.C. Heath.
   Terrell, Tracy (1990). Trends in the teaching of grammar in Spanish language textbooks. *Hispania, 73,* 201–209.
   Young, Dolly J., & Oxford, Rebecca (1993). Attending to learner reactions to introductory Spanish textbooks. *Hispania, 76,* 593–605.

   b. Compare your findings with those of others in your FL Methods class.
   c. Are there any general conclusions you can make about writing activities in the textbooks analyzed?
2. a. Administer Daly and Miller's Writing Apprehension Measure in Appendix G to three students in an FL or SL class; one should be a strong A student, one a strong B student, and one clearly a C/D student. Compare their scores and report the results to your classmates.
   b. Tally the results of the writing apprehension measure as they are reported in class. Are there any patterns? Discuss these in the context of this chapter and/or other articles you have read on this topic.
3. a. Use one of the writing techniques you designed for your portfolio (see activity **1** under **Portfolio Assignments**) with an FL or SL learner.
   b. Afterward, ask the student for his/her reactions to the techniques. For example, did the student feel that using the technique helped build writing confidence? Did it better prepare the student to write in the FL/SL? Would the student prefer to approach writing the way your activity does or some other way?
   c. In class, read each of the student's written comments to determine whether the majority of comments to the writing techniques were positive or negative.

REFERENCES

Chan, M. (1989). *Process and practice: Activities for composing in English.* New York: Collier MacMillan.

Cohen, A. D. (1987). Student processing of feedback on their papers. In A. L. Wenden & J. Rubinn (Eds.), *Research on learner strategies*. Upper Saddle River, NJ: Prentice Hall, pp. 57–69.

Daly, J. A., & Miller, M. (1975a). The empirical development of an instrument to measure writing apprehension. *Research in the Teaching of English, 9,* 242–249.

Daly, J. A., & Miller, M. (1975b). Further studies on writing apprehension: SAT scores, success expectations, willingness to take advanced courses, and sex differences. *Research in the Teaching of English, 9,* 250–256.

Daly, J. (1979). Writing apprehension in the classroom: Teacher role expectations of the apprehensive writer. *Research in the Teaching of English, 13,* 37–44.

Elbow, P. (1973). *Writing Without Teachers*. New York: Oxford University Press.

Friedlander, A. (1990). Composing in English: The effects of a first language on writing in English as a second language. In B. Kroll (Ed.), *Second language writing*. New York: Oxford University Press, pp. 109–125.

Fox, R. F. (1980). Treatment of writing apprehension and its effects on composition. *Research in the Teaching of English, 14,* 39–49.

Gungle, B. W., & Taylor, V. (1989). Writing apprehension and second language writers. In D. M. Johnson & D. Roen (Eds.), *Richness in writing*. New York: Longman, pp. 235–248.

Krashen, S. D. (1988). Do we learn to read by reading? The relationship between reading and reading ability. In D. Tannen (Ed.), *Linguistics in context: Connecting observation and understanding*. Norwood, NJ: Ablex, pp. 269–298.

Lay, N. (1982). Composing processes of adult ESL learners. *TESOL Quarterly, 16,* 406.

Lee, J. (1986). On the use of recall tasks to measure L2 reading comprehension. *Studies in Second Language Acquisition, 8,* 83–93.

Leki, I. (1991). The preferences of ESL students for error correction in college-level writing classes. *Foreign Language Annals, 24,* 203–218.

Leki, I. (1995). *Academic Writing*. New York: St. Martin's Press.

McCroskey, J. C. (1970). Measures of communication-bound anxiety. *Speech monographs, 37,* 269–277.

MacIntyre, P. D., & Gardner, R. C. (1994). The subtle effects of language anxiety on cognitive processing in the second language. *Language Learning, 44,* 283–305.

Miller, C. (1983). Speech exercises for the writing class. *Journal of Developmental and Remedial Education, 6,* 24–25.

Newkirk, T. (1979). *Why students find writing to be torture*. Paper presented at the annual Spring meeting of the NorthEast Modern Language Association, Hartford, Conn. March 29–31. ERIC Document No. ED169542.

Pajares, F., & Johnson, M. J. (1994). Confidence and competence in writing: The role of self-efficacy, outcome expectance, and apprehension. *Research in the Teaching of English, 28,* 313–331.

Radecki, P. M., & Swales, J. (1988). ESL students' reaction to written comments on their written work. *System, 16,* 355–365.

Raimes, A. (1983). *Techniques in teaching writing*. New York: Oxford.

Raimes, A. (1984). Anguish as a second language? Remedies for composition teachers. In S. McKay (Ed.), *Composing in a second language*. Boston: Newbury House, pp. 81–96.

Raisman, N. (1982). I just can't do English: Writing anxiety in the classroom. *Teaching English in the Two-Year College, 9,* 19–23.

Reid, J. (1987). *Basic writing*. Upper Saddle River, NJ: Prentice Hall.

Rico, G. L. (1986). Clustering: A pre-writing process. In C. B. Olson (Ed.), *Practical ideas for teaching writing as a process*. Sacramento: California State Department Education, pp. 17–20.

Segal, M. K., & Pavlik, C. (1985). *Interactions: A writing process book*. New York: Random House.

Shoemaker, C. (1985). *Write in the corner where you are*. New York: Holt, Rinehart and Winston.

Silva, T. (1993). L1 vs L2 writing: ESL graduate students' perceptions. *TESL Canada, 10*, 27–47.

Smith, M. W. (1984). *Reducing writing apprehension*. Urbana, IL: National Council of Teachers of English.

Spack, R. (1984). Invention strategies and the ESL college composition student. *TESOL Quarterly, 18*, 649–670.

White, R., & Arndt, V. (1991). *Process writing*. New York: Longman.

Zamel, V. (1985). Responding to student writing. *TESOL Quarterly, 19*, 79–101.

Grammar Learning as a Source of Language Anxiety: A Discussion

Bill VanPatten
The University of Illinois at Urbana-Champaign
William R. Glass
McGraw-Hill Higher Education

Personal Reflections

a. Think back to when you were learning grammar. Did you ever experience a feeling of simply "not getting it"? Was there ever a time when you felt there was too much to learn?

b. If you have been teaching for a while, have you ever felt that the textbook or syllabus was attempting to cover too much grammar in too short a period of time? Have your students ever expressed a similar concern?

c. Think about traditional approaches to grammar instruction in the language classroom. What does this look like? What are the steps involved? Do students get a chance to become familiar receptively with the grammar before being asked to produce it? In what way?

d. What does second language acquisition research have to say about grammar acquisition?

Fundamental Concepts

Potential sources of anxiety in grammar learning

a. too much
b. errors
c. evaluation
d. lack of congruence
e. lack of grammar instruction

Insights from second language acquisition

a. acquisition is slow
b. errors are natural and largely unavoidable
c. developmental stages and orders of acquisition
d. underlying knowledge versus performance
e. the role of input

The daisy analogy
Traditional instruction
Processing instruction
Principles of second language input processing
Structured input
Guidelines for constructing structured input activities

In the last decade, the growing interest in anxiety and second language learning has been documented by the number of scholarly publications appearing in professional journals and also in the form of edited volumes (e.g., Horwitz & Young 1991). Some researchers have endeavored to establish foreign language anxiety scales (Horwitz 1986; Horwitz, Horwitz, & Cope 1986; MacIntyre 1988), while others have examined the relationship between anxiety and second language cognitive processing (MacIntyre & Gardner 1991, 1994a, 1994b) and anxiety and learners' oral exam performance (Phillips 1992; Young 1986; see also Table 3.1 in MacIntyre, this volume).

Absent in the literature, however, is any discussion about anxiety and grammar learning. The language teaching profession's concern about grammar has been its role in communicative language teaching; for example, whether or not grammar needs to be explicitly taught, what grammar needs to be taught. (See Larsen-Freeman & Long 1991, Chapter 9; the special issue of *Studies in Second Language Acquisition*, June 1993.) In this essay we present a preliminary exploration of the relationship between anxiety and grammar learning as we postulate sources of anxiety and suggest ways to reduce anxiety in light of a particular approach to grammar instruction known as *processing instruction*.

ANXIETY IN GENERAL: WHY DO PEOPLE GET ANXIOUS?

Although grammar-associated language anxiety is the focus of this chapter, we preface our essay with a short discussion about anxiety in general. Although MacIntyre (this volume) provides a thorough discussion of anxiety, we need to reiterate here that anxiety is related to a combination of external (e.g., impending situations or tasks) and internal factors (e.g., self-evaluation, self-doubt, preoccupation about others' opinions) (Eysenck 1979; MacIntyre & Gardner 1994b). The anxious person is apprehensive not only about threatening situations in his or her environment but also about self-related concerns. Moreover, the convergence of these factors becomes evident when individuals confront something in their environment that they cannot easily control. Impending tasks, one's self-doubt, and the inability to negotiate tasks result in an anxiety-provoking context.

The logical question to ask is "How does grammar learning in the foreign language classroom relate to the construct of anxiety identified here?" That is, in what way does grammar learning present a situation of little or no control for the learner? Our focus, then, will be on the issue of learner control as it relates to learning grammar and the anxiety that may result.

ANXIETY AND GRAMMAR LEARNING

As stated earlier, there is to our knowledge no research on the relationship between grammar learning and anxiety. In this section we offer a series of possible explanations for why the learning of grammar may be anxiety provoking for some students of language.

Too Much Material

One reason that grammar learning can be anxiety provoking is that there may be too much material to learn. While the earliest lessons of a second language textbook may not contain much grammar (see, for example, the **Ante todo** of *Puntos de partida*, the **Pasos preliminares** of *Dos mundos*, the **Premier rendez-vous** of *Rendez-vous*), classroom learners may soon find that lessons are grammar heavy. Students and instructors alike have commented on the "terrible second semester" of typical grammar-driven college courses. In the second semester students are often expected to learn and be able to produce on tests a variety of compound tenses, the subjunctive tenses, **por** and **para** in Spanish, pronominal verbs in French, and other difficult grammatical items. Both of the present authors (and we are sure many readers as well) have heard from students that a particular part of the syllabus is "jam packed," "overwhelming," and "too focused on detail." These students are expressing a certain lack of control over their ability to learn grammar; they could learn it if simply given more time.

Errors

Some learners, if not many, are concerned about making errors in the second language. Embarrassed to speak in class for fear of not sounding as good as their peers and expressing less than they could in written work for the same reasons, these students are showing signs of anxiety induced by an inability to control their spontaneous output. If instructors also show a concern for errors through constant feedback and grading for errors in communicative tasks, then learners' anxiety will be heightened. We recall the words of Sandra Savignon who, in a published letter to her Spanish instructor, wrote the following about when she had to introduce her classmate to the rest of the class:

> When my turn came, I made my introduction more or less as I had practiced it. When you corrected an error I had made, I repeated after you the best I could, but I was really too flustered to understand what I was doing. The experience was simply too intense to allow me to focus on the form you were trying to teach me (Savignon 1997, p. 3).

In addition to perspectives such as Savignon's, there is also the issue that speaking in a language class often reduces the adult or adolescent into sounding like a child who makes simple utterances with simple ideas and is, for all intents and purposes, forced to make errors when attempting to communicate an idea. Adults in particular are used to expressing abstract and complex ideas in their first language using complex language without making errors in grammatical form or structure. In short, they have control over their expressive abilities in their native language. In a language classroom, adults must abandon this control if they are going to communicate any kind of message, a situation that may be unacceptable to or difficult for many.

Evaluation

This issue is related to the preceding two points. If most of a language learner's evaluation is based on grammatical performance, then testing and evaluation may induce anxiety. Students who consistently ask "Is this going to be on the test?" or "Do we need to know this for the quiz?" may be experiencing anxiety provoked by their perceptions of how the instructor evaluates them or what they think is important to know for a test.

Lack of Congruence Between Communicative Language Teaching and Traditional Grammar Instruction

This issue is related to the previous one. Some instructors embrace communicative approaches to the classroom with an emphasis on the expression of meaning, vocabulary development, discussion, listening comprehension, reading of authentic texts, and so on but engage in traditional grammar instruction and give more weight to grammar knowledge on tests and quizzes. Because of this lack of fit between communicative and so-called "traditional" approaches, and because testing may emphasize grammar, students may become anxious if they feel that the teaching and testing practices are not in synch. These students come to feel that the classroom is a waste of time or at best only marginally useful for the purpose of "learning the material" that will appear on the formal evaluation.

Lack of Grammar Instruction

Contrary to what we have been saying up to now, a source of both anxiety and frustration for a number of students comes from curricula in which grammar instruction is either absent or minimized. Many students enter a beginning language class with previous classroom language learning experience and have certain expectations about the class. These expectations include assuming that one of the instructor's primary roles is to teach grammar explicitly and that the students' role is to practice it. If such instruction is absent, these students become concerned about the nature of the instruction and what they are supposed to learn. VanPatten recalls one student who visited his office to express her distress over a first-year Spanish class. She expressed great worry over the fact that her instructor was not teaching grammar. As she said, "How can you learn a language without knowing its grammar thoroughly? That's how I learned French." Students like her feel that explicit grammatical instruction is not only beneficial but necessary and become anxious when they don't have access to it. As this student expressed to VanPatten, she didn't feel "in control" of her language learning. What may be the issue here (again) is that grammar is a tangible, quantifiable entity, and students can measure their "progress" with a grade and with performance on grammar-oriented tests. Classrooms in which grammar instruction and discrete point testing are not the emphasis may leave students wondering how they are to be evaluated and how progress is to be measured.

Summary

The picture that emerges from our brief discussion of possible sources of student anxiety over grammar ties into a global source of anxiety in humans; an inability to control what is happening to them. In some cases, the grammatical material to learn is too great or comes too fast and some learners can't keep up. Anxiety may be especially high if knowledge of grammar and ability to use it are important in evaluation of the students. In a few cases, learners can't gain control over their language learning because explicit grammar instruction is not provided. In this type of extreme communicative classroom, learners who "need" grammar have little to grab onto in the course and may not understand what is expected of them.

REDUCING ANXIETY ABOUT GRAMMAR

Beliefs about grammar learning and grammar instruction are deeply ingrained in the minds of both students and instructors. Likewise, the manner in which grammar is treated in materials and in many curricula reflects some strong beliefs. It may be difficult to effect any kind of change because of such beliefs;

what we offer here are suggestions about how we might begin the process of anxiety reduction related to grammar in the foreign language classroom. Our suggestion is two-part. The first involves informing students about second language acquisition. The second involves changing the type of grammar instruction that currently predominates in the profession.

Informing Students About Second Language Acquisition

As we have seen, students may experience anxiety owing to expectations about their performance. As intelligent adolescents and adults, they ask themselves "Why can't I do this? Why can't I get it right?" If learners understood something about the nature of second language acquisition, then they could gain increased self-confidence, which would cause a reduction in anxiety. We think that learners could benefit from a simple understanding of the following insights from second language acquisition research:

- Grammar acquisition is slow.
- Errors are natural and largely unavoidable.
- There are such things as developmental stages and orders.
- There is a difference between underlying knowledge and the ability to perform.
- Meaning-bearing input is a critical factor in grammar acquisition.

We will take each of the above points in turn.

Learners should understand that grammar acquisition is slow. Unimpaired children are uniformly successful in first language acquisition, but few people realize the thousands of hours that children spend in developing a native-like grammatical system. We know that most of a native-language grammar is acquired by the age of 7. If we assume that children really start to pick up words at around the age of 8 months, then this means that they spend roughly 6 years and 4 months acquiring the grammar. If we further assume that the child is exposed to language for at least 6 hours a day during this time period, this means that the child has spent some 13,797 hours learning and using language! If we look at the names that we give to the 3-year college-level language sequence—beginning, intermediate, advanced—we can easily see how learners may come to expect miraculous feats in a short amount of time.

Errors are natural and unavoidable. This is common knowledge in second language research. The brain organizes and stores language in ways that are not entirely clear to researchers, and this organization may result in nonnative grammatical knowledge. Overt discussion of the nature of errors can help students of a second language understand that a certain amount of language acquisition is beyond their control. One way in which an instructor might approach this topic is by leading a conversation about child-L1 acquisition. Have students noticed that children make errors when learning their first language? What are these errors like? (Instructors may want students to understand the difference between grammatical errors and sociolinguistic errors. The former are errors such as "wented" and "teeths," while the latter are errors children get corrected for such as "ain't" and double negatives.) How are these errors evidence of constraints on learning? Don't all children go on to acquire the language fully while making errors all along the way? We have found it useful to bring samples of L2-learner speech to class, samples from different levels, so that students can see how errors are natural and that improvement does happen over time.

There are predictable stages of development in the acquisition of grammar, and there are orders of acquisition for many surface features of language. Again, what learners need to know is that various aspects of grammar acquisition are indeed beyond their control. To offset the frustration that can result from students' feeling a "lack of control," teachers could address the root of these emotions. For example, a useful technique is to provide learners with information about the stages of acquisition in English L2 development. Stages in the acquisition of negation, WH-questions, auxiliaries, and other phenomena are well documented in the L2 literature and can serve as starting points for talking about stages in general, as well as possible stages in the L2 of the students. Knowledge that results from this discussion may help learners to understand that the brain often organizes language data outside their awareness and that much is happening subconsciously, even though they may not think so.

There is a difference between underlying competence and the ability to perform. Many students think that because they know a rule or structure explicitly that they should be able to use it in speech and writing. This may be reinforced by instructors and teaching practices in which learners are penalized for making errors during more spontaneous acts of communication, particularly if the forms/structures have been "taught" in class. In addition, many learners also think that learning grammar is a matter of memorization and rote practice, a belief that once again may be reinforced by certain teaching practices. What these learners need to understand is that underlying knowledge is not the same as the conscious rules that they learn from textbooks. The kind of competence that underlies language use is largely abstract and subconscious. Here learners could benefit from some simple examples from their native language. Using English as an example, we might ask why everyone says (1) and not (2)?

1. Where did you go?
2. Where you went?

(2) is correct in that the verb agrees with the subject, it is correctly formed as an irregular, and *where* appears at the beginning of the sentence. But no English speaker would say (2); we say only (1). Clearly our performance in English is not guided by conscious rules, and there is no reason to expect that in a second language it would be different.

Learners need to be aware of the important role that input plays in the acquisition of a second language grammar. It is universally accepted now in second language research circles that learners build their underlying competence in grammar based on the input they receive. By input, we mean comprehensible meaning-bearing input—language that the learner hears (or sees) that is communicative in nature. This input provides the internal processors with the kind of raw language data they need to construct the linguistic system. (For more detailed discussion of these insights, see Lee & VanPatten 1995, Chapters 2 and 3; VanPatten 1996.)

If we examine the preceding insights from second language acquisition research, we see that in each case information can be given to students concerning the limitations of explicit grammar learning. Since much of anxiety is a result of a sense of loss of control, learning that much of grammar acquisition is beyond their direct control can aid anxious students in dealing with the negative feelings they may have about learning grammar. One thing, however, is to know what information might be useful to students; another is to devise ways in which they can grasp it. To be sure, we cannot expect students to become experts in second language acquisition; indeed most of their instructors aren't either! We also don't want to induce added anxiety by introducing concepts that are beyond their reach. One technique that instructors might use to get learners to understand the nature of grammar acquisition involves analogy. Using their first language, learners discuss in groups the following:

Describe the growth of a daisy.

How does it go from seed to mature flowering plant?

What is necessary for its successful growth?

After small group discussions the instructor can then ask one group to share its discussion with the class. Afterward, the instructor can ask the class questions such as "What happens if sun or water or soil nutrients are withheld? Does the daisy control how much sun it gets? How much water?" The instructor can then establish the link for students: acquiring grammar is like the growth of a daisy. We all possess "grammar seeds" in our heads, parts of the brain that are responsible for the growth of grammar. These seeds lie in wait for something to trigger the growth of grammar. Various forms of input act like the sun, water, and nutrients so that the grammar can grow in our heads. If input is missing or deficient, grammatical growth will be stunted in the long run, just like a flower whose growth is stunted because of lack of sun, rain, or soil nutrients. And as a flower is limited in controlling its growth, we are limited in what we can do to make grammar grow in our heads. We cannot substitute anything for the three basic elements that the daisy needs. All we can do to help is to give it extra vitamins and nutrients and to water it when it doesn't rain. Likewise, explicit grammar knowledge and practice with grammar rules is no substitute for input. We can, however, enhance the input in certain ways, and we can certainly attempt to get as much input as possible for our developing grammar system by reading more, listening to people talk, and so on.

We can also use the daisy analogy to help students grasp other insights from second language acquisition mentioned previously. When the seed first comes to life, is the flower the first thing that emerges? No, first the seed must begin to grow roots. Do we see leaves and stems right away when the daisy plant first pokes its head out of the ground? No, we see a little green stalk that really doesn't look like a daisy at all. In fact, if we didn't know what it was, we might think it was a weed and pull it. How does the flower eventually appear on the daisy plant? First the plant sends up a stalk. As this stalk grows, a greenish bud appears on it. After some time, we begin to see the outlines (still green) of what will eventually be the white petals of the daisy flower itself. At some point, the bud begins to open, while at the same time the petals slowly turn from green to white. Finally, the flower is completely opened and we see the familiar white and yellow parts of the daisy flower.

What we have just described is akin to stages of development and orders of acquisition in the growth of grammar. Certain things must happen before other things, and at no point along the way does the developing grammatical system have the exact appearance of a native grammatical system. Just like the daisy that must undergo developmental stages and follow a certain chronological ordering of events, the developing grammatical system must also follow a path. We can't change the sequence of events for the daisy, though we might be able to speed it up (see previous discussion of nutrients). In a similar fashion, we cannot really change the sequence of events for the growth of grammar during second language acquisition. We might be able to speed up the acquisition of grammar, but we can't *prevent* stages of development, errors, and so on.

To summarize this section, we have suggested that anxiety induced by grammar learning may be reduced by giving learners a better understanding of what it means to acquire grammar. Using the daisy-growing analogy, we can provide students with the knowledge that grammar acquisition is slow, largely unmanipulable by external factors (i.e., explicit knowledge, practice, rote memorization), governed by predictable sequences and stages of development, and dependent on comprehensible meaning-bearing input for growth. Armed with this knowledge, anxious students can remind themselves of what they can control and what they cannot control.

Processing Instruction

A second and complementary approach to reducing anxiety about grammar learning involves altering both the way in which we teach grammar and the kinds of practices we ask of students. The particular approach to grammar instruction that we believe can help to reduce anxiety is called *processing instruction* (Cadierno 1995; Lee & VanPatten 1995, Chapters 5 and 6; VanPatten 1993, 1996, 1997; VanPatten & Cadierno 1993; VanPatten & Sanz 1995). Since processing instruction is relatively new and many readers may not be familiar with it and its theoretical and research support, we offer a detailed albeit brief description here. We will subsequently discuss its potential benefits for reducing learner anxiety about grammar and grammar learning.

Most foreign language textbooks (and instructors) continue to present grammar in a way that emphasizes the memorization of rules and paradigms, immediate oral production, and manipulation of form. Practice is based on the mechanical→meaningful→communicative grammar drill hierarchy (Paulston 1972), which has come to typify grammar instruction in this country. As noted, this treatment of grammar stresses immediate production/manipulation of form—a questionable practice in view of the research on the role of input. In addition, traditional treatment of grammar has tended to overwhelm the learner by presenting too much grammar in the form of complete verbal, nominal/adjectival paradigms, and lists of rules.

The learner's objective in such a situation becomes one of memorizing numerous forms. These forms are then "tested" in substitution and other mechanical drills that ignore meaning.

Based on general insights into second language acquisition, processing instruction recognizes that the development of learners' internal linguistic system is input-dependent. Second language learners must be exposed to comprehensible meaning-bearing input. Their internal language processors must process the input in particular ways so that form/meaning connections become available for accommodation by the developing system. In direct opposition to the drill-based nature of traditional instruction, processing instruction uses a particular type of input activity and thus helps to provide the type of linguistic data that learners' internal processors need for the (re)construction of the developing system.

Additionally, processing instruction is meaning-based in that it always requires learners to focus on the propositional content (i.e., the message) expressed in an utterance. As will be illustrated later, processing instruction activities always require learners to respond in some fashion to the message contained in the input, thereby maintaining the link between form and meaning.

Processing instruction also draws on the research on input processing for the formulation of activities that are maximally beneficial psycholinguistically speaking. In terms of input processing, VanPatten has proposed a set of principles that underlie learners' input processing. (See Table 6.1.) These principles not only inform us about how learners process incoming linguistic data, but they also provide important pedagogical implications with regard to the teaching of grammar from a processing approach. We turn our attention at this point to the concept of "structured input," the foundation of processing instruction.

TABLE 6.1. Some Principles Regarding L2 Input Processing

P1. Learners process input for meaning before they process it for form.
   P1a. Learners process content words in the input before anything else.
   P1b. Learners prefer processing lexical items to grammatical items (e.g., morphological markings) for semantic information.
   P1c. Learners prefer processing "more meaningful" morphology before "less" or "non-meaningful morphology."

P2. For learners to process form that is not meaningful, they must be able to process informational or communicative content at no or little cost to attention.

P3. Learners possess a default strategy that assigns the role of agent to the first noun (phrase) they encounter in a sentence. We call this the "first noun strategy."
   P3(a). The first noun strategy may be overriden by lexical semantics and event probabilities.
   P3(b). Learners will adopt other processing strategies for grammatical role assignment only after their developing system has incorporated other cues (e.g., case marking, acoustic stress).

Based on VanPatten (1996). *Input Processing and Grammar Instruction.* Norwood, NJ: Ablex Publishing Corporation.

Structured Input

As we have stressed in this chapter, learners need input for their grammatical system to develop. Thus, processing instruction incorporates a series of "structured input" activities for any grammatical feature. Structured input means (1) that during the activities, learners are not engaged in producing the target item but are engaged in processing it actively and (2) that the input is manipulated in certain ways as to make form/meaning connections more salient to the learner. The guidelines used in the development of such activities are as follows (Lee & VanPatten 1995, Chapter 5):

1. One thing at a time.
2. Keep meaning in focus.
3. Move from sentences to connected discourse.
4. Use both oral and written input.
5. The learner must do something with the input.
6. Keep the learner processing strategies in mind.

Guideline 1 captures the notion that input must be delivered to the learner's developing system efficiently. This is realized when one form and one function are the focus at any given time. To that end, traditional verbal and nominal/adjectival paradigms are broken up, as are rules of usage. To illustrate, rather than presenting the entire verbal paradigm of the Spanish imperfect tense along with all of the uses of the imperfect, the instructor would isolate a single form (e.g., third-person singular) and a single use (e.g., habitual actions in the past) at a given moment, subsequently adding more forms and rules of usage to the picture as the lesson continues.

The next guideline requires activities that push the learner to attend to both meaning and form. In essence, processing instruction avoids mechanical drills that separate meaning and form. A structured input activity would always require that the learner know what the sentence means and how grammar is encoding meaning.

Guideline 3 simply recognizes that initial input at the sentential level is less likely to overwhelm learners' processing capabilities than input that is paragraph-length in nature. Sentence-level activities provide processing time crucial to the initial attempt to link meaning and form in the input. However, this guideline also acknowledges the importance of activities at the level of connected discourse following sentential-level tasks. Thus, learners will work their way from sentence-level to discourse-level input activities in a given lesson.

Recognizing that some learners benefit from seeing the language (i.e., having it provided in written form) in addition to hearing it, the fourth guideline encourages the use of both oral and written input. This can occur in any combination across activities or within the same activity if it contains various steps/stages.

Guideline 5 requires that learners do something with the input—that is, that they not sit passively without having to respond in some fashion. In this way, learners' internal processors are more likely to attend to the relevant grammatical item as they attend to meaning. Note, however, that by "doing something" learners do not produce the grammatical feature. Rather, they respond to the input in some way: indicating yes/no or possible/impossible, matching phrases, ordering events, checking off things that apply to them or to someone else, among other response types.

The final guideline refers to VanPatten's principles of second language input processing. This guideline serves to ensure that the learner is indeed directing his attention to the grammatical feature rather than to some other part of the utterance when cues are in competition. To illustrate, Principle 1b states that "learners prefer processing lexical items to grammatical items (e.g., morphology) for semantic information." An implication of this is that beginning learners will attend to temporal adverbials (e.g., *yesterday, last week*) rather than morphological markers (e.g., past-tense endings) to process past-tense information. Thus, when both are available to beginning-level learners, they tend not to pay attention to the grammatical feature itself and instead rely on the temporal adverbials to grasp tense. Consequently, to circumvent this particular processing strategy, an instructor would create structured input activities that focus on past actions but that do not contain temporal adverbs. In this way, learners are pushed to attend to verb endings to grasp tense. To illustrate, we provide the following activity.

Activity A. ¿Actividades típicas?

Step 1. Listen as your instructor reads a series of statements about some activities that a friend did or is doing. For each, indicate whether the action occurred last week **(la semana pasada)** or is happening this week **(esta semana).**

	La semana pasada	Esta semana
1.	_____	_____
2.	_____	_____
3.	_____	_____
4.	_____	_____
5.	_____	_____
6.	_____	_____
7.	_____	_____
8.	_____	_____

Step 2. Now, write the name of a good friend below. Listen as your instructor reads the statements again and indicate whether they apply to your friend or not.

Mi amigo/a se llama _____.

	Sí	No
1.	_____	_____
2.	_____	_____
3.	_____	_____
4.	_____	_____
5.	_____	_____
6.	_____	_____
7.	_____	_____
8.	_____	_____

101

CHAPTER 6
*Grammar Learning
as a Source of
Language Anxiety:
A Discussion*

Step 3. Your instructor will read each of the statements again so that the class can compare and discuss their responses. For example, you might offer details about when, where, why, with whom, and so on to augment the sentence that your instructor reads.

Instructor's script

1. *Mi amigo se levantó a las siete de la mañana.*[1]
2. *Corrió 5 kilómetros.*
3. *Estudia en la biblioteca, no en casa.*
4. *Limpió su casa.*
5. *Lee una novela interesante.*
6. *No prepara la cena en casa. Va a un restaurante o pide una pizza por teléfono.*
7. *Sacó unos videos.*
8. *Corrigió unos exámenes.*

Note that in this activity learners are required to attend to the verbal inflections to assign tense. Since temporal adverbs are absent, there is nothing else in the utterances that would identify when the actions took place. Note also how the task requires attention to the message that is being communicated by asking learners to indicate whether each statement applies to their friend and to subsequently offer details.

PROCESSING INSTRUCTION AND ANXIETY

As one of the objectives of this chapter is to address how grammar-induced learner anxiety might be reduced, we return to our earlier speculations about the causes of anxiety and discuss them in light of processing instruction. We take these point by point.

1. Too much material. Processing instruction addresses this cause of anxiety by reducing the amount of grammatical information that is being presented and emphasized at a given time. A focus on one form and one meaning (Guideline 1) allows learners an opportunity to isolate features rather than trying to memorize a number of different forms and then substitute them in a mechanical drill. As a result, learners do not become overwhelmed by the amount of grammar and thus have more control over their learning.

2. Errors. Processing instruction addresses this by not requiring learners to produce the grammatical forms initially. Rather, as illustrated in the structured input guidelines above, learners first attend to the linguistic data contained in the input. The activities provide the learners an important opportunity to attend to grammatical features and begin to process them without forcing production. Naturally, this approach reduces the anxiety caused by having to speak or write with negligible control of the structures.

3. Evaluation. An approach to testing that evaluates input before output would provide cohesion between instructional and testing practices, as well as underscore communication owing to the meaning-based nature of structured input. Moreover, learners would be more likely to experience success in formal evaluations that used an input-based format.

4. Lack of congruence between communicative language teaching and traditional grammar instruction. Processing instruction always keeps meaning in focus and underscores how grammar assists in the conveyance of messages. Additionally, structured-input activities are engaging and thought provoking and require the learners' attention to the messages. They are not mechanical drills that run in opposition to a "communicative" classroom; that is, grammar is not reduced to meaningless drills that focus on form at the exclusion of message.

5. Lack of grammar instruction. Processing instruction reduces anxiety by providing learners with explicit grammar instruction—thus responding to certain affective concerns—yet at the same time presents grammar in a way that allows learners to feel in control and successful. Furthermore, processing instruction works with acquisition processes, as illustrated by its focus on comprehensible, meaning-bearing input and also by its consideration of how learners actually process input.

CONCLUSION

In the present essay, we have attempted to isolate some of the potential sources of anxiety in grammar learning. We have also offered two suggestions about how to reduce anxiety resulting from grammar learning. The first is to inform students about the nature of grammar acquisition. Knowing about certain processes can help learners come to grips with what they can control and not control when it comes to internalizing the grammar of a second language. Our second suggestion is to use processing instruction as an alternative to more traditional grammar instruction. While not developed specifically to address anxiety, processing instruction appears to contain a number of features that do directly address the sources of anxiety in grammar learning that we have postulated in this essay.

To be sure, we recognize that our discussion on the sources of anxiety resulting from grammar learning is largely speculative. However, the sources that we list are easily researchable. It may be the case that all provoke anxiety. Or, it may be the case that only one or two of them seem to be valid. In terms of our suggestions about reducing anxiety, since we have provided concrete suggestions, these, too, are imminently researchable. It would be interesting to document, for example, whether or not anxious grammar learners experience some reduction of anxiety over time by simply knowing about second language acquisition. In terms of processing instruction, quantitative measures of learners' reaction to this innovative input-based approach to grammar instruction may reveal that it indeed produces a much more positive affective reaction in learners than traditional instruction. VanPatten recalls that at the end of the instructional treatment sessions used in VanPatten and Cadierno (1993), a number of learners in the processing group rushed to the front of the room at the end of the lesson to mention the positive experience they had in this particular session on object pronouns in Spanish. As one learner put it, "I really liked this! I never understood this stuff in high school, and it used to frustrate me. Are we gonna do more of this?" There were absolutely no reactions from the learners in the traditional group. We think, then, that we have zeroed in on an approach to grammar in the classroom that is not only psycholinguistically valid but that at the same time addresses affective variables in language learning.

103

CHAPTER 6
Grammar Learning
as a Source of
Language Anxiety:
A Discussion

NOTES

1. Translation of sentences: 1. *My friend got up at 7:00 a.m.* 2. *He/She ran 5 kilometers.* 3. *He/She studies in the library, not at home.* 4. *He/She cleaned her house.* 5. *He/She is reading an interesting novel.* 6. *He/She does not cook dinner at home. He/She goes to a restaurant or orders a pizza on the phone.* 7. *He/She checked out some videos.* 8. *He/She corrected some exams.*

PORTFOLIO ASSIGNMENTS

1. In this essay, we use the daisy analogy to help students understand the insights from second language research about grammar acquisition. Are there any other analogies that work as well? If so, develop one into a discussion question for small groups, and include the follow-up questions that you would ask and the points that you would like to bring out so that students can grasp the nature of grammar acquisition.

2. Adapt the structured-input activity on the past tense that we used in the present essay to the language that you (will) teach. Then create a second structured-input activity that also works on third-person singular forms of the past tense. Keep the guidelines in mind that are presented on page 99. Note: You may wish to consult Chapter 5 of Lee and VanPatten (1995), since this chapter contains a detailed discussion of structured input with many practical suggestions.

ACTION RESEARCH

1. Interview a student who seems to have difficulty with grammar acquisition and has expressed some frustration to you. What strategies is this student using to study outside class? What are his or her beliefs about grammar learning, and how are they similar to or different from the insights about second language acquisition discussed in this essay? Then, work through the daisy analogy with this student. Do you see any visible signs of the frustration being relieved? How do the feelings and thoughts of this student change, if at all, with the information provided to him or her. Write your findings up as a brief report.

2. In a first-year language class, lead the students through two mechanical drills on the past tense (after appropriate explanation of course!). Mechanical drills include substitution drills, transformation drills, fill-in-the-blank written exercises, and other types of activities (see Chapter 5 of Lee & VanPatten 1995 for more help with these concepts). After leading your students through the drills, have them rate them in the following categories using the scale (4) very, (3) somewhat, (2) not too much, (1) not at all.

How enjoyable were these practices to you?

How valuable were these practices to you?

How comfortable did you feel being put on the spot during the practices?

Next, lead your class through the two structured-input activities that you developed for the preceding Portfolio section. After completing the activities, have students rate the two activities in the same way as they did the mechanical drills. Then ask them to write a brief paragraph to answer the questions: Which two activities did you like more? The first two or the second two? Or did you like them equally? Can you explain your response?

Then examine the results of your informal study. Does it reveal anything about student reactions to grammar activity types?

REFERENCES

Cadierno, T. (1995). Formal instruction from a processing perspective: An investigation into the Spanish past tense. *The Modern Language Journal, 79,* 153–165.

Eysenck, M. W. (1979). Anxiety, learning and memory: A reconceptualization. *Journal of Research in Personality, 13,* 363–385.

Horwitz, E. K. (1986). Preliminary evidence for the reliability and validity of a Foreign Language Anxiety Scale. *TESOL Quarterly, 20,* 559–562.

Horwitz, E. K., & Young, D. J. (Eds.) (1991). *Language anxiety: From theory and research to classroom implications.* Upper Saddle River, NJ: Prentice Hall.

Horwitz, E. K., Horwitz, M. B., & Cope, J. (1986). Foreign language classroom anxiety. *The Modern Language Journal, 70,* 125–132.

Larsen-Freeman, D., & Long, M. H. (1991). *An introduction to second language acquisition research.* London: Longman.

Lee, J. F., & VanPatten, B. (1995). *Making communicative language teaching happen.* San Francisco: McGraw-Hill.

Lightbown, P., Spada, N., & White, L. (Eds.) (1993). The role of instruction in second language acquisition. Special edition of *Studies in Second Language Acquisition,* June 1993.

MacIntyre, P. D., & Gardner, R. C. (1988). The measurement of anxiety and applications to second language learning: An annotated bibliography. *Research Bulletin No. 672.* London, Ontario: University of Western Ontario. Washington, DC: ERIC Clearinghouse on Languages and Linguistics (ERIC Document Reproduction Service, No. ED 301 040, 39pp.).

MacIntyre, P. D., & Gardner, R. C. (1991). Language anxiety: Its relationship to other anxieties and to processing in native and second languages. *Language Learning, 41,* 513–534.

MacIntyre, P. D., & Gardner, R. C. (1994a). The effects of induced anxiety on three stages of cognitive processing in computerized vocabulary learning. *Studies in Second Language Acquisition, 16,* 1–7.

MacIntyre, P. D., & Gardner, R. C. (1994b). The subtle effects of language anxiety on cognitive processing in the second language. *Language Learning, 44,* 283–305.

Musumeci, D. (1997). *Breaking tradition: An exploration of the historical relationship between theory and practice in second language teaching.* San Francisco: McGraw-Hill.

Paulston, C. B. (1972). Structural pattern drills. In H. B. Allen & R. N. Campbell (Eds.), *Teaching English as a second language.* New York: McGraw-Hill, pp. 129–138.

105

CHAPTER 6
*Grammar Learning
as a Source of
Language Anxiety:
A Discussion*

Phillips, E. M. (1992). The effects of language anxiety on student oral test performance and attitudes. *The Modern Language Journal, 76*, 14–26.

Savignon, S. J. (1997). *Communicative competence: Theory and classroom practice.* (2d. ed.). San Francisco: McGraw-Hill.

VanPatten, B. (1992a). Second language acquisition and foreign language teaching: Part I. *The ADFL Bulletin, 23*, 52–56.

VanPatten, B. (1992b). Second language acquisition research and foreign language teaching: Part II. *The ADFL Bulletin, 23*, 23–27.

VanPatten, B. (1993). Grammar teaching for the acquisition-rich classroom. *Foreign Language Annals, 26*, 435–450.

VanPatten, B. (1995). Cognitive aspects of input processing in second language acquisition. In P. Hashemipour, R. Maldonado, M. van Naerssen (Eds.), *Studies in language learning and Spanish linguistics in honor of Tracy D. Terrell.* New York: McGraw-Hill, pp. 170–183.

VanPatten, B. (1996). *Input processing and grammar instruction: Theory and research.* Norwood, NJ: Ablex.

VanPatten, B. (1997). The relevance of input processing to second language theory and second language teaching. In W. R. Glass & A. T. Pérez-Leroux (Eds.), *Contemporary perspectives on the acquisition of Spanish, volume 2: Production, processing and comprehension.* Somerville, MA: Cascadilla Press, pp. 93–108.

VanPatten, B., & Cadierno, T. (1993). Explicit instruction and input processing. *Studies in Second Language Acquisition, 15*, 225–241.

VanPatten, B., & Sanz, C. (1995). From input to output: Processing instruction and communicative tasks. In F. Eckman, Highland, Lee, Mileham, & Rutkowski Weber (Eds.), *Second language acquisition theory and pedagogy.* Hillsdale, NJ: Earlbaum, pp. 169–185.

Young, D. J. (1986). The relationship between anxiety and foreign language oral proficiency ratings. *Foreign Language Annals, 19*, 439–445.

Addressing Listening Comprehension Anxiety

Anita Vogely
The State University of New York, Binghamton

Personal Reflections

a. Have you ever experienced frustration or anxiety because you couldn't understand your FL teacher? What did you do?
b. Have you ever felt frustrated with professionally made audio- or video-taped material? If so, what was the source of your frustration?
c. Do you listen strategically, or do you try to understand every word the FL teacher says?
d. Can you recall an FL teacher who was particularly effective in making herself or himself understood? What did he or she do to make the FL comprehensible?

Fundamental Concepts

Input processing

Nature of speech

Comprehensible versus incomprehensible input

Structured LC tasks

Degree of attention

Strategy training

Activating background knowledge

Layers of processing input

*You freeze up, knowing that you won't get
to go back to the question.*
—SECOND-YEAR UNIVERSITY SPANISH STUDENT

107

CHAPTER *7*
*Addressing Listening
Comprehension
Anxiety*

One of the most innocuous but potentially one of the most debilitating types of anxiety is the anxiety accompanying listening comprehension (LC) tasks. With reading and writing, students have time to stop and consider what they are trying to write or read; however, with listening, students can be presented with information delivered swiftly, just once, and then can be asked to quickly respond. With speaking, students do stumble and hesitate, and teachers, who expect this, can reduce the anxiety this creates for students by having them engage in structured practice to overcome their fear of speaking (see Phillips in this volume). Unfortunately, too many teachers assume, erroneously, that students do not feel that same anxiety with listening tasks and treat listening as a "passive" skill that will "happen" magically during or as a result of regular classroom activities and routine. However, learners do not develop listening-comprehension skills by osmosis. For learners to become effective listeners, research indicates they must actively and strategically participate in listening.

To provide the kind of learning atmosphere that encourages students to participate actively, we must create a learner-centered, low-anxiety classroom environment. If we do not, comprehension-related anxiety can directly undermine motivation, cause students to dislike the FL (Gardner et al. 1987), and thereby inhibit the listening-comprehension process.

The language teaching profession needs to develop effective listening-comprehension activities that also alleviate anxiety associated with listening comprehension, for all the following reasons:

1. Listening comprehension is the most frequently used language skill in the classroom.
2. Listening skills have been shown to contribute to academic success more than reading or aptitude (Conaway 1982).
3. Input (comprehended aurally) is fundamental to second language acquisition (VanPatten 1996).
4. Listening-comprehension anxiety can short-circuit the entire language-learning process from processing input to producing output.

LISTENING-COMPREHENSION (LC) ANXIETY

In most of the literature on language-learning anxiety, students report that speaking in the FL produces the most anxiety (Phillips 1992; Young 1990). Slowly, however, LC has begun to surface as a problematic area for students. Krashen (in Young 1992) acknowledged that, although speaking is cited as the skill that most produces anxiety, LC is also "highly anxiety provoking if it [the discourse] is incomprehensible" (p. 168). In her study on the relationship between gender differences and language anxiety, Campbell (in this volume) found that "both males and females are more anxious about listening than the other skills both before a course begins and after 60 hours of instruction" (pp. 200–201).

According to Scarcella and Oxford (1992), listening anxiety occurs when students face a task they feel is too difficult or unfamiliar. If the listeners believe that they must understand every word they hear, their anxiety is exacerbated. Joiner (1986) contends that the anxiety arising during the listening process often springs from a negative "listening self-concept"—that is, from low self-esteem in the area of listening. In addition to difficult listening tasks and low self-esteem, Vogely (1997) has identified other sources of LC anxiety. The most salient sources of LC anxiety were reported to be, in the order listed here, (1) the nature of the speaking (voice clarity and enunciation, speed of speech, and variation in pronunciation), (2) inappropriate strategy use, (3) level of difficulty of a LC passage, and (4) fear of failure. Less common sources of LC anxiety included lack of visual support to accompany input, lack of repetition of input, lack of time to process input, and lack of LC practice.

The remainder of this chapter offers suggestions and sample activities to address sources of LC anxiety that have been documented in research.

RECOGNIZE CHARACTERISTICS OF OUR SPEECH

> *People speak too quickly, and you panic that*
> *you won't catch it all.*
> —SECOND-YEAR UNIVERSITY SPANISH STUDENT

In the Vogely study, a little over half the students reported a source of anxiety to be the nature of the speaking, which refers to the speed of the speech, the enunciation, the different accents (pronunciation), and the quality of the voice (high versus low, low versus soft, monotonous versus varied, among other qualities). Although many of these students reported that their anxiety would be alleviated if the instructor would speak more slowly, to do so would support the belief that listening comprehension is equivalent to word-for-word translation. Rather than speaking more slowly, a more effective technique would be to break the discourse down into natural segments, or phrases, and deliver them as "chunks" of speech, each presenting an idea unit while maintaining all the natural intonations, emphases, and pauses (Lee & VanPatten 1995).

Teachers can develop an awareness of their enunciation, pronunciation, and voice quality, which may lead to changes that could reduce LC anxiety in learners. For example, teachers can tape themselves to observe characteristics of their speech such as mumbling, tone of voice, volume of speech, and speed of speech. Based on these observations, teachers may want to alter their speech, although not to such an extent that speech becomes unnatural. Furthermore, as native speakers, some teachers may reflect specific dialects in their pronunciation. By overtly illustrating dialectal variations in a teacher's pronunciation, such as aspirating the /s/, using the /θ/ instead of the /z/ sound, or dropping final consonants, learners can more easily recognize and therefore process meaning based on the sounds they hear.

*I'm afraid I might hear the wrong thing and
think the teacher is talking about a different
topic than she is.*

—SECOND-YEAR UNIVERSITY SPANISH STUDENT

To address LC anxiety that stems from a passage's level of difficulty, we must examine ways to make LC material comprehensible and encourage students to use strategies in LC tasks. The difficulty level of an LC passage does not depend exclusively on the passage's language such as the vocabulary or syntax; several variables function together to make a passage comprehensible or incomprehensible. Although many students feel that the solution to LC anxiety involves simplifying the speaking to accommodate their skill level, too much of the research in SLA suggests that simplifying alone is not the solution. The following list highlights alternative suggestions rooted in LC research:

1. Use students' background knowledge (Anderson 1985; Phillips 1984; Young 1989, 1991a).
2. Use L1 knowledge (Yano, Long, & Ross 1994).
3. Use clearly and concisely structured tasks (Lee & VanPatten 1995).

As instructors, we must make speech more accessible to the students, and the list above represents only some of the ways in which an instructor can make input more comprehensible. A closer examination of these suggestions, followed by classroom ideas or activities, is intended to offer some insight into LC to help understand the complexity of this skill.

Use students' background knowledge. According to Ausubel (1968), "the most important single factor influencing learning is what the learner already knows. Ascertain this and teach accordingly" (p. vi). Young (1991b) notes, however, that it is virtually impossible to ascertain a student's background knowledge. She suggests several prereading strategies geared to activate all types of knowledge that are just as relevant to the listening task. The following suggestions are a combination of ones Young offers for prereading that are appropriate for prelistening (Young 1991b, p. 1125) and ones that come from listening-comprehension research.

1. Provide a summary or outline of the text to be heard.
2. Offer prelistening organizers, such as allowing learners to review comprehension questions or other elements of a task to be completed (e.g., a chart to be filled out or a map in which items are to be drawn), or offer a discussion that will activate appropriate schema (Berne 1995).
3. Talk to students to find what they know about a topic.
4. Use analogies to help develop schemata for cultural information that the learner may not know (Shook 1997).
5. Use texts with content and/or rhetorical structures with which students are familiar.

In the classroom, both task schemata and topic schemata should be considered. For example, once the listeners know the conversation they will be hearing is taking place in a restaurant, they immediately have an imaginable stage on which the action can occur, and the task should be more easily approached. The task and topic schema become even more accessible if the restaurant is specified by type, such as fast food or fancy, so students can draw on their knowledge of the cuisine available in each type of restaurant, as well as serving procedures.

Use L1 knowledge. All learners come to an FL class with linguistic knowledge of their own native language, and this can be accessed to facilitate learning the FL. For example, students recognize exaggerated intonation and use of gestures. They know how to request repetition and restatements. They have experienced conversational adjustments in their native language. An instructor's task would be to help them recognize their L1 skills as strategies that could potentially facilitate comprehension of the FL. Yano, Long, and Ross (1994) summarized the linguistic and conversational adjustments native speakers use in their native language with non-native speakers. Teachers can use these same linguistic and conversational adjustments in the target language input to facilitate LC and help decrease learners' anxiety. (See their summary in Table 7.1). The following is a listening-comprehension activity with a prelistening step that attempts to activate the appropriate background knowledge and, at the same time, makes use of students' L1 linguistic knowledge (in this case L1 would be English).

Activity A. Thumbs up or thumbs down?

Prelistening tasks

Step 1. You are about to hear a movie review on the radio. You must determine if the review is a positive one (thumbs up) or a negative one (thumbs down). Recall what you know about reviews. Brainstorm the various features of movie reviews.

Step 2. To help you attend to words or phrases that signal the type of review this critic offers, mark with an X the words that could be used to reflect negative attributes in a movie review and with a check ones that could represent positive attributes. Remember that many of these words are cognates.

❑ ser estimulante   ❑ satisfacer su curiosidad   ❑ no tener trama
❑ ser interesante   ❑ tener fascinación   ❑ ser espectacular
❑ aburrir   ❑ detestar   ❑ devastar
❑ encantar   ❑ ser demente   ❑ gustar

Listening tasks

Step 3. Listen to the movie review, which also includes many cognates. This first time, circle the words in the preceding list that you hear in the review.

Step 4. Now listen to the review a second time. This time listen for other words or phrases that indicate whether the review is a positive or a negative one. Write a few of those on the following blank.

_____

TABLE 7.1

Characteristics of linguistic adjustments and conversational adjustments between native speakers (NS) and non-native speakers (NNS).

Linguistic adjustments can occur in all domains and affect the forms the learner hears (or reads).

Phonological adjustments:

a. Slower rate of delivery
b. More careful articulation
c. Stress of key words and pauses before and after them
d. More full forms and fewer contractions

Morphological adjustments and syntactic changes:

a. Use of fewer words and clauses per utterance
b. Preference for canonical word order
c. Retention of usually deleted optional constituents
d. Overt marking of grammatical relations
e. Higher frequencies of certain types of questions

Semantic changes:

a. More overt marking of semantic relations
b. Lower type-token ration
c. Fewer idiomatic expressions (occasionally resulting in marked uses of lexical items, such as *to have*, rather than *earn money*)
d. Noun phrases over pronouns
e. Concrete over dummy verbs (like *do*)

Conversational adjustments affect both the content and the interactional structure of foreign talk.

Where content is concerned, conversational adjustments with NNSs tend:

a. To have more of a here and now orientation
b. To treat a more predictable, narrower range of topics more briefly—for example, by dealing with fewer information bits
c. By maintaining a lower ration of topic-initiating to topic-continuing moves

The interactional structure of NS-NNS conversation is marked by:

a. More abrupt topic-shifts
b. More use of questions for topic-initiating moves
c. More repetition of various kinds (including semantic repetition, or paraphrase)
d. More comprehension checks
e. Confirmation checks
f. Clarification requests
g. Expansions
h. Question-and-answer strings
i. Decomposition

Postlistening task

Step 5. On the basis of the review, is this a movie that merits a thumbs-up or a thumbs-down reaction? Would you go see it?

Use clearly and concisely structured tasks. Structured-input activities "guide and focus learners' attention when they process input" (Lee & VanPatten 1995). Structured tasks effectively alleviate LC anxiety because the listeners know why they are listening, where to begin, and in what direction to go. By starting an LC activity with tasks that allow students to experience successes, then increasing the level of difficulty through a sequenced structure, the activity boosts students' confidence and reduces their anxiety.

To process information effectively, listeners must pay close attention to speech if they are to comprehend. For example, structuring a practice listening activity for specific verb morphology in speech could help students associate the necessary changes in meaning triggered by that morphology. In designing structured input for LC, the instructor must first determine the purpose and the task of the LC activity. The following example illustrates an LC task designed to identify changes in meaning triggered by verb morphology.

Activity B. Listening for time reference

Step 1. Listen to each sentence taken from a weather report. Indicate whether the weather report refers to yesterday's (Y), today's (TD), or tomorrow's (TM) weather.
1. _____ In Mexico, it was unexpectantly cold.
2. _____ Temperatures are going to rise.
3. _____ It is sunny and cool for the moment.
4. _____ It rained for an entire week.
5. _____ Snow will arrive soon in the higher elevations.

Step 2. Once again listen to each sentence. This time select the appropriate time-related adverbial that can be added to the sentence you hear.

MODEL: (you hear) The temperature continues to be mild. (you select from)
a. later this week
b. today
c. last night

According to Cohen (1990) depth of attention is crucial to the listening process, but students will feel overwhelmed if they have to listen for several specific pieces of information simultaneously. However, by breaking down an LC task into smaller processing units, we can increase LC and consequently contribute to students' feelings of success. The next activity illustrates an example of a structured LC task designed to enhance learners' comprehension and reduce LC anxiety by breaking down the listening task into several steps.

Activity C. When can we study together?

Ramón, Alicia, and Tomás are taking a Spanish class together, and they have an exam in 1 week. Listen to them as they discuss their schedules with one another for the purpose of finding a specific time when all three can get together. (Students have a weekly calendar that reflects the class times of their school.)

Step 1. The first time you hear their schedules, fill in the calendar with the times that each of them are in class (see Appendix B at the end of this chapter for teacher's script). Write R in the time slots that Ramón is in class, A for Alicia's class schedule, and T for Tomás.

Step 2. The second time you hear their schedule, take notes on the information requested in the blanks below the schedule. Make sure you know what information you are asked to provide before the second listening.

Step 3. Your instructor will read the text to you one last time to verify your work. Once you have all the information on the calendar, determine the day and time all three will be able to get together to study for their Spanish exam.

	el lunes	el martes	el miércoles	el jueves	el domingo
8:00–8:50					
9:05–9:55					
10:10–11:00					
11:15–12:05					
12:20–1:10					
1:25–2:15					
2:30–3:20					
3:35–4:25					

Notes:

What are the activities that each does after 4:25 in the afternoon?

R: _____

A: _____

T: _____

What day and time will all three be able to meet to study at least for an hour for the Spanish exam?

Day and Time: _____

In this activity, when the learners hear the passage for the first time, they should focus on specific lexical items in order to fill in the calendar (the times that Ramón, Alicia, and Tomás are in class). The second time they hear the passage, they should listen for chunks of language that will provide the information they need to complete the second task (determine what they do when not attending class).

When they hear the passage the last time, they can attend to more detail and confirm or correct their prior comprehension. In this last task, students must synthesize the information to indicate a day and time when Ramón, Alicia, and Tomás are free to study together. If they had been asked to listen for class times, to listen for out-of-class activities, and to determine when Ramón, Alicia, and Tomás were all free to study together, many students would probably be unable to process quickly enough to take in all the information they needed. Their processing capacity would overload.

Guiding students through an LC text by focusing their attention on one thing at a time, as we do when we listen to an announcement at the airport to determine whether it has information relevant to our flight, students get practice with a variety of real-world listening-comprehension tasks. At the same time, teachers help students avoid being overwhelmed by too much information. Rather than struggling to understand everything in order to comprehend, students can be encouraged to see comprehension as a progressive process and to understand how the passage fits together. As Omaggio Hadley (1993) states, listening skills can be developed by progressing through functions in a cyclic rather than linear manner. This can be done by using texts "recurrently" (p. 173). Moreover, if students are required to support their findings with textual evidence, rather than simply offering an opinion on the topic, they can be encouraged to be more accountable for the information the text provides.

When LC instruction includes structured-input tasks, several sources of LC anxiety can be addressed at the same time. For example, students get the repetition they often need; they are asked to listen for specific items of information, one at a time, so they have time to process texts; and the texts are chunked so the tasks are less complicated, thus alleviating students' anxiety caused by difficult LC texts and tasks.

PROVIDE INSTRUCTION IN STRATEGY-USE

> *Sometimes it is difficult for me to get a hold of the words being spoken let alone understand them.*
>
> —SECOND-YEAR UNIVERSITY SPANISH STUDENT

Instructors should not assume that learners know what it means to be a strategic listener. Class time should be dedicated to discussing aspects of the listening process and listening strategies, as well as applying LC strategies. By sensitizing learners to the use of LC strategies, we can alleviate another source of anxiety and simultaneously improve their LC skills. The following is a possible sequence of activities that can be used to help students become aware of the role of strategy-use in LC. It is followed by a list of strategies that can be used to enhance LC.

Activity D. Learning how to listen

Step 1. Have the students explore and articulate their own definition of aural comprehension. What does it mean to "understand" what you hear? To help them determine what their "listening process" is, have them close their eyes while you read a passage to them. Instruct them to concentrate on what they are doing to understand the passage rather than the information that is being transmitted. Give them 5 minutes to jot down (in English) what they perceived themselves doing to understand the passage; then repeat the exercise. The second time, they will be more attuned to what it is they do. Compare notes either as a class or in small groups.

Step 2. In small groups, have students elaborate on strategies that seem appropriate for different listening tasks. These exercises should create a listening strategy list, grouped by type of task, that can be referred to in future activities. Explain that this list should be seen as descriptive rather than prescriptive and that it might change as they gain more experience.

Step 3. Provide the students practice with strategies and allow time to get feedback on the effectiveness of the strategies. For example, ask listeners to listen for main ideas, as opposed to specific details, and/or vice versa. Then, ask them to discuss what strategies they used and whether they felt the use of those particular strategies helped them understand what they heard.

Sample LC Strategies

- Guess the meaning of words through context.
- Use existing knowledge of the world.
- Make use of visual cues.
- Recognize cognates.
- Listen for specific information.
- Listen for the main idea.
- Recognize the structural format of the discourse.
- Recognize the function of the discourse.
- Recognize transitional words and phrases.

Many of the students in the recent Vogely study cited their lack of LC "strategies" as one source of anxiety. In their own words, they struggled with the context in which what they were listening to occurred, or they felt they did not understand key words. Others feared they would hear the "wrong thing" and assume the discourse was about one topic when it was actually about something else. For these students, confusion and panic would set in and make them even more anxious. If we teach students to be strategic listeners, we may help them approach LC texts with less anxiety. For example, we can teach students to listen for cues that would lead them to assume the correct context for an LC text. By providing excerpts from authentic contexts—such as radio broadcasting of weather reports, movie reviews, national and local news, and sports news—and then asking students to identify the context in which the text occurs, we give students practice in contextualizing an aural text. Students in a foreign language class are also faced with aural texts that are academic in nature. The following activity illustrates how we can have various layers of comprehension and of strategy-use. The LC strategies practiced in this activity include activating background knowledge, listening for the main idea, and listening for specific detail.

Activity E. Sports in the Hispanic world

A. Prelistening: Phase I

Step 1. In a moment, your instructor will read a passage about sports in the Hispanic world (see Appendix C at the end of this chapter for teacher's script). Before he or she reads this passage, jot down a list of the sports or physical activities that you think might be popular in the Hispanic culture (in Spanish or English). Write down at least three. If you can think of more, write them down as well.

Step 2. Do you think the same sports are popular in the Hispanic world that are popular in the United States? Why or why not?

B. Further explorations: Phase II

Step 1. Listen to the passage one time without writing anything down. Try to determine if the sports you wrote down in your prelistening list are mentioned. Also, try to determine if it seems that the activities mentioned are different from or similar to those that are popular in the United States.
Were your sports mentioned?   ❑ Yes   ❑ No
Are the activities mentioned similar to or different from those that are popular in the United States?

Step 2. Listen to the passage a second time. This time you may wish to take some notes. Just try to get the gist of what the passage is saying. After you have listened, decide if the following activities are mentioned.

		Sí	No
a.	el fútbol	❑	❑
b.	el béisbol	❑	❑
c.	el básquetbol	❑	❑
d.	el esquí	❑	❑
e.	el tenis	❑	❑
f.	el vólibol	❑	❑

Step 3. This will be the third and final time you will hear the passage. Listen this time to get more detail. You may wish to take notes. After you have listened, decide if the following statements are true or false based on what is said in the passage. Be prepared to explain why a statement is false and offer a true statement.

a. El deporte más popular en los EE.UU. y el mundo hispano es el
   fútbol.
b. El béisbol es muy popular en el Caribe.
c. Los hispanos no practican deportes individuales.
d. Se puede esquiar en España, Chile y Argentina.
e. No hay gimnasios en muchas ciudades hispanas.
f. Los hispanos no tienen entusiasmo por los deportes.

Note that the activity began by activating what knowledge the listeners
might have about sports. Those who do not follow sports have an opportunity
to ask questions and learn from the sports fans what background they may
need for the LC task. Each time the passage was read, students were asked to
focus their attention on one particular item, to complete only one particular
task, and to practice a particular strategy or combination of strategies.

First, they listened to compare their predictions to those in the LC passage.
Then, they focused their attention on the actual sports mentioned in the task
(listening for specific information). In these two steps, students are guided to
build meaning from the text by tapping their own knowledge and verifying
what they know with what they hear (using background knowledge). The last
task asks students, after they have built some lexical skills, to focus on the content of the passage in order to understand the main idea. Each time they listened, they attended to a particular level of detail, they attended to one thing
at a time, and they practiced different listening strategies.

Once this kind of strategy training takes place, instructors will need only
to reactivate students' knowledge about LC strategies before beginning an LC
task. By training students to use strategies in LC tasks, we sensitize them to
tools that can empower them, facilitate their LC comprehension, and ultimately reduce their LC anxiety.

Make Use of Visuals

Although visual stimulus is not an inherent part of LC activities, it can be a
beneficial addition to any listening task, especially to beginning language
learners. According to some neuroscientists (Fiske & Taylor 1984; Nisbett &
Ross 1980), concrete, vivid images exert the most powerful influences on a
learner's behavior. In the classroom, visual stimuli can take many forms, including spatial and bodily-kinesthetic. The more varied the stimuli used, the
more likely the instructor will accommodate different learning styles and individual preferences.

To be effective, the visuals do not have to be the activity's focus; peripheral
materials, like posters and models, can have as strong an impact as centrally lo-
cated visual stimuli (Caine & Caine 1994). Instructors can enhance LC by accompanying any listening tasks with one or more of the following visuals.

1. Entire videos or video clips
2. Taped or live television programs
3. The actual object or a model of the object discussed
4. Photographs, drawings, or paintings
5. Posters

6. Overhead transparencies
7. Pantomime, body language, or role playing
8. Facial expressions
9. Lip movements
10. Semantic maps

Visual support not only makes the topic of the listening task *more accessible* for these listeners who are visual and spatial learners, it also helps all listeners relate personally to the topic, thus reducing the anxiety that can occur when they think they do not know what is being discussed. The following activity illustrates one way to use visuals in listening-comprehension tasks.

Activity F. Homes for sale

Step 1. Brainstorm the various pieces of information usually found in a description of a home for sale—that is, price, number of rooms, number of bathrooms, and so on. Write them on the board.

Step 2. Hand out five brochures of homes for sale and allow learners 2 minutes to review the descriptions of the homes.

Step 3. Now watch and listen to four televised homes for sale and match each home to its written counterpart (the brochure).

Step 4. Discuss how students arrived at their answers.

Language learners in the Vogely study also indicated that they would feel less anxious about LC tasks if they could practice LC more often in class; however, dedicating more class time to LC activities will be effective only if appropriate activities are used. In this chapter, I have highlighted various characteristics of LC activities that produce LC anxiety and have suggested ways the instructor can address those anxieties in practical ways. One source of LC anxiety students report, and not yet discussed, is LC anxiety stemming from their fear of failure.

RECOGNIZE LEARNERS' FEARS OF FAILURE

> *I feel like everyone else except me*
> *understands perfectly.*
> —SECOND-YEAR UNIVERSITY SPANISH STUDENT

According to McKeachie (1994), an important instructor characteristic that can do much to relieve student anxiety is a sympathetic attitude toward students' problems and fears. Beginning FL students find it difficult to accept that they are back in a state of infancy when it comes to understanding a spoken FL; therefore, an important step is to create a positive, nonthreatening atmosphere in the classroom. The climate of the classroom is directly related to the instructor's attitudes, expectations, and physical presence, which in turn determine the way in which the instructor and the student interact. If we want students to succeed in FL learning, we must not ignore their beliefs, perceptions, fears, obstacles, and anxieties.

Actively addressing listening anxiety will empower both the teacher and the listener. One way to address students' fears about FL learning, and LC in particular, would be to have students list sources of LC anxiety on the board. Students would see that everyone shares LC anxiety and that many of the other students experience similar fears of failure. Knowing that others share their beliefs can motivate students to overcome their own anxiety. Moreover, when teachers and students make the shift from listening for correctness or listening to understand word for word, to listening for a message, the motivation to understand increases and the fear of being "wrong" decreases.

To minimize further the LC anxiety stemming from fear of failure, it is crucial to begin developing students' LC skills at a level where they can experience small successes, as previously mentioned in this chapter. Reactivating the knowledge gained through those successes and expanding them could prove to be an effective approach to developing LC skills in learners. If students feel like they are progressing within their LC ability, they will be more motivated to stretch themselves and feel more relaxed.

CONCLUSION

In this chapter, I have discussed sources of LC anxiety reported through research and have offered practical activities designed to alleviate LC anxiety stemming from the major sources of anxiety that students report. The limited activities and suggestions presented here can be modified to fit the dynamics of most FL classes. By increasing opportunities for students to experience small successes in the FL classroom, we help reduce their LC anxiety and we help them acquire a second language less painfully.

PORTFOLIO ASSIGNMENTS

1. a. Design an LC activity that structures aural input and increases the possibility of comprehension.
   b. Share your activity with the class, or turn it in to your instructor.
2. a. Since strategy-use in LC may lead to better comprehension and thus less frustration with LC tasks, design an LC task that encourages students to listen strategically.
   b. Share your activity with two other classmates. Which strategies did the LC activities invoke? Do the activities appear to be well thought out?

ACTION RESEARCH

1. a. Administer the following Anxiety Thermometer to an FL class.

Listening Comprehension Anxiety

Indicate how much anxiety you experience during listening comprehension tasks in your FL class.

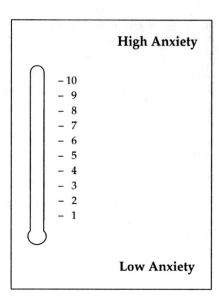

b. Tally the results to determine the number of students who reported 6 or higher on the thermometer.

c. Share your findings with the class to ascertain whether LC anxiety is experienced by a high percentage of language learners.

2. a. Interview a language learner who has expressed frustration and anxiety because of not being able to understand the FL teacher. (You may need to have an instructor identify a student in class if you do not teach.) In the interview, identify the student's sources of LC anxiety and ask him or her to suggest ways the teacher can help reduce the anxiety. Take copious notes during the interview.

b. Examine your notes to ascertain whether the sources of LC anxiety were ones already identified in this chapter. Were there other sources that the student mentioned that were not mentioned in this chapter?

c. Share your results with your class.

REFERENCES

Anderson, R. C. (1985). Role of the reader's schema in comprehension. In H. Singer & R. B. Ruddell (Eds.), *Theoretical models and processing of reading* (3rd ed.). Newark: International Reading Association, pp. 372–384.

Ausubel, D. P. (1968). *Educational psychology: A cognitive view.* New York: Holt, Rinehart & Winston.

Berne, J. (1995). How does varying pre-listening activities affect L2 listening comprehension? *Hispania, 78,* 316–329.

Caine, R. N., & Caine, G. (1994). *Making connections: Teaching and the human brain* (2nd ed.). Reading, MA: Addison-Wesley.

Campbell, C. (1997). Language anxiety in men and women: Dealing with gender difference in the language classroom. In D. J. Young (Ed.), *Affect in foreign language and second language learning: A practical guide to creating a low-anxiety classroom atmosphere.* San Francisco: McGraw-Hill, pp. 191–209.

Cohen, A. D. (1990). *Language learning: Insight for learners, teachers, and researchers.* Boston: Heinle & Heinle.

Conaway, M. (1982). Listening: Learning tool and retention agent. In A. S. Algier & K. W. Algier (Eds.), *Improving reading and study skills.* San Francisco: Jossey-Bass.

Fiske, S. T., & Taylor, S. E. (1984). *Social cognition.* Reading, MA: Addison-Wesley.

Gardner, R. C., Lalande, R. N., Moorcroft, R., & Evers, F. T. (1987). Second language attrition: The role of motivation and use. *Journal of Language and Social Psychology, 6,* 29–47.

Joiner, E. (1986). Listening in the foreign language. In B. H. Wing (Ed.), *Listening, reading, and writing: Analysis and application.* Middlebury, VT: Northeast Conference on the Teaching of Foreign Languages, pp. 43–70.

Lee, J. F., & VanPatten, B. (1995). *Making communicative language teaching happen.* New York: McGraw-Hill.

Mendelsohn, D. J., (1984). There ARE strategies for listening. *TEAL Occasional Papers, 8,* 63–76.

McKeachie, W. J. (1994). *Teaching tips* (9th ed.). Lexington, MA: D. C. Heath.

Nisbett, R. E., & Ross, L. D. (1980). *Human inference: Strategies and shortcomings of social judgement.* Englewood Cliffs, NJ: Prentice Hall.

Omaggio Hadley, A. (1993). *Teaching language in context* (2nd ed.). Boston: Heinle & Heinle.

Phillips, E. (1992). The effects of language anxiety on students' oral test performance and attitudes. *The Modern Language Journal, 76,* 14–26.

Phillips, J. (1984). Practical implications of recent research in reading. *Foreign Language Annals, 17,* 285–296.

Scarcella, R. C., & Oxford, R. L. (1992). *The tapestry of language learning: The individual in the communicative classroom.* Boston: Heinle & Heinle.

Shook, D. (1997). Identifying and overcoming possible mismatches in the beginning reader-literary text interaction. *Hispania, 80,* 234–243.

VanPatten, B. (1996). *Input processing and grammar instruction.* Norwood, NJ: Ablex.

Vogely, A. J. (1997). Listening comprehension anxiety: Students' reported sources and solutions. *Foreign Language Annals, 31,* 67–80.

Yano, Y., Long, M., & Ross, S. (1994). The effects of simplified and elaborated texts on foreign language reading comprehension. *Language Learning, 44,* 189–219.

Young, D. J. (1989). A systematic approach to foreign language reading: What does the research suggest? *Hispania, 72,* 755–762.

Young, D. J. (1990). An investigation of students' perspectives on anxiety and speaking. *Foreign Language Annals, 23,* 539–553.

Young, D. J. (1991a). Activating student background knowledge in a take charge approach to foreign language reading. *Hispania, 74,* 1124–1132.

Young, D. J. (1991b). Creating a low anxiety classroom environment: What does language anxiety research suggest? *The Modern Language Journal, 75,* 426–437.

Young, D. J. (1992). Language anxiety from the foreign language specialist's perspective: Interviews with Krashen, Omaggio Hadley, Terrell, and Rardin. *Foreign Language Annals, 25,* 157–172.

APPENDIX A

Teacher's script for Activity A, p. 110

El público de hoy tiene mucha fascinación con los desastres naturales. Le encantan películas con mucha acción y destrucción. Pues aquí les presento

la película con ambas. En esta película, el personaje central es una tempestad que es muy común en muchas partes del mundo: el tornado. Varios actores dinámicos luchan contra el viento y la lluvia para satisfacer su curiosidad científica, y para encontrar al verdadero amor. A la vez, la audiencia satisface su curiosidad hacia los efectos de un tornado. Todos pueden disfrutar de carros y animales que vuelan y de tornados que tocan a la tierra con dedos de destrucción. Al que le guste lo espectacular, hay que llevar su paraguas y ponerse su cinturón de seguridad.

APPENDIX B

Teacher's script for Activity C, p. 112

Ramón tiene cinco clases este semestre. Los lunes, martes y miércoles asiste a su clase de español a las 9:05 de la mañana. Despúes va a su clase de literatura a las 10:10. Por la tarde tiene una clase a la 1:25 donde estudia administración de empresas. A las 2:30 tiene una clase de composición. Ramón hace una carrera en computación. No le gusta estudiar literatura ni composición. Trabaja en Taco Bell los martes, jueves y sábados. Sale de su trabajo a las 5:30 de la tarde. Estudia en la biblioteca los martes y jueves por la noche.

Alicia hace una carrera en las ciencias políticas. Tiene tres clases este semestre porque trabaja en la librería todas las tardes de la 1:00 hasta las 5:00. Los lunes, martes y jueves asiste a su clase de economía a las 8:00 de la mañana e inmediatamente después va a su clase de español. Tiene la clase de ingeniería los martes desde las 10:10 hasta las 12:05. Alicia visita a su familia en Boston los fines de semana.

Tomás estudia teatro. Tiene cuatro clases este semestre. Tiene una clase de periodismo a las 9:00 hasta las 11:00 los martes y jueves. Los lunes, miércoles y viernes tiene una clase de música a las 10:10. Su clase de arte es después de su clase de español. Tomás practica en un teatro con otros dramaturgos todas las tardes, desde la 1:30 hasta las 5:00. Tomás no tiene mucho dinero y tiene que trabajar en McDonalds los sábados y domingos.

The instructor may tailor the content of the script to a particular audience and refer to places with which their learners are familiar, courses that are popular, and hours that correspond to the class times with which the learners are familiar.

APPENDIX C

Teacher's script for Activity E, p. 116

A los hispanos les gustan mucho los deportes, especialmente el fútbol, que es el deporte más popular en el mundo hispano. Hay muchos equipos en las escuelas, en los clubes y en las vecindades.

Otro de los deportes que los hispanos practican mucho es el béisbol. Este deporte, de origen norteamericano, es muy popular en Puerto Rico, Cuba, Venezuela y la República Dominicana.

Los hispanos también practican deportes individuales, el esquí y la natación, por ejemplo. Hay lugares en España, como Baqueira de los Pirineos, adonde va mucha gente a esquiar. Y en Chile y Argentina también se practica mucho el esquí.

Un deporte muy popular en España y Latinoamérica es el jai alai, un juego de origen vasco. En el jai alai participan sólo dos jugadores, que tienen que ser ágiles y rápidos. El jai alai es un deporte que requiere mucha destreza.

En muchas ciudades del mundo hispano hay gimnasios donde es posible jugar al ráquetbol y al tenis, nadar, darse un baño de vapor, correr, levantar pesas, hacer gimnasia y hacer ejercicios aeróbicos.

El entusiasmo por los deportes es sin duda un rasgo importante del carácter hispano.

Script taken from *Dos mundos*, 1st edition, by Tracy D. Terrell, Magdalena Andrade, Jeanne Egasse, and Elías Miguel Muñoz. Published by Random House/McGraw-Hill in New York, 1986.

Decreasing Language Anxiety: Practical Techniques for Oral Activities

Elaine M. Phillips
Southwest Educational Development Laboratory

Personal Reflections

a. Do you recall ever comparing your language ability with that of other students? How did this make you feel?
b. What emotions do you associate with speaking in your FL/SL class? Do you feel the same way when you speak in public in your native language?
c. Were there any particular oral activities you found most unpleasant in language class? What kinds did you find least stressful?

Fundamental Concepts

Realistic expectations

Self-esteem

Community of learners

Group/paired activities

Communication strategies

Overt correction versus modeling

Oral evaluation

125

CHAPTER 8
*Decreasing Language
Anxiety: Practical
Techniques for Oral
Activities*

Research has consistently shown that anxious language students suffer significantly during oral activities and that anxiety has a negative impact on students' attitudes toward language study (Phillips 1990). For instance, Young (1990) found that the language students she surveyed were most anxious when they had to speak in front of their peers, and Horwitz, Horwitz, and Cope (1986) reported that concern about speaking in the foreign language was expressed most frequently by university language students who visited their learning skills center for help. In addition, Price (1991) reports on interviews with highly anxious, former language students who agreed unanimously that speaking the target language generated the greatest anxiety. Based on consistent results showing that the speaking skill is the most frequently cited source of anxiety among language students, one might posit that today's emphasis on the development of communicative competence will exacerbate students' anxiety about speaking (Phillips 1991). If teachers are unwilling to renounce the goals of the oral proficiency movement, they must seek a resolution to the apparent conflict between those goals and the negative affective reactions engendered by oral practice. The purpose of this chapter is to help practitioners better understand some of the variables related to anxiety and the oral skill and to offer teachers strategies for lowering the levels of stress in their classroom through the use of anxiety-management tools and activities that encourage authentic communication within a warm and supportive community of learners.

A brief review of the literature shows that researchers have examined the relationship between language anxiety and numerous variables such as classroom activity (Crookall & Oxford 1991; Koch & Terrell 1991; Young 1990), competitiveness (Bailey 1983), learning styles (Ehrman & Oxford 1990), risk-taking (Ely 1986), attitudes (Phillips 1992; Price 1991) and, in particular, beliefs about language learning (Horwitz 1988), self-esteem (Horwitz et al. 1986; Phillips 1990; Price 1991; Young 1990), and even the conflict between effort and reward (Price 1991; Speiller 1988). This conflict, for example, may contribute to heightened anxiety because ability and effort are not necessarily rewarded quickly or in the same manner in language learning as they may be in other academic domains. Imagine, for instance, the frustration of the student with perfect scores on discrete-point tests who suddenly discovers during an oral exam the difference in what she *knows* and what she can *use* to communicate with the teacher. Phillips (1992) notes that, although the correlation between anxiety levels and oral exam scores is modest at best, students often believe that their anxiety affects their oral performance, and she suggests that psychological factors play an important role in determining whether students continue their study of a language. Learning another language is a lengthy process, especially for those who study in a "foreign" language environment. Speiller (1988), for example, found that high school students who chose not to continue their language study often mentioned lack of progress as a contributing factor. According to Price (1991), "the discrepancy between effort and results" was especially frustrating for high achievers. Only recently this writer had a student, a presidential scholar at the university, who confessed her frustration at not being able to do better on tests and not feeling more confident in class in spite of the hours she spent preparing. She also confessed, "I'm afraid it's affecting my attitude, too."

Another variable often mentioned as contributing to heightened language anxiety is low self-esteem. Because one's self-image is closely associated with the ability to express oneself through language (Guiora et al. 1972), it is understandable that language students, particularly beginners, develop a negative self-image in the classroom when they do not have the linguistic skills necessary to express themselves in an authentic manner (Horwitz et al. 1986). For example, students often do not learn simple expressions for reacting to the comments of others—such as expressing surprise, joy, anger, indifference, and so on. In addition, they are often self-conscious about their accents (Price 1991), and, if they are competitive by nature, their perceived lack of ability to compete with other students may also engender anxiety (Bailey 1983). In fact, Young (1990) found that students' concern about making mistakes was the primary reason they were reticent about speaking in class. According to Krashen (in Young 1992), students with low self-esteem are more likely to be concerned with what their classmates think about them; thus, fear of making a mistake or appearing foolish in front of peers heightens their anxiety. Unfortunately, common error-correction methods tend to put individual students "on the spot." Foss and Reitzel (1988) also suggest that "[p]erception of self plays a key role in how students approach the acquisition and use of a second language" (p. 440). For example, if students suffer from a negative self-image in language class, they may see their contributions as less important than those of other students and thus be less willing to speak out, to practice speaking. Indeed, Price's interviewees confirm this assertion, speaking uniformly of their fear about "being laughed at by the others, of making a fool of themselves in public" (p. 105).

Students' self-image can also be indirectly affected by their expectations related to their language class. Most learners usually arrive the first day with some preconceived notions regarding the process on which they are about to embark—whether or not they have ever studied another language. Research shows that many of these beliefs and expectations may be unrealistic and suggests that these beliefs can contribute to heightened anxiety in the language classroom. In the most detailed study of student beliefs about language learning, Horwitz (1988) used the *Beliefs About Language Learning Inventory* (BALLI) to interview learners of French, German, and Spanish. She found that 30% or more of the students agreed or strongly agreed that learning a foreign language involved primarily learning a lot of vocabulary words, learning a lot of grammar rules, or translating from English. In fact, 72% of Spanish and German students agreed with the statement on translation. Furthermore, 37% of the students believed it would take them 1 to 2 years to become fluent in another language spending 1 hour a day! Armed with these unrealistic expectations and incomplete ideas about the language-learning process, it is not surprising that a student's anxiety heightens when his or her expectations go unfulfilled or when the preferred learning strategies fail to produce the desired results.

Understanding some of the underlying factors associated with language anxiety is essential for practitioners because language teachers, as a whole, are a self-selected group. That is, if they had suffered greatly from classroom anxiety themselves, they would not likely have become language educators. Consequently, to help anxious learners in their classrooms, teachers need to begin with a great deal of concern and empathy for the negative affect students may experience. They must talk openly with their students about realistic expectations for the course and about the nature of language anxiety. Most importantly, they must develop strategies for developing a sense of community among learners, activities that allow students a great deal of non-threatening oral practice, and evaluation techniques designed to reduce learner anxiety.

Understanding some of the factors that can raise anxiety levels of language students is important. Knowing what to do to reduce stress in the classroom, however, is the issue of primary concern to most practitioners. The next section of this chapter provides teachers with practical suggestions that can be implemented in the classroom without special training or expertise. The first part introduces two instruments for leading students in a discussion of their anxieties about language learning; the second presents classroom activities designed to lower students' stress about speaking in the target language; the third addresses error correction; and the final part suggests ways to reduce the anxiety associated with the evaluation of oral performance.

TALKING ABOUT STUDENTS' FEARS

Although a few students may experience little anxiety related to oral performance in the language classroom, the large majority confess to some degree of nervousness related to the speaking skill. Teachers should therefore begin from the first day of class to reach out to students and acknowledge their fears, openly admitting that language learning does make many people anxious to one degree or another. Instructors need not be trained in psychotherapy to use the tools presented below to generate discussion in the classroom. Without dwelling unnecessarily on the negative, teachers can provide an outlet for students to express their feelings and to recognize that there are others in the class who share their concerns.

Beliefs About Language Learning Inventory (BALLI)

The results from Horwitz' survey (1988) mentioned earlier reveal that many students operate under a highly unrealistic belief system when it comes to the nature of language acquisition. To rectify students' erroneous assumptions and to help them develop reasonable criteria for evaluating their own progress, teachers themselves must be armed with some basic information suggested by the research. First, students need to know that while aptitude plays an important role in one's ability to speak another language, there are many other variables associated with language learning, such as attitude, motivation, anxiety, learning style, tolerance for ambiguity, and risk-taking. Risk-taking, for example, can be as important as accuracy in language learning because students who risk speaking, even when they are unsure of themselves, generally receive more feedback, hence get further exposure to comprehensible input (Rubin 1975). Second, students should understand that there are many ways to go about learning another language. Although traditional learning activities that focus on the mechanics of language and the lexicon (memorizing vocabulary lists, translating, learning grammar rules) have their place in the learning process, students should also realize that *acquisition* activities (reading and listening for meaning where attention is on the message, not form) likewise play a substantive role. Finally, teachers should state honestly that learning another language, especially in a non-target-language environment, is a lengthy process. If the Foreign Service Institute believes it takes at least 240 hours to produce an intermediate level speaker under ideal circumstances (small, intensive classes with highly motivated learners), students' goals of becoming fluent in a year or two certainly need to be revised!

Armed with factual information, teachers can use the BALLI to generate classroom discussion about the language-learning process. A BALLI survey will provide teachers a composite picture of the nature of their students' beliefs about language learning and also present them with an excellent opportunity to instruct students about the nature of language learning.

Foreign Language Classroom Anxiety Scale

Students' concerns related to their self-image can be addressed in a similar manner using the *Foreign Language Classroom Anxiety Scale* (FLCAS) (Horwitz, 1984; see Appendix B, pp. 248–249), which can also be used to identify students mostly likely to suffer from language anxiety related to speaking the target language. Having learners react to statements such as "I never feel quite sure of myself when I am speaking in my foreign language class," "I start to panic when I have to speak without preparation in language class," and "I can feel my heart pounding when I'm going to be called on in language class" allows them to express their concerns openly. Simply telling students they should not be anxious about speaking in class is not as effective at lowering anxiety as showing them that they are not alone in their fears, that others in the class are also anxious about speaking the target language.

Both the BALLI and the FLCAS can be treated in a variety of ways, preferably at the beginning of the semester or school year. The teacher can have students fill out the survey, then collect and review the results. Once the worst distortions in students' beliefs about language learning have been identified, the instructor should spend some class time discussing, for instance, realistic expectations for the course or the fact that a variety of strategies and techniques are required to become fluent in another language. A second approach is to have students complete the questionnaires and discuss their reactions with another student. After the individual discussion period, students come together and share with the rest of the class. At this time, the teacher elicits students' reactions to the cues and provides a necessary counterbalance when highly unrealistic beliefs or expectation are expressed, thereby adding to students' knowledge base as well as providing them an outlet for expressing their emotions and an opportunity to see that many of their classmates feel as they do.

TECHNIQUES AND ACTIVITIES THAT DEVELOP COMMUNITY AND REDUCE ANXIETY

129

CHAPTER 8
Decreasing Language
Anxiety: Practical
Techniques for Oral
Activities

The dilemma for language teachers is how to reduce anxiety while practicing the oral skill—when research suggests that it is oral work that produces the most anxiety. The recommendations so far have addressed attempts to deal with language anxiety on a cognitive level. Attempts to lower anxiety through cognitive restructuring will be less effective, however, if traditional activities and classroom behaviors that are the source of much of the students' original fear remain unchanged. This section discusses the importance of developing a classroom community, of teaching communicative gambits, and of using non-threatening group/paired activities that increase the amount of time individual students spend communicating in the target language.

As in any domain, performance anxiety can usually be reduced through repetition of a task. Although practice may make perfect, we are now aware that practice in the mechanical manipulation of language does not make for perfect authentic communication—that is, communication where meaning is a key ingredient. Little and Sanders (1989) suggest, in fact, that before authentic communication can take place, the students must constitute a community of learners because "the existence of a classroom community *feeds* the desire for authentic communication" (emphasis added, p. 279). *Community* in this context implies learners who "support each other and act collaboratively to construct meaningful utterances" (p. 280). Simply put, in a community, students listen and care about the personalized responses generated by their classmates, and that information becomes part of the collective knowledge referred to by the class. Certainly a teacher cannot declare the class a community; the impetus must come from the learners themselves. Nevertheless, there are certain steps the instructor can take to foster an environment where a community can develop.

Conversation Gambits

One technique for cultivating a community is to provide learners a common language—that is, a corpus of communicative gambits or expressions useful for classroom activities and for helping students feel that they are carrying on a "natural" conversation. For example, students will need to know expressions showing interest, surprise, indifference, and so on if they are to spend much time interviewing their classmates. These communicative gambits can be taught lexically and give an authentic feel to the task. They also allow students to feel more comfortable with their ability to proceed with oral activities and to work with a partner who may have a different skill level. Rather than identifying particular key expressions, the following list suggests types of expressions (with examples) that can help students respond appropriately to their classmates.

Conversation cues

Starting a conversation:
By the way,
Listen,
Well, I think that . . .

Stalling for time:
  Uh,
  Let's see . . .
  Well . . .
  You know,
  So . . .
Getting your partner involved:
  How about you?
  Do you agree?
  What do you think?
  Who . . .? When . . .?
  What . . .? Where . . .?

Reactions

Recognition:
  Yes, yes . . .
  I understand.
Clarification:
  For example?
  I don't understand.
  Huh?
  Pardon?
  You mean . . .
Agreement/Positive:
  Absolutely!
  You're right.
  I agree.
  That's great!
  Super!
  Really?
  No kidding!
Disagreement/Negative:
  I don't agree.
  No way!
  Absolutely not!
  I don't like that idea.
  Too bad!
  I'm sorry.
  Rats!
Indecision:
  Well . . .
  It's possible, but . . .
  I don't know . . .
  It depends.

Since learners usually develop confidence the more they practice, the use of the target language for classroom management purposes is also encouraged. The following lists were generated by third-semester college students. Some of the questions/statements are ones students generally direct to the teacher. More importantly, however, students want to know how to conduct simple interactions with other students about what is taking place in the classroom. Instructors are encouraged to have their students devise their own classroom vocabulary lists by asking them to note instances when they have to resort to their native language during group work. Students are then taught how to express those ideas in the target language.

131

CHAPTER 8
*Decreasing Language
Anxiety: Practical
Techniques for Oral
Activities*

Interaction with the teacher

> I don't know.
> I don't understand.
> What does _____ mean?
> How do you say _____?

Interaction with other students

> Do (did) you understand?
> I understood it all / a little / most.
> I don't (didn't) understand anything.
> What are we supposed to do?
> What do you have for number 10?
> I guessed.
> You start.
> Go on!
> You're right/wrong.

In addition to equipping students with a common communicative vocabulary, community may be developed and anxiety lowered by providing learners ample opportunity to get to know one another through oral activities with partners and in small groups. When students work in groups, they often feel safer and are less self-conscious and embarrassed to speak out because reporting on a group response is less threatening than giving an answer for which only the individual student is responsible. Furthermore, as Vande Berg (1993) points out, students are generally less timid about speaking in front of a small group than they are about speaking to a large group. Reticent students speak more freely, and community is fostered when learners must depend on their partner or partners to complete a task. Ensuring that all students know the names of their classmates, have the opportunity to work with each of them, and can provide some bit of personalized information about them may seem a daunting task for instructors whose classes number thirty or more. But group and partner work is exactly what is needed to provide adequate oral practice for all students and to encourage active involvement, especially in large classes.

The following activity types are offered as models for group and partner work and are contrasted with more traditional activities. They have been used in lower-division college French courses.[1] Most can be adapted to many structures and semantic fields to suit the needs of the class.

Recognition Activity

The use of a recognition activity for introducing new items is recommended as a means of lowering anxiety even though the activity is not necessarily a group exercise. Learners will be less anxious if they are allowed to react to the input before being required to produce the new structure. Mechanical exercises such as verb substitution drills require students to produce new structures immediately after being introduced to them when they have had no time to process the forms. Since the goal of the activity is to produce the correct form, students feel pressured (and embarrassed), and anxiety is heightened. In the following activity, note that students are asked to recognize input before being asked to produce it.

THINGS TO DO

Date *September 1*

Priority   Completed ✔

8:30 *math*	☐
10:00 *history*	☐
	☐
11:30 *geography* *—Test!!*	☐
	☐
12:00 *meet Hélène at Le Bistrot*	☐
	☐
2:00 *French*	☐
3:30 *gymnastics*	☐
	☐
call Anne about *7:45*	☐
	☐
	☐
8:30 *Concert!*	☐
	☐

Activity A. Audrey's personal agenda

133

CHAPTER 8
*Decreasing Language
Anxiety: Practical
Techniques for Oral
Activities*

Step 1. As the teacher reads the cues to the class, look at Audrey's personal agenda and indicate whether the statements the teacher reads are true or false based on Audrey's schedule.

Step 2. As the teacher repeats the cues, respond orally whether the statement is true or false.

Teacher cues: (1) Audrey has her math class at 8:30. (2) At 9:45 she has her history class. (3) Her geography class is at 12:45. (4) At midnight, she's eating with Hélène. (5) French is at 2:00. (6) Audrey does gymnastics at 2:45. (7) She has to call Anne at 6:00. (8) The concert begins at 8:30.

1. vrai ❑	faux ❑		**5.** vrai ❑	faux ❑
2. vrai ❑	faux ❑		**6.** vrai ❑	faux ❑
3. vrai ❑	faux ❑		**7.** vrai ❑	faux ❑
4. vrai ❑	faux ❑		**8.** vrai ❑	faux ❑

The instructor may give the correct time for false statements or allow volunteers to answer. Anxiety is minimized in this activity because students need not produce the new structure, only react to it. When mistakes naturally occur at this early stage, they are not apparent to other students.

Cued Response

Contextualized cued-response activities are also useful during the early production stage when cognitive overload heightens stress. They give students alternatives while providing the option of an original response. Traditional cued activities provide students one right answer in parentheses, once again raising anxiety by making form the sole focus of the activity and eliminating any creativity on the part of the learner. In the following example, the instructor first answers any questions about vocabulary, verifying that learners understand the example and directions.

Activity B. This weekend

Step 1. Work with another classmate to complete this next task.

Step 2. The following people have some free time this weekend, and they are going to do exactly what they want. Imagine their plans and say whether or not they're going to do the following activities. Add an activity of your own.

EXAMPLE: my brother: shave / comb his hair / have breakfast?
My brother's not going to shave or comb his hair. He's going to have breakfast at noon, and he's going to go to bed at 8:00 p.m.

1. my roommate: wash up / put on make-up (shave) / get dressed?
2. the professor: have fun / go to bed early / hurry?
3. my friends: get together / get married / take a walk?
4. my family and I: talk to each other / relax / get up early?

Although this activity can be done with the whole class, students get more practice if they first go through the activity with a partner, each student responding to each cue. Partner work reduces the pressure to perform perfectly and gives students more time to come up with original answers. In addition, the cues provided serve to alleviate the frustration that occurs when students try to focus on meaning and form in the early stages of learning. Once partners complete their work, volunteers share their best responses with the class.

Information Gap Activities

Another common format that increases tension is the teacher question/student response activity that places the responsibility for answering squarely on the individual student. While the entire class waits silently to hear the answer, seconds seem like minutes, and anxiety increases exponentially for the learner who has been singled out. In contrast, with information gap activities, whereby each person receives a part of the information needed to solve a puzzle, students have time to formulate responses, and the solutions come from the "team," not the individual. A further advantage is the ease with which, for example, a chart completion activity may be constructed for any number of semantic fields or grammatical structures. The learners' goal in the following activity is to find out where the International School students come from and in which countries they have lived and traveled. Each partner receives a different version of the chart containing half the information sought. They can complete the chart only by asking each other questions designed to elicit the missing information. They must not show their charts to each other! The instructor begins by eliciting the questions students will need: "How can you ask where someone is from? where they have lived? where they have traveled?" When students report back to the class, anxiety is lowered because the answers are verifiable and come from the team, not the individual.

Activity C. Completing data sheets

Step 1. Work with a partner to complete the data sheet.
Step 2. Your partner's data sheet contains the information missing in your data sheet, and vice versa. Ask your partner questions that will enable you to complete your data sheet.
Step 3. Compare your data sheets with those of another pair of students in class.
Step 4. As a class, verify your answers.

All information gap activities involve an exchange of information, but not all require a chart completion. Students may be asked to identify the location of various pieces of furniture missing from a house plan, for example, or to identify unknown buildings on a map. They may be asked to find their "long-lost relative" by interviewing classmates and matching biographical data, and so forth. Although teachers hope students use pertinent structures correctly, the focus of all information gap activities is on the task rather than on form, a factor that helps decrease anxiety.

Students at the International School (A)

135

*CHAPTER 8
Decreasing Language
Anxiety: Practical
Techniques for Oral
Activities*

name	comes from	lived in	traveled in
Mariette	Belgium		Netherlands, Germany
Fahrid		USA	Tunisia, Algeria, Canada
Kofi			Mali, Libya, Ivory Coast
Nancy	Louisiana		
Robert	Quebec	Manitoba	

Students at the International School (B)

name	comes from	lived in	traveled in
Mariette		Spain	
Fahrid	Morocco		
Kofi	Mauritania	Senegal	
Nancy		New York	Chile, Portugal, Venezuela
Robert			USA, Israel, Philippines

Interviews and Surveys

Interviews and surveys are also recommended for lowering anxiety because, as Young (1990) has pointed out, students generally feel more comfortable talking about the familiar: their feelings, attitudes, opinions, and habits. Students find these affective activities more stimulating than those that simply ask them to practice a particular structure by reconstructing sentences about Alexis or Marie-Pierre, whom they do not know. They are more relaxed because they know the answers and can focus their attention on producing them in the target language.

The following activity allows the students to talk about what they have done recently; it also provides an opportunity to interact with a number of their classmates. For the following survey, the students' goal is to find at least one classmate who answers *yes* to each question. The instructor first passes out the directed questions, verifying that students understand the vocabulary and what types of questions are required. All students stand so that they can circulate freely about the room, moving from one partner to another. They are to question one classmate at a time until that person gives a *yes* answer. They then write that person's name beside the cue and look for another partner, repeating the process with a new question. To encourage as much oral practice as possible, students should ask an appropriate follow-up to each question. Group interviews are not allowed, and only the target language is to be used. (Groups of threes may occur as students separate at different times in search of other partners. Simply discourage "crowds" where only one student is actually asking the questions.) When students complete their surveys or when time is called, volunteers report to the class on what they found out about their classmates—for example, "Susan didn't sleep well last night. She drank too much coffee."

Activity D. Find someone who . . .

Step 1. You will be looking for at least one classmate who can answer truthfully *yes* to a question you will ask. The information you seek is listed in items **a** through **h.**
    a. stayed at home Saturday
    b. saw a good film last week
    c. went out last night
    d. got home very late
    e. didn't sleep well
    f. left for class at 8:00 this morning
    g. arrived on time for French class
    h. brought a chocolate cake for the teacher

Step 2. For each of the preceding items, think of a way to ask a question that will give you a *yes* or *no* answer.

Step 3. If you have problems remembering how to ask a particular question, consult with your teacher.

Step 4. Circulate around the room so you can ask individual classmates (not crowds or groups) one question at a time. Remember, one classmate, one question. If an individual answers *yes* to your question, write that person's name next to the item and probe for more information. For example, if the classmate responds *yes* to the question, "Did you see a good film last week?", ask the person for the name of the film, or who was in it, or whether the classmate went alone to see it.

Step 5. Once you have completed your survey, go to your desk and prepare to share orally with the rest of the class what you learned about your classmates.

This activity offers students a great deal of practice with the *passé composé* while still focusing on the task, getting information. Students feel more comfortable because their mistakes are not corrected in front of other students and because they have used the structure numerous times in interviewing their classmates.

Cartoon Stories and Role Play

Finally, cartoon stories and role plays are examples of open-ended group activities that allow humor, a natural tension-reliever, to be injected into the classroom and students' creativity to be encouraged. Once again, the team is responsible for the end product as opposed to the familiar oral report, whereby the often insecure student gets all the credit or blame for the performance. Furthermore, the cartoon story can be used at many levels depending on the simplicity or complexity of the sequence selected. To begin, a picture sequence (preferably without captions) is selected and photocopied, and the panels are cut apart with pieces arranged so that each group of students receives the full set of panels. If the number of students in each group does not match the number of panels, some students can be given more than one panel. The group's goal is to arrange the panels in an appropriate order, telling the story as they go. To this end, each student describes what is happening in his/her panel without showing it to the other group members. Once all panels have been described, the group, still without looking at the pictures, decides on an appropriate sequence by trying out various possibilities orally. Only after the group has reached its conclusion may students lay out the panels for all to see to verify that their decision was logical. Since humor can help relieve tension, the use of cartoons is especially appropriate.

Like cartoon stories, role play can also be used to add levity to classroom activities, and role play is particularly useful because situations can be readily concocted to review a large number of vocabulary units, language functions, or grammatical structures. Each group gets a copy of the role-play situation, which they are free to interpret in a creative manner. It is important to allow plenty of time for group planning and practice to attenuate anxiety. Characters can be added or eliminated to the role play to match the number of students in each group. The following role-play situation provides practice in agreeing and disagreeing, describing and narrating in the past, and talking about vacations.

Activity E. Memories

Step 1. You will need to have four partners for this role play. You and your partners are going to play the role of a family that is reminiscing about a family vacation of 10 years ago when you stayed in a small coastal town on the Mediterranean.

Grandma remembers the house where you stayed; Mom, the various activities the family engaged in; John, what you ate (of course!); and Bernadette, the people that you met at the beach. Dad remembers the long car trip. Unfortunately, for each family member who recalls a detail, there is another member who remembers things differently.

Step 2. Decide which role you will play, then write down five "memories" according to your role.

Step 3. Now share—and compare—your recollections with the other members of your "family," who are never in agreement on the facts!

Although some students may find role play stressful, others enjoy the opportunity to use their creative abilities and will frequently inject humor into the skit. The shared responsibility inherent in group work also helps students feel more comfortable as long as they have adequate time to prepare.

137

CHAPTER 8
Decreasing Language
Anxiety: Practical
Techniques for Oral
Activities

ERROR CORRECTION

Since learners (like the rest of us) are concerned with their self-image and since many students are embarrassed and feel stupid when their errors are corrected, it is not surprising that their anxiety is heightened when speaking because their mistakes are most obvious to other students. This section discusses techniques for error correction that are designed to reduce learners' anxiety with regard to speaking in the foreign language.

In the classroom, teachers can reduce students' stress to a degree simply by continually reminding them that mistakes are a natural part of the language-learning process. Reassurances will have little or no effect, however, if instructors are then over-vigilant in correcting every mistake in form. Once again a dilemma occurs because teachers feel a responsibility not only to help students communicate but to help them communicate with a certain degree of linguistic accuracy. At the same time, they realize that error correction heightens anxiety. The compromise recommended here is to use different methods of correction for different circumstances.

First, because overt correction is directed at errors in form, its use should be limited to mechanical practice in which attention is also placed only on form. However, if a learner is responding to what she believes is authentic communication, overt correction may be entirely inappropriate. Examine the following exchange:

TEACHER: What did you do last night, Susan?
SUSAN: I goed to the movie *Captain Hook.*

The student has obviously committed an error in verb form that the instructor can correct with question intonation ("Goed?") or by saying, "I went to the movie." But does Susan necessarily understand these responses as attempts at correction? If she assumes the teacher is *communicating,* she may actually think the teacher went to the movie, too! The teacher could make the correction more obvious by asking, "What is the past tense of *go?*" But in this case, Susan has attempted to communicate (just what the teacher says is important!) and the teacher has not responded to her message—only to the form. Furthermore, Susan may feel singled out and embarrassed—and possibly frustrated and resentful. Certainly her anxiety about speaking the target language has not been lowered.

However, if most class time is spent on communicative activities, overt error correction is not the most effective tool. Another technique known as *modeling* is preferred when students are engaged in activities that require them to attend to meaning, whether or not form is also being practiced. In modeling, the teacher responds most importantly to what the student has said while at the same time modeling the correct form or vocabulary item. To respond to Susan's answer in the example given above, the teacher can say, "Oh, you went to the movie. I went to see *Captain Hook,* too. What a coincidence! We went to the same movie." Now the teacher has not only modeled the correct verb form several times; more importantly, she has responded to what the student said. Furthermore, the student has not been put on the spot or embarrassed. Although some teachers may be concerned about whether the learner actually "gets it" when indirect correction is used, anecdotal evidence suggests that this method is at least as effective as overt correction; that is, students who are not ready to internalize a structure will continue to make periodic mistakes no matter what correction method is used. (One educator was overheard to muse that error correction did more for the teacher than the students anyway.)

At times, a teacher may feel that overt instruction is necessary but may not want to interrupt students who are working on a communicative activity. In these instances, the instructor should note the mistakes that are relevant to the day's lesson and wait until the activity is completed to review rules and so on with the class. This technique can also reduce students' anxiety because individual learners are not singled out.

139

CHAPTER 8
Decreasing Language
Anxiety: Practical
Techniques for Oral
Activities

ORAL EVALUATION

Oral evaluation is, without doubt, the most anxiety-inducing situation that occurs in language classrooms, for it is during oral testing that numerous types of anxiety identified in the literature can come into play: language anxiety, test anxiety, communication anxiety, and fear-of-negative-evaluation anxiety. No wonder some students are overwrought at the thought of taking an oral exam in another language. Reducing students' anxiety related to oral testing is a difficult task because so many of the students' fears are brought into play at once. Although some students will never feel at ease during oral evaluation, there are steps teachers can take to reduce the inherent tension. Many of these are the same techniques used to reduce anxiety about oral activities in class. First, provide students ample opportunity for oral practice, and test them using the same types of activities they have practiced in class. If partner and group work is used for oral practice in class, test students in pairs or in small groups as well. Classroom activities such as role plays are also excellent tools for evaluating communicative competence. If the instructor uses humor effectively in the class to reduce tension, humorous role plays should be incorporated into the testing situation. Practitioners should also encourage students to use conversation strategies and expressions for reacting during tests, just as they do during class. Role plays such as the examples that follow can recombine functions, structures, and vocabulary studied in class in an original or different context. The task is specific, and numerous suggestions are given. For intermediate students, details are left to the students' imagination.

Level: First year, college

Functions: Asking/answering questions; talking about preferences

Vocabulary: Favorite activities (sports, music, family, other)

Task: You've just met the two roommates you will have at camp for the next few weeks. Ask them questions to get to know them better and find out how you will get along.

Ask about their family (names, ages, ?),
their favorite school subjects (math, French, ?),
the kind of music they prefer (rock, jazz, ?),

how they spend their free time (movies, sports, art, ?),
and anything else you think important.

Answer the questions they ask you. Give as much information as possible.
When you finish, don't forget to say your good-byes.

Level: Third semester, college

Functions: Describing; talking about relationships; asking questions

Vocabulary: Physical traits; personality traits

Task: You and your good friend are having a serious discussion about the future. Ask your partner what he or she would like in an "ideal mate"—a person he or she would like to meet and perhaps marry one day. Ask followup questions to get all the details. Your partner will ask you questions on the same topic. You may wish to include physical characteristics (hair, eyes, age, size, and so on) and personality traits. What characteristics must he or she *not* have, and so forth? When you finish, say your good-byes.

Finally, in addition to choosing appropriate tasks for oral testing, the teacher may need to re-evaluate the evaluation instrument itself. If communicative competence is really a goal of the course, then communicative competence—not just accuracy—must be rewarded during testing. An important percentage of the students' grades should be based on whether or not they are able to complete the assigned task. Although most beginning language learners are unable to communicate in the target language with a great deal of linguistic accuracy, most can, with sufficient and appropriate practice, learn to get their meaning across. Their anxiety about the evaluation process can be reduced if they realize this ability, too, will be rewarded.

CONCLUSION

Practitioners are encouraged to heighten their awareness of students' anxiety about language learning to better help them manage their anxiety. Developing activities that encourage students to cooperate and depend on their classmates fosters an environment conducive to the development of a community and allows learners to feel more at ease, as do communicative activities that encourage oral practice in a nonthreatening manner. The teacher also must develop techniques and strategies for error correction and oral evaluation that reduce negative affect and improve low self-esteem. The importance of reducing students' anxiety related to oral activities cannot be overstated if language educators are to maintain the development of communicative competence as a goal and if practitioners wish to see their students continue language study beyond the level of lower division.

PORTFOLIO ASSIGNMENTS

1. In this chapter, Phillips suggests that one way to create a comfortable atmosphere in class is by helping language learners get to know their

classmates better. Create an activity for use at the beginning of the semester whereby students must interact with several of their classmates—but on an individual basis—finding out information about their preferences, interests, families, and personal lives.

141

CHAPTER 8
Decreasing Language
Anxiety: Practical
Techniques for Oral
Activities

2. a. To reduce anxiety and encourage a sense of community, design one original oral activity from the following list of oral activity types Phillips discusses in this chapter, remembering to focus on pair/group work, familiar topics, and personalized responses.

   —a recognition activity (p. 131)

   —a cued-response activity (p. 133)

   —an information gap activity (p. 134)

   —an interview or survey activity (p. 135)

   —an activity using cartoon stories or role play (p. 136)

   b. Make sure to mention the structure, function, or semantic field you have targeted in this activity.

3. a. Take a structure, function, and semantic field from a chapter in the language textbook you currently use and prepare a role play that could be used as part of an oral exam. To reduce students' anxiety, the role-play tasks should be reminiscent of but not identical to classroom activities.

   b. Exchange your role-play activity with another classmate.

ACTION RESEARCH

1. a. Administer McCroskey's Personal Report of Communication Apprehension (PRCA) found in Appendix H (pp. 259–261) to a classmate to ascertain whether he or she suffers from communication apprehension in the native language.

   b. Now, administer Horwitz' (1984) Foreign Language Classroom Anxiety Scale (FLCAS) found in Appendix B (pp. 248–249) to the same classmate to ascertain whether he or she experiences much language anxiety.

   c. Compare your results. Pay particular attention to items 1, 2, 3, 5, 9, 13, 14, 18, 20, 23, 24, 27, 31, and 33 on the FLCAS.

   d. Based on your results, is there a relationship between fear of public speaking in the native language and in the FL/SL?

   e. Discuss your findings with the class.

2. a. Take the language textbook you currently use and examine the activities in Chapter 5 to identify any activities that might heighten anxiety in students. The following questions may serve as a guide to your analysis.

   • How many activities for speaking does this chapter contain?
   • Of the total number of activites designed to promote speaking, how many activities allow students to respond to input before having to produce?

- How many are personalized activities?
- How many are based on paired and group work?

b. Share your findings with two other classmates and then report your general findings to the class.

3. a. Interview a language learner who attends class, does well on written tests, and completes all homework on time but who does not speak much in class to determine (1) whether the learner experiences communication apprehension in the FL/SL and (2), if applicable, the sources of his or her anxiety.

b. If the student does experience language anxiety, try to dispel certain erroneous beliefs about language learning that students may hold, such as:

- They probably will have native-like fluency after four semesters.
- As adult learners, their pronunciation should sound native-like.
- Mistakes are not part of the acquisition process.
- Learning a language is a matter of acquiring vocabulary.

c. After the interview and discussion, have the student write, as though writing in a journal, about whether the interview helped to establish more realistic expectations about speaking in the FL/SL and consequently reduced his or her apprehension associated with speaking.

d. Share your findings with the class to ascertain whether helping students set realistic expectations about speaking in an FL/SL is useful and helps them reduce their anxiety about speaking.

NOTE

1. Several examples are from *Mais Oui*, a first-year, college-level French textbook published by Houghton Mifflin. They are used with the permission of the publisher and authors, Chantal Thompson and Elaine Phillips.

REFERENCES

Bailey, K. M. (1983). Competitiveness and anxiety in adult second language learning: Looking *at* and through the diary studies. In H. W. Seliger & M. H. Long (Eds.), *Classroom-oriented research in second language acquisition*. Rowley, MA: Newbury House, pp. 67–102.

Crookall, D., & Oxford, R. (1991). Dealing with anxiety: Some practical activities for language learners and teacher trainees. In E. K. Horwitz & D. J. Young (Eds.), *Language anxiety: From theory and research to classroom implications*. Upper Saddle River, NJ: Prentice Hall, pp. 141–150.

Ehrman, M., & Oxford, R. (1990). Adult language learning styles and strategies in an intensive training setting. *Modern Language Journal, 73*, 311–327.

Ely, C. (1986). An analysis of discomfort, risktaking, sociability, and motivation in the L2 classroom. *Language Learning, 36*, 1–25.

Foreign Service Institute (1973). *Expected levels of absolute speaking proficiency in languages taught at the Foreign Service Institute*. Roslyn, VA: Foreign Service Institute.

143

CHAPTER 8
*Decreasing Language
Anxiety: Practical
Techniques for Oral
Activities*

Foss, K. A., & Reitzel, A. C. (1988). A relational model for managing second language anxiety. *TESOL Quarterly, 22,* 437–454.

Guiora, A. Z., Beit-Hallahmi, B., Brannon, R. C. L., Dull, C. Y., & Scovel, T. (1972). The effects of experimentally induced changes in ego states on pronunciation ability in a second language: An exploratory study. *Comprehensive Psychiatry, 13,* 421–428.

Horwitz, E. K. (1984). *Scale of reactions to foreign language class.* Unpublished manuscript, University of Texas at Austin.

Horwitz, E. K. (1988). The beliefs about language learning of beginning university foreign language students. *Modern Language Journal, 70,* 283–293.

Horwitz, E. K., Horwitz, M. B., & Cope, J. (1986). Foreign language classroom anxiety. *Modern Language Journal, 70,* 125–132.

Koch, A. S., & Terrell, T.D. (1991). Affective reactions of foreign language students to Natural Approach activities and teaching techniques. In E. K. Horwitz & D. J. Young (Eds.), *Language anxiety: From theory and research to classroom implications.* Upper Saddle River, NJ: Prentice Hall, pp. 109–126.

Little, G. D., & Sanders, S. L. (1989). Classroom community: A prerequisite for communication. *Foreign Language Annals, 22,* 277–281.

Phillips, E. M. (1990). The effects of anxiety on performance and achievement in an oral test of French (doctoral dissertation, University of Texas at Austin, 1990). *Dissertation Abstracts International, 51,* 1941A.

Phillips, E. M. (1991). Anxiety and oral competence: Classroom dilemma. *French Review, 65,* 1–14.

Phillips, E. M. (1992). The effects of language anxiety on students' oral test performance and attitudes. *Modern Language Journal, 76,* 14–26.

Price, M. L. (1991). The subjective experiences of foreign language anxiety: Interviews with anxious students. In E. K. Horwitz & D. J. Young (Eds.), *Language anxiety: From theory and research to classroom implications.* Upper Saddle River, NJ: Prentice Hall, pp. 101–108.

Rubin, J. (1975). What the "good language learner" can teach us. *TESOL Quarterly, 9,* 41–51.

Speiller, J. (1988). Factors that influence high school students' decision to continue or discontinue the study of French and Spanish after levels II, III, and IV. *Foreign Language Annals, 21,* 535–545.

Vande Berg, C. K. (1993). Managing learner anxiety in literature courses. *French Review, 67,* 27–36.

Young, D. J. (1990). An investigation of students' perspectives on anxiety and speaking. *Foreign Language Annals, 23,* 539–553.

Young, D. J. (1992). Language anxiety from the foreign language specialist's perspective: Interviews with Krashen, Omaggio Hadley, Terrell, and Rardin. *Foreign Language Annals, 25,* 157–172.

Computer-Mediated Communication: Reducing Anxiety and Building Community

Margaret Beauvois
The University of Tennessee

Personal Reflections

a. Have you used a computer in a language class or for any other subject? Write five adjectives that you associate with using a computer to learn.
b. Do you experience a sense of community in your current classes? Or, have you ever experienced a sense of community in a course? If so, in which? Can you describe to what you attribute the feelings of community membership?
c. Would you use computer-mediated instruction in your foreign language class if the hardware and software were made available to you? Why? Why not?

Fundamental Concepts

LAN	Interlanguage
CMC	Real-time, synchronous
ENFIs	computer messaging
DIWE	Internet
InterChange	Flaming
Computer transcripts	

145

CHAPTER 9
Computer-Mediated
Communication:
Reducing Anxiety
and Building
Community

Language teachers are acutely aware of the stress involved in learning a second language—most of us have experienced the anxiety firsthand. As we move toward the increasing use of communicative activities in our language courses, much of that stress seems to revolve around the oral production that is increasingly required of students (Phillips 1991). Verbal practice in the target language tends to augment anxiety in many students, as documented by Horwitz' Foreign Language Classroom Anxiety Scale (Horwitz et al. 1986). In a study in which forty intermediate French students at the university level were asked to respond to a questionnaire about learning French, 90% of them responded that they were most ill at ease when asked to speak the language in the classroom (Beauvois 1994). And yet speaking remains an essential part of learning a modern foreign language. Getting students to use meaningful target language in the classroom is probably the greatest challenge language teachers face. One of the ways in which good instructors compensate for the anxiety evoked by the "on-the-spot" syndrome is by putting students in small discussion/work groups. One problem in such a system is that the teacher cannot be in five to seven groups at the same time, so inevitably much conversation gets off task. In truth, most of that conversation also goes on in English, when the teacher is out of earshot (Kinginger 1990).

But imagine for a moment a language classroom in which all the students are willing to interact (negotiate meaning) with one another and with the teacher in the target language; in which even the most shy students dare to express an opinion; in which the students have time to think quietly about their responses before communicating anything, and yet no one seems bored or acts impatient waiting for a response. Although it may sound too good to be true, this scene is not atypical in some language courses at the University of Tennessee, Knoxville, and elsewhere that are taught in a computer laboratory/classroom on a local area network (LAN).

In this chapter the focus will be on the reduction of anxiety and the creation of community experienced by students in French classes using a LAN and a program that allows synchronous real-time computer conferencing. Students' evaluations, journal entries, self-report instruments, and interviews with the researcher form the data discussed in this chapter. The quotes used in this chapter are from actual foreign language (FL) students who offer their perspectives on computer-mediated communication (CMC). This data was collected over a three-year period in three studies conducted in a variety of academic settings: one large public university, one medium-size state university, and one small private university. Subjects were enrolled in courses that used CMC at different levels of the universities' French curriculum: elementary, intermediate, and intermediate–advanced (300 level).

BACKGROUND

Electronic Networks used For Interaction (ENFIs) originated at Gallaudet University, Washington, DC, as part of a project to teach English expression and composition to deaf students. Professor of English Trent Batson was looking for a way of bridging the gap between American Sign Language used by the students at Gallaudet and more mainstream English when he had the idea of putting his students on a local area network to have them communicate with one another in writing. His experiment proved to be successful (Batson 1988). Students responded well to the medium, and their written English showed improvement. An unexpected bonus from the writing class was that Batson noticed progress not only in the students' writing ability but also in their sense of confidence in expressing their ideas, even when not communicating on the LAN. Since the medium allows for no real control on the part of the instructor, apart from the initial questions or other input, students are relatively free to take the discussion where they want it to go. Batson began to notice that his students would initiate ideas instead of waiting for him to bring up topics for discussion. They became more willing to carry the conversational burden by answering and asking one another questions and by not relying always on directions from him. Subsequent use of ENFIs has proven to be effective in encouraging and motivating student writers/communicators, thereby opening the door to more study of this interesting hybrid communicative process (Batson 1988; Bruce & Batson 1992; Bruce & Rubin 1992).

Batson's experiment caught the attention of some graduate students in the Department of English at the University of Texas who were looking for a way to use computers to teach English composition. In their desire to turn word processing into process writing, they developed the Daedalus Integrated Writing Environment (DIWE) software, and, with a computer lab funded by IBM, they began teaching English composition and literature on the LAN. That was in 1987. Since that time, many classes have been taught in the English Department's experimental lab at the University of Texas at Austin. In addition to improving their writing skills, students have demonstrated a lack of stress in the lab environment, an openness and honesty of communication, and a sense of comfort not observed to the same extent in the regular classroom (Bump 1990; Faigley 1990; Kinneavy 1991; Peterson 1989; Slatin 1991).

INITIAL LAN RESEARCH
IN FOREIGN LANGUAGES

Research into the use of LANs to teach foreign languages began in 1991 in Portuguese (Kelm 1992) and in French (Beauvois 1992). Follow-up studies confirmed previous findings that computer-mediated communication does seem to reduce learner classroom-performance anxiety (Beauvois 1993, 1994). The high student-approval rates found in most of general CMC research compel us as language professionals to take note and explore the potential of this motivating process in terms of second-language learning. The module of the software package used in this process is called InterChange. InterChange facilitates student interaction in synchronist real-time communication. An increasing body of research is accumulating that examines CMC in the foreign language classroom, and from this initial research in the area of student-student interaction via LANs, the following tendencies can be documented.

1. Students claim to experience less stress in the lab environment.
2. All the students can and generally do participate in any given class period.

3. All the students can and generally do read the discussion as it scrolls in front of their eyes.
4. There tends to be more student production in a typical LAN session than orally in the classroom (words, phrases, and sentences).
5. When the fear of oral speech is removed, students tend to delve into subjects they do not otherwise choose to discuss (Kelm 1992; Peterson 1989).

147

CHAPTER 9
Computer-Mediated
Communication:
Reducing Anxiety
and Building
Community

Students' positive reactions to CMC reverberate throughout the interview data. Of the seventy-six student interviews examined for this chapter, only four expressed a negative reaction to using LAN discussion in French class: one student was a graduate student in an intermediate course who found the undergraduates' comments trite and trivial; one was a dominant student whose oral French was stronger than that of the other members of the class. He was not happy with the "leveling effect of the computer" whereby his "voice" had less impact; and the last two were students who thought the process was too much "fun" and not a serious use of class time, in which formal grammar study should be stressed.

In addition to the positive affective aspects of CMC, some research has found academic advantages. In a comparison study of student production in two environments, the conversation generated in the computer lab was superior to general classroom discussion on the same topics in French in both quantity and quality (Beauvois 1996). Recent studies have shown a link between oral skill acquisition and CMC to enhance student interaction (Beauvois 1997, 1998a, 1998b, 1998c). While it is likely that CMC may be an effective means for language learning, the main point here is to propose an additional way of reducing students' anxiety while at the same time developing their language skills.

A DESCRIPTION OF SYNCHRONOUS, REAL-TIME, COMPUTER MEDIATED COMMUNICATION

In synchronous, real-time computer-mediated communication, students engage in an electronic discussion of a text. Although we use the words "discussion" and "communication," this medium does not provide face-to-face oral practice; thus there can be, of course, no evaluation of pronunciation. However, by providing a setting in which real-time communication can take place, albeit electronically, the network allows students to brainstorm, to express their own ideas, to see the thoughts of their classmates/instructor in a concrete way, and to negotiate meaning in a mode in which learners have time to process input and monitor output. They can take their time to compose messages in the privacy of their edit boxes, re-read them, and then send them when they are ready. At the end of the class, students can make a hard copy or download the discussion to their own diskettes for later review. Re-reading the discussion can serve to sensitize learners to accuracy issues, or it can be used as a source of content, ideas, and different perspectives from which students could glean information.

In the regular university classroom, oral discussion is often carried on by the instructor with a few brave students who dare to risk showing their knowledge (or lack thereof) in the foreign language before their classmates. Many students are too often left out of such discussions because of timidity, lack of skill, or perceived faults in their linguistic ability. Even with the emphasis on communicative methodology, there is still in many foreign language classrooms, at the university level in particular, a definite silent minority. The instructor rarely knows what these students think until quiz, test, or exam time and then only after the grade is given, can he or she alter misconceptions and correct errors.

In contrast, in a typical CMC foreign language class, the students have read the text to be discussed before coming to class, just as they might do for an oral discussion class. As the lab session begins, students are given four to eight written questions in French about the previous night's reading assignment and asked to address these questions as they discuss the text on networked computers. They begin by writing a message—a greeting, a response to one of the questions, or a comment—in the lower half, the "edit box," of the divided screen on the computer monitor in front of them. When the students have completed their messages and are satisfied with the content, they click on the "send" button. In seconds, the sent messages appear on the screens of all the linked computers on the LAN for the entire class to see and read. The students continue to compose and send their messages in response to any number of stimuli: a message from the instructor, questions about the text, a comment or response from another student. They often express their thoughts or ideas stimulated by reading the on-going discussion scrolling on the screen in front of them. The entire exercise takes place in the target language.

This intra-class communication via networked computers is facilitated by the software package mentioned previously, called DIWE. DIWE takes the student through the whole writing process beginning with InterChange, the brainstorming/discussion module mentioned above, through a refining, structuring module (Invent), then through a question series to guide the peer critiquing process (Respond), and finally, through a simple word processing module (Write) to enable the student to compose a rough draft and the final product of a paper, if one is desired. There is also an e-mail module (Mail) for asynchronous communication between the members of the class and a module (Bibliocite) to organize the bibliography of the final paper in APA or MLA styles.

An example of the process in a 300 (third-year) level composition/conversation course in French follows, in the order in which the messages were sent. In all excerpts in this chapter, only the student names have been changed to protect their anonymity.

Start of Conference MAIN

MARK STEVENS: Bonjour!
Hello!

INSTRUCTOR: Bonjour tout le monde! Commençons cette discussion avec la première question: Avez-vous ressenti un certain malaise en lisant cette histoire? Si oui, pourquoi?
Hello everyone! Let's begin this discussion with the first question: Did you feel a certain discomfort in reading this story? If yes, why?

MARK STEVENS: Les Villes?
The Cities? [Name of the story]

149

CHAPTER 9
Computer-Mediated
Communication:
Reducing Anxiety
and Building
Community

JAMES SMITH: Oui, dans le texte de cette histoire, il manque de humaintie.
Yes, in the text of this story, it lacks humanity.

JIM FERGUSON: Moi, j'ai ressenti un certain malaise dans cette histoire parceque je crois que l'auteur veux dire que notre monde sera comm ca dans quelques ans.
I felt a certain discomfort in this story because I think that the author means that our world will be like that in a few years.

MARK STEVENS: Il a un air de vieux (grammaire?). Cette machine mysterieuse qui roder (ou rodir) les chemins. Comme Star Trek maintenant, on peut essayer faire les estimations de l'avenir, mais ils ne sont jamais correct.
It seems old (grammar?). This mysterious machine that to wander (to winder?) the roads. Like Star Trek now, you can try to make predictions [estimations] but they are never right.

CATHY CRAIG: Oui, j'ai ressenti un sens de malaise en lisant cette histoire. Tout est impersonnel et on ne connait pas ses voisins. (p. 156, l. 38) Une machine dirige la ville, pas de personne.
Yes, I felt a sense of discomfort in reading this story. Everything is impersonal and you don't even know your neighbors. (page 156, line 38). A machine is running the city, not a person.

MELISSA JONES: Oui, j'ai ressenti un certain malaise en lisent cette histoire. J'attribute ma inquietude a la connaissance que nous dependond beaucoup a les machines. Monsieur Ferrier a dit que la machine connait tout dans la page 152, ligne 33–40. Il a beaucoup de confiance en la machine et il ne question pas si il est un bon idee.
Yes, I felt a certain discomfort in read this story. I attribute my anxiety to the knowledge that we depends a lot on the machines. Mr. Ferrier said that the machine knows everything in page 152, line 33–40. He has lots of confidence in the machine and does not question if it is a good idea.

Only the IBM version of this software numbers the messages, an advantage in a rather chaotic "conversational" mode. The Mac version of the software does not number the messages, and students must restate the previous message as a point of reference. This latter strategy has certain advantages for the elementary language learner.

The following is a short printout sample of students' electronic discussion of "L'Attaque du Moulin" *(The Attack of the Mill)* by Emile Zola (pp. 105–139) in *Panache Littéraire*, edited by Mary Baker and J. P. Cauvin (1995). Student intitials replace their real names. The English translation in italics attempts to convey the student's use of French Interlanguage—that is, sometimes with errors and somewhat unclear sentence structure:

PROFESSEUR: Le ton de ce conte peut nous sembler exageré . . . mais le message de Zola est très claire! Qu'en pensez-vous?
The tone of the story may seem exaggerated to us . . . but Zola's message is very clear! What do you think?

L. H.: Bonjour!
Hello!

J'aime cet histoire beaucoup. Il est tres interessant et il y a beacoup d'action. Des images sont belles aussi.
I like this story a lot. It is very interesting and there is a lot of action. The images are beautiful also.

R. R.: Je m'en reve que j'ai pu vivre aux ces annees.
I dream to myself that I was able to live at those years.

L. V.: Le plus grand contrast que je vois dans le conte est avec la description de le moulin. Le ligne 7 le decrit comme une vraie gaiete, et par le fin Zola a dit "le pauvre moulin" ligne 938. C'est une grand changement dans le tone.
The greatest contrast that I see in the story is with the description of the mill. Line 7 describes it as a real gaity, and by the end Zola said "the poor mill" line 938. It is a great change in the tone.

S. A.: Le message de Zola est la brutalite de la guerre. La guerre destruit tout, meme ce vieux moulin et la vieux nature.
The message of Zola is the brutality of war. War destroys everything, even this old mill and old nature.

R. J. T.: Bonjour tous les mode!! *Hello everyone!!*
Je ne comprendre la derniere histoire tres bien. J'etais un peu perde a la fin. Je sais que Dominique est fusille, et que le pere Merlier est tue, mais je ne comprends exactement qui. C'est qu j'etais un peu perde.
I don't understand the last story very well. I was a bit lost at the end. I know that Dominique is shot down, and that the old man Merlier is killed, but I don't understand exactly who. I was just a bit lost.

PROFESSOR: Oui, L—tout le ton change—et en quoi consiste ce "ton"—par quelles images est-ce que Zola nous fait comprendre son message—Quel est son message?
Yes, L. the entire tone changes—and what does this "tone" consist of— by what images does Zola convey his message—what is his message?

S. A: Au debut du texte, on voit une veille nature, qui est tranquille et dure longetemps. Le moulin est un batiment tellement vieux et il a une personalite. Zola le compare avec une femme. A la fin du recit la beaute est disparu. La nature et le moulin est destruit. Meme le temps fait mal. L'orage nous montre la destruction et le fin dramatique.
At the beginning of the text, one sees old nature, which is calm and lasting a long time. The mill is a very old building and it has a personality. Zola compares it to a woman. At the end of the story, the beauty has disappeared. Nature and the mill is destroyed. Even the weather is bad. The storm shows us the destruction and the dramatic end.

L. H.: Cet histoire compare la paix et la guerre. L'autour utilisait les images de nature pour juxtiposer les deux.
This story compares peace and war. The author used images of nature to juxtapose the two.

After reading these students' messages, the professor becomes aware of the participants' comprehension of a given text as well as their individual

151

CHAPTER 9
Computer-Mediated
Communication:
Reducing Anxiety
and Building
Community

problems with the language. A copy of the entire discussion is available at the end of the session for study and instructor's comments. In addition to the synchronous communication of messages, the software provides a sorted copy of each student's participation in the discussion—that is, each student's individual contributions can be printed out. These copies can then be corrected by the instructor and returned to the students as feedback.

The following is an example of a sorted copy of an individual student's participation (only the student's name has been changed). The instructor in this instance chose to write the corrections on the sorted copy. Another option would be to simply highlight errors or to indicate the sentence in which the structure is awkward and not give the corrected version. Students could then make corrections and return their copies to the instructor.

InterChange The following messages are one student's sorted copy of a discussion on Ionesco's short story *Conte pour enfants de moins de trois ans*. The instructor's corrections are in italics but on the students' papers they were highlighted in yellow.

KATIE MARTIN: *une*   *aime beaucoup manger*
    Un gourmand est un personne qui veut beaucoup, especiallement beaucoup de nourriture.
KATIE MARTIN: Je ne comprends "faire des commissions."
KATIE MARTIN: *la petite fille*
    Robert, oui. Josette attend a la porte et, puis, Jaqueline laisse la
    entrer dans
    fille a la chambre.
KATIE MARTIN: *une toilette*
    Je pense que le petit pot est un "toilet."
KATIE MARTIN: *que*
    Je pense que la femme de menage est sarcastique parce qu'elle
    les parents se levent.   *peuvent*
    veut les parents enlever. Ils ne peut pas garder Josette au lit et Jaqueline ne veut pas garder Josette.
KATIE MARTIN: *de la*   *oui!*
    Je pense que le job de Jaqueline est faire le cuisine et nettoyer ("clean"?), pas garder Josette.
KATIE MARTIN: *l'histoire*   *ecrite*
    Est-ce que le histoire est ecrivee pour les enfants ou pour les adultes. Ce n'est pas typique des histoires pour les enfants.
KATIE MARTIN: Robert, l'histoire du pere etait folle. Je pense que le pere a
       raconte une   *pour que Josette le laisse*
    voulu dormir; il a dit un histoire folle si Josette le laisse a
    dormir.
    dormir.

[Instructor's comment—handwritten on document]
Bien fait, Katie! Vous avez bien saisi les idées générales du texte. Bonne participation à la discussion. Bravo!

STUDENTS' VOICES AND PERSPECTIVES
ABOUT CMC IN THE FL CLASS

Based on a total of 76 students interviewed over a three-year period, student responses to CMC have been unanimously positive on the question of stress. No students interviewed stated a feeling of performance anxiety in the lab environment. On an evaluative instrument given at the end of the semester to all students in the three levels of French (elementary, intermediate, and intermediate–advanced) the following items (**2**, **12**, and **15**) asked students to rate their anxiety in the lab using a 5-point Likert Scale (from "A," strongly agree, to "E," strongly disagree):

2. _____ I am more comfortable speaking French in class than in lab.

12. _____ I usually get anxious when I am writing responses in the computer lab.

15. _____ I am generally tense when participating in the computer lab.

Responses to **2** were consistently C, D, or E ("no opinion" to "strongly disagree"). Responses to **12** were unanimously D, "disagree," or E, "strongly disagree." Responses to **15** were also unanimously D or E.

A sampling of student responses to follow-up questions to these instruments follows. Two specific interview questions, designed to determine both the individual affective response and the social effects of the exercise, served to evaluate the computer-mediated communication process. The voices we hear in this chapter are student perceptions from their exit interviews. The two patterns that emerge from these interviews are as follows:

1. A stress-free environment is experienced in the computer lab.
2. Computer-mediated communication creates a sense of community.

Novice Learner Perceptions

Before examining the responses of intermediate and advanced students to the question of anxiety, we must first look at the true beginning language student. The novice learner faces a particularly difficult situation in terms of language-learning anxiety. Most beginning college-level French classes always have a few students with prior exposure to French who end up in an elementary French course with real beginners in the language. The true novice learner is often anxious because others in the class sound as if they are much more proficient or better language learners; they seem to understand more quickly and respond more easily. This situation was particularly well expressed by a novice French student in her exit interview:

RESEARCHER: On the questionnaire, you say that the primary advantage of using the computer lab in French class is that it "is easier for me to write than to speak. I wasn't worried about making mistakes." So why do you think it is "easier" for you?

CARRIE: Just because I don't have the pressure of being in a class where I felt there were more people further ahead of where I was. I felt I was too far behind to speak up. Just being self-conscious because

of that. Being on the computer, even though I wasn't able to respond as quickly or as well as other people did, I did make relevant remarks to the conversation.

RESEARCHER: What did you think about the flow of the conversation in the lab?

CARRIE: I liked it a lot. It was kind of fast for me but that is just because I
have no background in the language whatsoever. . . . In [the
regular] class I kind of got lost. I wasn't able to say something before the topic changed. . . . I felt that for the last few weeks I
was using the program, I got more out of class and was able to
retain more information from one week to the next because I was
writing it out. Having it available for students to use on their
own by a group or whatever would be nice. I definitely think it
should be incorporated into the course.

153

CHAPTER 9
Computer-Mediated
Communication:
Reducing Anxiety
and Building
Community

What this student seems to be defining is a way in which the communication on the LAN can help bridge the gap for the student who is struggling
with fluency in the language. The delayed response possible in computer communication provided this true novice with time to compose her message and
freedom from the pressure of oral performance. Other students in the class
echoed her feelings.

First-Year Students (French 102, Second Semester)

In response to the specific question "How would you compare your own level
of stress when communicating in French in the computer lab and in classroom oral discussion?", student's opinions varied in content but were unani-
mous in affirming a positive reaction to the low-anxiety atmosphere of the
lab. As stated previously, not one student said he or she felt more stress in the
lab than in the classroom. The sample comments that follow reflect the general attitudes of the *elementary* French students relating their lab experience in
their own words.

JIM: "I didn't feel like someone was waiting for me to answer. It was a
slow motion conversation—one you could prepare for ahead of time,
but not rushed, like in the classroom.

JANE: It felt like I was speaking in my head and writing it down—so I think
it did help carry over into the oral classroom.

BRENDA: It's easier to express yourself in a written way—you can see the
structure. I *think* more in the lab. It helped the structural part of my
speaking.

BRIAN: I like the lab because you have time to get your ideas across. I can't
speak French well enough to carry on a conversation [orally].

AMY: I really looked forward to the lab sessions all semester long. I'd say
"Yay! Today we go to the lab!" It was fun!

Second-Year Students (French 201, First Semester)

Intermediate students' comments reflected their more advanced stage of
language learning but gave evidence also of the underlying tension associated

with oral performance even with their increased experience with the language:

STEVE: I participated a lot more in InterChange [sessions] with a lot less anxiety.

KATIE: I am most at ease in my French class when we are at the computers.

JIM: Conversations in the lab tend to be slightly more intense and involved. I got the other students' opinions and could pick apart pieces of the texts. It was fun—a change of pace—even relaxing!

Intermediate–Advanced Students
(Sixth Semester French)

Comments from these advanced students revolved more around the interactive process than those of the intermediate classes, but mention was still made of the low-anxiety atmosphere they experienced in the lab.

COLLIN: This gives time for all of us to exercise what they've learned [*sic*]. It's a good use of time. A lot of learning and reviewing takes place during that 50 minutes since everyone is on task, and everyone is being monitored—very efficient.

ERIC: It's so anonymous . . . It's the fact that people aren't so self-conscious. Also they have more time to sit and compose something and they can double check themselves. They don't have to stumble all over themselves. Usually in class, I'm too embarrassed to talk because I know I'll stumble all over myself, but on the InterChange I don't have time. If I didn't know the conjugation of a certain word, I could look it up. And then later when we had the [oral] discussions I felt confident. I felt I had a carry over from the written talk to the oral talk.

One student's comment was particularly intriguing as she tried to explain the process to me:

MEGAN: When you are on the computer, it's much easier because your brain is in a different mode when you write something versus when you say it. There isn't that attention and everyone looking directly at you and you feel the pressure to say something. In the lab, I think everyone expressed their opinions. I think the lab exposed more than the classroom.

Her observation that your "brain is in a different mode" is the subject of much interest now as those involved in computer communications explore this new medium and all the aspects of virtual reality and virtual communities (Faigley 1992; Hawisher & Selfe 1989; Rheingold 1993; Selfe & Hilligoss 1994; Walthers 1994).

In sum, both on the written evaluations and informally in class, students commented on the lack of stress they felt when communicating in French in the lab. Even those who began the course with little or no skill in keyboarding, remarked that only at first did they feel a bit slow typing their messages. In going discussion. All expressed the point of view that the relative anonymity of CMC, the time to think, to process input and to edit output, and the relaxed atmosphere they experienced in the lab reduced their communication anxiety significantly, all the while enabling them to participate fully in the electronic discussion. A class of twenty elementary students typically generated more than 150 messages (often composed of several sentences) per session. Many sessions in the intermediate and advanced courses (fifteen to twenty students per class) went well over 200 messages per session.

155

CHAPTER 9
Computer-Mediated
Communication:
Reducing Anxiety
and Building
Community

Another thread discerned in the voices and perspectives of the students had to do with the social aspects of classroom network communication in a foreign language. The following section will illustrate this more clearly.

SOCIAL ASPECTS OF COMPUTER-MEDIATED COMMUNICATION

We are all aware of the wide area network called the Internet. This network connects us to the entire world; thus the possibilities the Internet offers language teachers are limited only by our imagination. In the light of this information explosion, classroom use of a local area network for intense interaction might seem limiting and relatively unexciting. However, it is perhaps because of the seeming limitlessness amount of information that the Internet provides that we need the LAN to "offer more intimate local area occasions for students to find their center again" (Peterson 1995). The use of the module InterChange allows free-flowing exchange of ideas and feelings within a community of learners and their instructor "where they can be actually heard and physically recognized" (Peterson 1995).

As students begin to experience the freedom of being able to say what they want when they want, even in their varying stages of Interlanguage French, they begin to see themselves as a community of speakers of this language; no longer is language learning relegated to "book" French. Even simple phrases that would often be said in English in the regular classroom—such as "What are you doing this weekend?"—are written in French on the network. Students begin to use the target language for all communication and often refer to the bonds and spirit of community that develop in the CMC class.

A sense of community is what many students identified as evolving from the intensity of their interactions on the network. In a limited sense, this phenomenon resembles the virtual communities described by Harold Rheingold in his 1993 book *Virtual Community: Homesteading on the Cyberspace Frontier* in which he describes the honesty of communication and the connection that occurs between members of computer-networked communities. The spirit of a community of speakers of a second language also seems to alleviate the fear of ridicule associated with expressing oneself in a foreign language (Young 1992). With the increased knowledge of one another through their written interactions and discussion of ideas and dialogue (polylogue), the students exhibit a supportive attitude toward one another that is not always obvious in the classroom. Students frequently sent affirming messages such as **J'aime la reponse**

de Jenny a ce [*sic*] **question!** *(I like Jenny's answer to that question!)*, **Je suis d'accord avec tu** [*sic*], **Tom!** *(I agree with you, Tom!)*, and **Tu as raison, Jane!** *(You are right, Jane!)*, and even **C'est un** [*sic*] **idee interessant, Mary!** *(That is an interesting idea, Mary!)* Even the fact of having one's name mentioned in a message, or having a message addressed to one, was brought up by the students as making them feel good.

A comment that reveals the bonds that develop in the French class follows.

LISA: In the lab, usually I try to answer the [teacher's] questions first and to get them out of the way and just have a free conversation. If there was a comment that I really liked, I wanted to answer it right away. Then I would try to read everyone else's thoughts and if there was something within the answers that they had given that I reacted to, a whole different conversation spun off from that. . . . You begin to notice more about what they say versus speaking to someone face to face. People feel much more free to speak their mind over the computer, so you can learn more about their personalities than in class.

A focus on using French almost exclusively is another thread that surfaced in students' comments. As you can see in the following students' comments, the students frequently mentioned the fact that most participants made the effort to use only French. This meant 50 minutes of focused, communicative French. The students put it this way:

MARK: In the lab, if you use English instead of French, it's a whole sentence on the screen—for everybody to see. That's bad. In the classroom, you just blurt it out in English fast and then it's gone—and forgotten.

JENNY: It almost felt like cheating to use English in the lab . . . it would have been too easy.

PETE: The best thing about this course is . . . getting to know other students by speaking French . . . It creates a whole new attitude to learning French and meeting different people with different backgrounds.

KATHY: It allows us to talk to each other in French for extended periods of time without the pressure of the classroom.

Perhaps this lack of code-switching was due to some kind of real or imagined peer pressure, teacher pressure, or just a desire to "play the game."

The honesty and the sometimes too straightforward quality of CMC was consistently mentioned in students responses to CMC instruction.

BETSY: People say what they want to say and although we know who says what, there is no one who is shy about their opinions because of the impersonality of the computer.

TIM: I feel that sometimes I would go off the handle and get irritated with people, but I participate a heck of a lot more in lab than in class!

A changing of teacher/student roles in this new electronic community was another area to emerge from the discussion using CMC. This feeling could be explained in several ways. First, there is no front of the room, and no sound of voices even though everyone is communicating in French. The teacher can even be in another room and yet be fully engaged in discussion with a class-room full of students. The teacher is not there to correct errors or put someone on the spot. Instead, the focus is on the exchange of ideas and information. The following comments illustrate these points.

157

CHAPTER 9
Computer-Mediated
Communication:
Reducing Anxiety
and Building
Community

KERRY: Students feel less restrained by possible errors in lab . . . Also the teacher is not so in control and a fun aspect to the language can emerge.

SANDY: Students are friendlier, and teachers can ask/respond more personally when the teacher is not the focus of the class. The screen is there and there is nothing to compete with the teacher or the students.

Communicating ideas and feelings allows for increased extensive knowl-edge of the members of the classroom community, and honesty and self-revelation are born from the bonding between members of the community. If we take the social constructivist's perspective that knowledge is constructed through social interaction, then we can understand why the communication that occurs in the computer lab setting seems to encourage students' higher-order thinking skills—that through argument, ideas become clear, and opin-ions are forged, defended, and perhaps on occasion even changed.

In sum, students are saying that even in the communicative classroom of the 90s, there is still stress about speaking up in class. They are also saying that there is less stress associated with electronic discussion. Because of the lowered levels of anxiety, students tend to participate more, and this in-creased participation leads to more communication with their peers. In light of the praise from the students for this computer intervention, it is neverthe-less important to remember that one approach to language learning is just that: one approach. What this chapter illustrates is that computer-mediated classroom discussion is one way to have students communicate with one an-other meaningfully in the foreign language and in a nonthreatening environ-ment. Only more research, both qualitative and quantitative, will help us de-termine long-term linguistic benefits that these inital findings seem to indicate. As instructors become willing to include computer-mediated com-munication in their curriculum, the data will help demonstrate the efficacy of the process.

If CMC reduces learner anxiety and offers one additional approach to lan-guage instruction that is effective, what do we need to know to use it in the FL class? The following section offers practical suggestions and raises important issues in CMC.

IMPLEMENTING CMC IN THE FOREIGN LANGUAGE CLASS

For teachers willing to try CMC in the foreign language class, information about access to the software, pedagogical suggestions, and sample exercises will prove useful, particularly because CMC is still in its infancy and most teachers are not yet familiar with this type of CMC.

Software

Readers with access to a local area network and some interest in exploring the effectiveness of CMC can examine the Daedalus software by ordering a demo from the company that produced the Daedalus Integrated Writing Environment.[1] The software runs on a network file server using either a PC or a Macintosh platform. The software creates an environment in which students use a module called *Invent* to initiate their writing process and the *Respond* module to critique the writings of their peers. It includes an e-mail module called *Mail*, as well as a *BiblioCite* module for posting "works cited" entries.

The software module InterChange allows for classroom discussion (probably best with twenty-five students or less), as well as small-group or conference discussion with only five to eight students per conference. This latter option is useful for indepth exploration of a topic followed perhaps by a larger class discussion for which the small conferences serve as background brainstorming.

Setting the Task

Experimentation with vague instructions for discussion contrasted with structured approaches have led this researcher to believe that using CMC is most effective when students have a definite task to accomplish, especially at the lower levels of intruction. The following example illustrates one way to set a task. These directions were given to an intermediate undergraduate class for the first InterChange session of the semester.

Structured Instructions for a CMC Task

Welcome to InterChange! Today we are going to discuss the story in *le Petit Nicolas* called "C'est Papa Qui Décide!"

Voilà les règles du jeux *(Here are the rules of the game):*

1. Read the questions about the content of the story. Please answer the five content questions first. Each participant is required to produce a minimum of five messages regarding the content of the story. The maximum number of messages is up to you!
2. The remaining three questions have to do with your personal reaction to the ideas expressed in the story. You must send a minimum of two messages in response to the personal questions. Feel free to ask and answer questions. Please use the person's name to whom you are addressing the message and a reference if you are writing about a previous message. For example: "John, I agree with you when you say Nicolas' mother is manipulative." Don't just say: "John, I agree with you." John may not know to which message you are referring.
3. For a better "conversation," keep your messages short, to the point, and on the subject! You may of course refer to your dictionaries or to the text whenever you need to.

Remember, this exercise is part of your oral participation grade, so do the best you can at exchanging ideas and information with your classmates.

159

CHAPTER 9
Computer-Mediated
Communication:
Reducing Anxiety
and Building
Community

In spite of these cautionary instructions, the teacher may still run into two kinds of problems in this student-focused environment: off-task comments and "flaming." If in the course of the discussion, there are students who wander off task and begin "talking" about matters having nothing to do with the lesson, you may send them a subtle message by asking them one of the questions from the list (via the LAN) directly. If they ignore your message, then you may have to go to them and ask that they return to the discussion in an appropriate manner. Generally, the latter solution is not necessary. If someone is off task, a question from the instructor or from another student usually brings the person back.

The freeing atmosphere of computer conferencing sometimes encourages students to express their feelings in a more verbal student-to-student fashion than is suitable for classroom discourse. Flaming, the use of inappropriate language, is a more difficult situation to deal with—although, once again, its occurrence is rare if the proper tone and parameters for LAN discussion are firmly established from the beginning. Sometimes if only one student becomes aggressive and begins to use strong language or attacks another student, the teacher can address that student individually and insist that he or she stop such behavior. Outbursts are best dealt with on a face-to-face basis.

The next section offers language teachers concrete examples of how CMC, and in particular the Daedalus software, can be used in the foreign language class at varying levels of instruction.

Exercises using InterChange

The following examples describe exercises used for first-year, second-year, and third-year university French courses. These descriptions of CMC on the LAN using the Daedalus software can be adapted for use in other languages:

Sample Exercises

Beginning level: French 111

At least once toward the end of the first semester, French students go to the lab just for conversation in preparation for their final oral exam. Students report that the exercise helps them prepare for orally expressing their ideas. As has been shown before, the process of slowing down student output, allowing time for composition of each message, enables the student to communicate without the pressure of others' attention and with less fear of failure (Beauvois 1994).

This initial exercise can be as brief as 20 minutes or last for a full period of 45–50 minutes.

Introduction:

In this first lab experience students must become acquainted with the software and the log-in process. The manuals and on-line help from Daedalus provide sufficient explanation. I would caution the instructor to spend the time to fully acquaint himself or herself with the materials before coming to the lab with a class for the first time.

Process:

1. Students log in. On-screen instructions explain in French that they are going to have **une conversation** similar to e-mail **(courrier electronique)** and that they may respond to the following questions and then to each others' messages at will. If the lab is equipped with an overhead projector, the instructor can demonstrate how to type a message and send it, but generally students understand the process without further explanation.

2. Students receive a sheet of paper with three questions (translations are in italics):

   a. Qui êtes-vous? Donnez une petite description de vous-même, physiquement et au morale.

   a. *Who are you? Give a small description of yourself physically and personality-wise.*

   b. Qu'est-ce que vous aimez faire? passe-temps? sports? études?

   b. *What do you like to do? hobbies? sports? studies?*

   c. Parlez un peu de votre famille... Est-elle grande ou petite? Etes-vous enfant unique ou avez-vous des frères et soeurs?

   c. *Talk about your family . . . Is it big or small? Are you an only child, or do you have brothers and sisters?*

   (These questions relate to Chapters 2–8 of *French in Action* [program used at the University of Tennessee for first and second year French] and are therefore good preparation for the final oral exam in French 111.)

3. Follow-up: The instructor returns the sorted copies of the discussion to the students with corrections highlighted. Students use these copies in preparing for their upcoming oral exam.

Intermediate level: French 211

Introduction:

Before going to the lab students will have viewed video 25 in the *French in Action* series and will have gone over the basic vocabulary and grammar structures of the lesson. The purpose of the lab session is to review this recently presented material and use what has been taught in a new context, that of the students' own experience. The questions, therefore, are designed to encourage student discussion on the same theme as the video lesson.

Process:

1. Students log on and read the following questions.

2. They answer the questions and "discuss" the ideas with one another and with the instructor if he or she wishes to participate. (I often reserve my participation to restate a sentence that is not clear, to ask a question to a quiet student, and to share my own experience, briefly, with the class. But just as often, I allow them the full range of conversation without my intervention.)

   a. **Dans cette video, Tante Georgette dit qu'elle n'est pas "rouspéteuse." Est-ce qu'elle dit la vérité? Est-ce qu'elle est rouspeteuse? Pourquoi?**

161

CHAPTER 9
Computer-Mediated
Communication:
Reducing Anxiety
and Building
Community

In this video, Aunt Georgette says she is not a "complainer." Is she telling the truth? Is she a complainer? Why?

b. **Est-ce que Tante Georgette a raison de se plaindre?**
Is Aunt Georgette right to complain?

c. **Et vous? Si vous êtes au restaurant, et il y a des problèmes, que faites-vous? Est-ce que vous vous plaignez? Qu'est-ce qui vous pousse à vous plaindre au restaurant?**
And you? If you are in a restaurant and there are problems, what do you do? Do you complain? What pushes you to complain in a restaurant?

d. **Racontez un incident au restaurant ou vous, ou quelqu'un d'autre, avez rouspété à cause du service, ou d'un problème avec la cuisine, etc.**
Tell about an incident in a restaurant where you, or someone else, complained because of the service, or a problem with the food, etc.

3. Follow-up: At the end of the session, students download the discussion to their own disks and review the ideas for the next lesson. For the first 15–20 minutes of the following class period, the instructor and students talk about the amusing or not-so-amusing things that can happen to make people complain in restaurants. The instructor will also return the sorted copies of the discussion to the students for them to look at and correct in class.

Intermediate Advanced: French 342 Conversation and Composition

Introduction:

In the Conversation and Composition course, students read a certain number of texts that serve as the springboard for oral and written activities. In the following example, the students do some prereading activities and read the short story *Les Villes* by Gerard Klein, in which a futuristic city and its life are described.

Process:

1. Prereading exercise: There is a classroom discussion of modern cities, the pros and cons of city living and possible solutions to some of the big-city problems. Relevant vocabulary is discussed, perhaps even written on the board.

2. Homework: Students are assigned to read the short story and to come to the next class period prepared to discuss the text.

3. In class: In the next class meeting, the students log on to the network and access the module InterChange.

4. They then read and respond to the following questions:

a. **Avez-vous ressenti un certain malaise en lisant cette histoire? Si oui, pourquoi? (Soyez précis! Donnez la page et la ligne qui soutiennent votre commentaire.)**
Did you feel a certain discomfort while reading this story? If yes, why? (Be precise! Give the page and the line that support your comment.)

b. **Est-ce qu'il y certains aspects du gouvernement des "Villes" qui vous font penser à notre société aujourd'hui aux Etats-Unis ou en générale dans l'Ouest? (Soutenez vos idées avec les citations précises du texte.)**

Are there certain aspects of the government of the "Cities" that make you think of our society today in the United States or in general in the West? (Support your ideas with exact quotes from the text.)

c. **Analysez le rôle des bruits et des silences dans cette histoire—comment est-ce qu'ils contribuent au dénouement de l'histoire?**
Analyze the role of the sounds and silences in this story—How do they contribute to the climax of the story?

d. **Quels avertissements et quelles critiques y a-t-il dans l'histoire:**
1. **du point de vue des valeurs humains.**
2. **du point de vue du rôle de la technologie dans la société.**
3. **du point de vue politique.**
What warnings and what criticisms are there in the story:
1. on human values.
2. on the role of technology in society.
3. on politics.

These are only a few possible types of activities that could be used with CMC in a foreign language class. As more research in this field develops, we will no doubt be able to offer a wider breadth of activities that promote language learning.

CONCLUSION

Through exploring the potential of computer-mediated communication, we have discovered that this unique activity slows down student interaction to allow more input and output processing time, more time for thought, more control of the utterance, and therefore, less performance anxiety in the language classroom than in any other setting. We have a sense that there is a socially supportive environment created by better communication among the members of a class in this lab environment. Whether the process will result in eventual acquisition of the foreign language is still to be proved. Issues such as improved accuracy and more fluent oral skills in the language as effects of CMC must be resolved by further research. What we do know now is that, for the reasons cited by the students in this chapter, we can use networked computers in our classrooms without activating anxiety in our students and without inhibiting their participation. The method requires some experimentation regarding the most effective tasks and structures to be used with different groups and different levels of linguistic ability. The technology has the potential to radically change the way student interaction takes place in the classroom. It is the language professional's challenge to use that potential to its full advantage.

PORTFOLIO ASSIGNMENTS

1. a. Investigate software programs designed to promote writing skills in the FL/SL (see the two that follow, but remember you are not limited to these two). Be prepared to discuss in detail at least one program with a

fellow classmate in the same way you would were you interviewing for a teaching position at an institution that emphasizes computer-mediated language learning. (Should these software programs not be available, contact the following distributors for information about them.)

163

CHAPTER 9
Computer-Mediated
Communication:
Reducing Anxiety
and Building
Community

Systéme D: Virginia Scott
Department of French
Vanderbilt University
Nashville, TN 37232
Atajo: Heile & Heinle
20 Park Plaza
Boston, MA 02116

   b. Once you have shared your observations with a classmate, write a formal review of the program, making sure to include information about the strengths of the program and/or potential learner frustrations with it, and turn it in to your instructor.

   c. Remember to place a copy of the review in your portfolio.

2. Throughout the remainder of the semester, collect flyers, brochures, advertisements, or any such other information about CMC. Based on the desciptions offered in the flyers and brochures, predict whether the programs might offer similar affective benefits as does the Daedalus program described in this chapter.

ACTION RESEARCH

1. a. Interview an instructor at your institution who has worked with computer-mediated communication. Investigate the instructor's perceptions about CMC. Are students excited about using the hardware (the computer), or is it the program that motivates them (or maybe both). Do students participate more when they use CMC? Do they appear to have a sense of group membership when they use CMC? Do students appear less anxious when they use CMC as opposed to when they experience traditional classroom instruction?

   b. Share your findings with the class. How similar are the perceptions about CMC across interviewees?

2. a. Obtain, orally or in writing, ten students' reactions to computer-aided language learning, real or projected.

   b. Be sure to investigate how many of the students' reactions are based on actual experiences and how many on predictions (how they think they would react).

   c. Does the topic of increasing a sense of community in the class or decreasing anxiety come up in their comments? If so, what do students say about these two areas?

   d. Write your findings in a paper and share it with your classmates and/or turn it in to your instructor.

My thanks to the Spencer Foundation Small Grants for funding my research, thereby making it possible for me to contribute this chapter to this volume.

Grateful appreciation also goes to Dolly Young for advice and editing and to Lisa Beauvois for her assistance.

NOTES

1. The Daedalus Integrated Writing Environment (DIWE) is designed to take the student through the writing process from initial rough draft to final copy. DIWE can be purchased or ordered for a 30-day demo. Contact:
Daedalus
1106 Clayton Lane #280 W
Austin, TX 78723
1-800-879-2144

REFERENCES

Baker, M., & Cauvin, J. P. (1995). *Panache Littéraire*. Boston: Heinle & Heinle.

Batson, Trent (1988). The ENFI project: A networked classroom approach to writing instruction. *Academic Computing*, February, 32–33, 55–56.

Beauvois, M. H. (1992). Computer-assisted discussion in the foreign language classroom: Conversation in slow motion. *Foreign Language Annals, 25*, 455–464.

Beauvois, M. H. (1993). E-talk: Empowering students through electronic discussion in the foreign language classroom. *The Ram's Horn*, Volume VII, August, 41–47.

Beauvois, M. H. (1994). E-talk: Attitudes and motivation in computer-assisted classroom discussion. *Computers and the Humanities, 28*, 177–190.

Beauvois, M. H. (1997). Computer-mediated communication (CMC): A link to second language learning. In Michael Bush (Ed.), *The ACTFL Volume on Technology*. Lincolnwood, IL: National Textbook Company, pp. 165–184.

Beauvois, M. H. (1998a). Conversation in slow-motion revisited. *Canadian Modern Language Review*, Spring 1998.

Beauvois, M. H. (1998b). E-talk: Computer-assisted classroom attitudes and motivation. In Swaffar, Romano, Markely, & Arens (Eds.), *E-talk: Computer-assisted classroom attitudes and motivation*. Austin, TX: Labyrinth Publications, pp. 120–140.

Beauvois, M. H. (1998c). Write to speak: The effects of electronic communication on the oral achievement of fourth semester French students. In Judith Muyskens (Eds.), *New ways of learning and teaching*. Boston: Heinle & Heinle, pp. 93–115.

Beauvois, M. H., & Elledge, J. (1996). Personality types and megabytes: Student attitudes toward computer-mediated communication (CMC) in the language classroom. *CALICO Journal, 13*, 27–49.

Bruce, B., & Batson, T. (Eds.) (1992). *Networked-based classrooms: Promises and realities*. New York: Cambridge University Press.

Bruce, B., & Rubin, A. (1992). *Electronic quills: A situated evaluation of using computers for teaching writing in classrooms*. Hillsdale, NJ: Lawrence Erlbaum Associates.

Bump, J. (1990). Radical changes in class discussion using networked computers. *Computers and the Humanities, 24*, 49–65.

Faigley, L. (1990). Subverting the electronic workbook: Teaching writing using networked computers. In Heineman-Boynton, *The writing teacher as researcher: Essays in the theory of class-based writing*. Upper-Montclair, NJ: Athlestan Press, 290–312.

Faigley, L. (1992). *Fragments of rationality: Postmodernity and the subject of composition*. Pittsburgh, PA: University of Pittsburgh Press.

Hawisher, Gail, & Selfe, Cynthia (1989). *Critical perspectives on computers and composition instruction*. New York: Teachers College Press, Columbia University.

165

CHAPTER 9
Computer-Mediated
Communication:
Reducing Anxiety
and Building
Community

Horwitz, Elaine K., Horwitz, Michael B., & Cope, Joann (1986). Foreign language classroom anxiety. *Modern Language Journal, 70*, 125–132.

Kelm, Orlando (1992). The use of synchronous computer networks in second language instruction: A preliminary report. *Foreign Language Annals, 25*, 441–454.

Kinneavy, James L. (1991). *I won't teach again without computers.* Invited paper, Conference on College Communication and Composition. Boston, March 1991.

Kinginger, Celeste S. (1990). *Task variation and classroom learner discourse.* Dissertation, the University of Illinois at Urbana-Champagne.

Peterson, Nancy (1989). The sounds of silence: Listening for difference in the computer-networked collaborative writing classroom. In T. W. Batson (Ed.), *Proposal abstracts from the 5th computers and writing conference, University of Minnesota, Minneapolis. May 12–14.* Washington, DC: Gallaudet University, pp. 6–8.

Peterson, Nancy (1995). InterChange: Local conversations, global concerns. *WINGS, 3*, 1.

Phillips, Elaine M. (1991). Anxiety and oral competence: Classroom dilemma. *The French Review, 65*, 1–14.

Rheingold, Howard (1993). *The virtual community.* Reading, MA: Addison-Wesley.

Selfe, Cynthia, & Hilligoss, Susan (1994). *Literacy and computers.* New York: Modern Language Association of America.

Slatin, John (1991). Is there a text in the class? In Edward Barrett (Ed.), *Sociomedia: Multimedia, hypermedia, and the social creation of knowledge.* Boston: MIT Press, 27–53.

Walthers, J. B. (1994). Anticipated ongoing interaction versus channel effects on relational communication in computer-mediated interaction. *Human Communication Research, 4*, 473–501.

Young, Dolly J. (1992). Language anxiety from the foreign language specialist's perspective: Interviews with Krashen, Omaggio Hadley, Terrell, and Rardin. *Foreign Language Annals, 25*, 157–172.

PART IV

Language Anxiety and Individual Differences

Native Language Skills, Foreign Language Aptitude, and Anxiety About Foreign Language Learning

Richard L. Sparks
College of Mount St. Joseph
Leonore Ganschow
Miami University

Personal Reflections

a. Have you ever tutored a language learner? What kinds of problems did he or she present?

b. Have you ever known someone to expend innumerable hours studying only to experience repeated failure? To what can you attribute the failure?

c. In your opinion, what are some characteristics of "good" versus "poor" language learners?

d. Do you believe that some individuals have a harder time learning a foreign language than others? To what would you attribute this difference?

Fundamental Concepts

Learning disability (LD)

Native language skills

Foreign language aptitude

Phonology/orthography

Phonological coding

Inductive language learning

Linguistic coding differences hypothesis (LCDH)

Semantics

Syntax

Low-risk foreign language learners

High-risk foreign language learners

Affective filter

Verbal memory

FLSI

FLAPS

To what extent does anxiety contribute to the learning problems of individuals with histories of difficulties learning to read, write, and spell? In this chapter we focus on the relationships among language learning and aptitude for learning languages and foreign language (FL) anxiety. We propose that students' relative overall language skills (listening, speaking, reading, and/or writing) are likely to affect their levels of anxiety about language learning. An FL instructor might reasonably expect to find several students in his or her classes for whom FL learning is difficult. Some of these students may have been diagnosed as having specific learning disabilities (LD) (see, for example, Ganschow & Sparks 1987; Lerner 1993), but most cannot be diagnosed as LD according to accepted identification criteria. We would expect their anxiety level to be somewhat proportionate to their language skills.

For the most part, researchers on FL anxiety have not examined the role of anxiety within the context of students' levels of language skill. Our purpose here is to present research supporting the relationship between native and FL learning and its effect on anxiety and to make suggestions to FL instructors about how to identify and accommodate these at-risk FL learners in their classrooms.

RELATIONSHIP BETWEEN NATIVE LANGUAGE
AND FOREIGN LANGUAGE LEARNING

171

CHAPTER *10*
*Native Language
Skills, Foreign
Language Aptitude,
and Anxiety About
Foreign Language
Learning*

More than two dozen years ago, several researchers hypothesized a link between native (L1) and foreign (L2) language learning. John Carroll and Stanley Sapon used native language abilities as the basis for the Modern Language Aptitude Test (MLAT) (Carroll & Sapon 1959). They suggested that four variables were predictive of FL learning aptitude: (1) phonetic coding—the ability to identify distinct sounds, to form associations between those sounds and the symbols representing them, and to retain those associations in memory; (2) grammatical sensitivity—the ability to recognize the grammatical functions of words in sentence structures; (3) rote memory—the ability to learn, retain, and recall foreign language material; and (4) inductive language learning ability—the ability to induce the rules of language intuitively (see also Carroll 1962). Carroll (1973) stated that FL aptitude is generally the "residue" of native language ability, inferring that one's FL ability is linked to one's first language ability. Pimsleur and his colleagues (Pimsleur 1966a; Pimsleur, Sundland, & McIntyre 1964) also related FL learning to native language ability. They studied individuals who did poorly in FL learning and devised an FL aptitude test, the Pimsleur Language Aptitude Battery (LAB) (Pimsleur 1966b). Pimsleur and his colleagues found that these "underachievers" lacked "auditory ability"; that is, they experienced the most difficulty with sound discrimination and sound-symbol learning. In our view, these language aptitude measures, though dated and not commonly used by FL educators today, provide some measure of students' aptitude for learning language in classrooms and, especially, their ability to induce the rules of the language (see Skehan 1991; Sparks, Ganschow, & Patton 1995).

More recent evidence for native and FL linkages comes from two FL researchers. Skehan (1986a) performed follow-up testing with children who had been a part of the Bristol Language Project in England (see Wells 1985). Results of the Bristol Project indicated that there was wide variation in the speed at which children acquire their first language, and Skehan (1986b) suggested that these differences were likely to be connected to their FL learning ability. His follow-up testing showed that children who developed more quickly in their first language had higher FL aptitude. Skehan agreed with Carroll's "residue" speculation in saying that "aptitude, it would seem, is the second or foreign language equivalent of a first language learning capacity" (1986b, pp. 200–201). In his book, *Conditions for Second Language Learning*, Spolsky (1989) speculates that "any physiological or biological limitations that block the learning of a first language will similarly block the learning of a second language" (p. 19). Necessary conditions for FL learning, in his view, include ability to make sound discriminations, strong verbal memory, and grammatical sensitivity.

Sparks, Ganschow, and a colleague (Sparks 1995; Sparks & Ganschow 1991, 1993a, 1995a; Sparks, Ganschow, & Pohlman 1989) have also hypothesized that there are linkages between native language and FL learning. In their Linguistic Coding Differences Hypothesis (LCDH), they speculated that one's native language skills serve as the foundation for successful FL learning.[1] In other words, the degree of success in internalizing, systematizing, and developing one's first language strongly correlates to the same in the FL. Initially, the LCDH was used to explain the FL learning problems of students with documented histories of overt learning problems in oral and written language—students classified as learning disabled (LD).[2] Early case study evidence showed that students classified as LD who had failed or experienced inordinate difficulty with FL learning exhibited problems in the phonological/orthographic (sound/symbol), syntactic (grammar), and/or semantic (meaning) "codes" of language (Ganschow & Sparks 1986; Sparks, Ganschow, & Pohlman 1989).[3] Results of psychoeducational evaluations with these students showed that most displayed phonological/orthographic deficits (for example, problems with spelling, pseudoword recognition, word recognition); many of the students also displayed concomitant deficits in syntax and/or semantics. All of these students scored in the low average or below average range on the MLAT, a finding that supported a study by Gajar (1987), who found that postsecondary students with and without LD exhibited significant differences on the MLAT Long Form and all of its five subtests.

Since the introduction of the LCDH, we have extended our research to students who are successful and unsuccessful in FL classes and have conducted a series of empirical studies supporting the premise that native language skills are related to FL learning. These studies have shown that successful (good) and unsuccessful (poor) FL learners exhibit: (1) no significant differences in IQ; (2) significant differences on an FL aptitude test (that is, the MLAT); (3) significant differences on native language measures of phonology/orthography and phonological processing (that is, word recognition, pseudoword reading, spelling, phonemic awareness); (4) no significant differences generally on native language measures of semantics (for instance, vocabulary, reading comprehension) (Ganschow & Sparks 1991, 1995, 1996; Ganschow et al. 1991, 1994; Sparks & Ganschow 1993c, 1995b, 1996, 1997; Sparks, Ganschow et al. 1997; Sparks et al. 1992a, 1992b). The studies show that students with significantly lower levels of native language skill and FL aptitude have poorer self-perception about their FL learning skills than students with significantly higher levels of language skill and FL aptitude (Javorsky, Sparks, & Ganschow 1992; Sparks, Ganschow, & Javorsky 1993). The studies have also shown that FL teachers report that students with low levels of native language skill and FL aptitude have high levels of anxiety, poor attitudes, and low motivation in the FL classroom (Sparks & Ganschow 1996). Likewise, parents of students enrolled in FL classes who have low levels of native language skill and FL aptitude report that these students have significantly more problems with native oral and written language before entering high school (Sparks & Ganschow 1995b). Finally, a recent study showed that students with significantly lower levels of native oral and written language skills and FL aptitude achieve lower levels of oral and written proficiency in an FL and significantly lower end-of-year FL grades than students with significantly higher language skills and FL aptitude (Sparks et al. in press).

The results of these studies have led the authors to draw the following four inferences, the last of which relates to the focus of this book. First, a large percentage of poor FL learners likely will display an overt or subtle deficit in the phonological/orthographic code of language. This deficit is demonstrated by students who have difficulties with skills such as spelling words, decoding (reading) real and nonsense words, learning sound/symbol relationships, making sound discriminations, and breaking the stream of language into meaningful units or chunks. Second, a poor FL learner does not have to be diagnosed as LD to exhibit problems with FL learning. Most poor FL learners will not meet accepted criteria for LD (that is, significant discrepancies between scores on IQ and academic achievement measures). Third, there is probably not a distinct entity such as a "foreign language learning disability"; FL learning likely runs on a continuum from very proficient to very weak learners. (See Ganschow, Sparks, & Javorsky 1998; Sparks, Ganschow, & Javorsky 1993, 1995; Sparks, Javorsky, & Ganschow 1995 for a discussion of this issue.) Fourth, affective differences between good and poor FL learners may be a consequence of differences in native language skill and FL aptitude. Poor FL learners with low motivation, poor attitudes, and high levels of anxiety are likely to be those who have a history of and current difficulty with some aspect of their native language skills (i.e., in the phonological/orthographic, syntactic, and/or semantic codes).

DISTINCTIONS BETWEEN ANXIETY AND FL LEARNING PROBLEMS

Several studies conducted by the authors have supported the speculation that affective differences such as anxiety may be the result of language skill differences (Ganschow & Sparks 1996; Ganschow et al. 1994; Javorsky, Sparks, & Ganschow 1992; Sparks & Ganschow 1996; Sparks, Ganschow, & Javorsky 1993; Sparks et al. 1997). The results of these studies have shown that students with high levels of anxiety generally have significantly lower levels of native language skill (that is, reading, spelling, writing, listening, speaking) and FL aptitude (on the MLAT) than students with low levels of anxiety. Admittedly, a good number of individuals who have language difficulties will also experience FL anxiety. How, then, does one distinguish between a learner whose sole problem is anxiety and one whose anxiety is likely to be secondary to his/her language difficulties? Is such a distinction necessary? That is, would the intervention be the same for the anxious FL learner as for the individual who experiences language problems?

In an attempt to sort out these distinctions, Ganschow et al. (1994) examined the self-perceptions of college students enrolled in first-year Spanish about their own FL anxiety in relation to their perceptions of the degree of difficulty they had learning an FL. Figure 10.1 presents a diagram of four groups of students categorized by both anxiety level on Horwitz's Foreign Language Classroom Anxiety Scale (FLCAS) (Horwitz, Horwitz, & Cope 1986) (low or high anxiety) and by their self-perception about the ease or difficulty they were experiencing learning an FL (very easy or moderately easy; very difficult or moderately difficult). Forty out of 174 students (23% in group 1) said that they experienced high anxiety and yet found FL learning relatively easy. The authors hypothesized that this group, in particular, might benefit most from

173

CHAPTER 10
Native Language
Skills, Foreign
Language Aptitude,
and Anxiety About
Foreign Language
Learning

FIGURE 10.1. Anxiety Level in Relation to Student Perceptions of FL Course Ease/Difficulty* (N = 174)

Group	Anxiety Level on Horwitz's Anxiety Scale	Students' Perceptions of Ease/Difficulty of FL Course	Number	Percent
1	Low anxiety	Perceive FL course as difficult	14	8%
2	High anxiety	Perceive FL course as easy	40	23%
3	Low anxiety	Perceive FL course as easy	59	34%
4	High anxiety	Perceive FL course as difficult	61	35%

*Subjects here represent a subset of the original population of students (N = 501) enrolled in first-year college Spanish (Ganschow et al. 1994). The students not included here either had rated their overall anxiety level on Horwitz's FL anxiety scale in the "neither disagree or agree" range or had rated their perception of the ease of learning an FL in the "average" range.

the anxiety-reducing exercises recommended by Horwitz and her colleagues. They also suggested that the other high anxiety group (group 4) might benefit from Horwitz's program. However, group 4 is more likely to be highly anxious because of overt or subtle native language learning difficulties that affect their learning of an FL.

ASSESSING STUDENTS WITH FL LEARNING PROBLEMS

What can FL teachers do to identify and distinguish between students whose FL learning difficulties are due primarily to problems with native language learning and those whose FL learning difficulties are the result of affective differences (for example, high anxiety, lack of motivation)? Even though FL educators are not trained as diagnosticians, it is possible for them to conduct a brief assessment procedure that involves three components: (1) classroom observation; (2) personal interview/review of FL learning history; and (3) administration of formal and informal measures of native language skill and FL aptitude. Each component is briefly outlined here.

Classroom Observation

As Figure 10.2 indicates, a screening and assessment continuum for students with suspected FL learning problems begins with teacher observation of classroom behaviors in relation to other students in the class. The characteristics in the first part of Figure 10.2 are among the most common language problems the authors have encountered in their studies of at-risk FL learners. If the instructor notes a substantial difference between the student and others in the class on these characteristics, in particular, a personal interview with the student is warranted. (See Ganschow & Sparks 1993 for a description of classroom problems of students with FL learning difficulties.)

FIGURE 10.2. Screening and Assessment Continuum for Students with Suspected FL Learning Problems

175

*CHAPTER 10
Native Language
Skills, Foreign
Language Aptitude,
and Anxiety About
Foreign Language
Learning*

Classroom Observations by FL Instructor

In relation to other students in the class, this student:

- has unusually poor spelling—often, letters are missing or wrong orthographic rule is used, even on regularly spelled words.
- has poor pronunciation.
- has poor memory for verbal material.
- has difficulty breaking down sentences into separate words.
- exhibits an inordinately slow pace of learning (always behind).

Personal Interview with Student by FL Instructor

The student:

- reports a history of difficulties learning to read, write, and spell.
- admits to being lost most of the time (after the point at which most of the class has begun to be comfortable with the class).
- reports an early history of speech/language therapy.
- doesn't like to read; is a poor reader.
- reports poorer grades in English (and, sometimes, courses requiring heavy reading loads) relative to other subjects.

Classroom Interventions, Adaptations, and Modifications (see Figure 10.3)

The FL teacher:

- obtains grades in previous FL courses.
- talks with student's previous FL teacher(s).
- asks student to describe his/her FL learning problems. Common problems include difficulty with:
  —comprehending sentences or questions in the FL.
  —formulating oral responses in the FL.
  —pace of the FL course (that is, time limits).
  —grammar.
  —spelling.
  —amount of material to learn.

Personal Interview/Review of FL Learning History

Before the interview, the instructor might administer one or more FL self-perception instruments in order to obtain the student's views of himself or herself as an FL learner. The authors, along with another colleague, have designed two instruments that can be used for this purpose. One is the Foreign Language Screening Instrument, or FLSI (Ganschow & Sparks 1991). This instrument (see Appendix A, p. 188) takes only about 10 minutes to complete and is designed to elicit self-perceptions in four areas: (1) FL learning history; (2) developmental history; (3) academic coursework; and (4) study habits. The authors also conducted a study in which the FLSI was adapted so that it could be completed by parents of students enrolled in FL courses (Sparks & Ganschow 1995b). The second is the Foreign Language Learning Skills and

Attitude Inventory, or FL-LSA (Javorsky, Sparks, & Ganschow 1992; Sparks, Ganschow, & Javorsky 1993), a quick screening measure designed to elicit self-perceptions in three areas: (1) academic history, (2) FL learning attitudes, and (3) FL academic perceptions (see Appendix B, p. 189, for a revised version of this instrument). These surveys can also be adapted by instructors and used informally as instructor questions in the interview. In addition, the instructor could determine anxiety level about FL learning by administering Horwitz's FLCAS (Horwitz, Horwitz, & Cope 1986). Talking to the student about both his or her anxiety and his or her difficulties with language may, in itself, help to reduce the student's apprehensions about learning an FL.

In the interview, the FL teacher should ask the student if he or she has or has had problems with native language learning. Often, students with FL learning difficulties report that they have problems with English and/or other courses with large amounts of reading. Many students report that they have reading and spelling problems in English. The teacher can verify students' self-reports by obtaining their current and previous grades in both native language (for example, English) and FL courses. The student should also be asked to describe his or her current problems in the FL course. In most cases, students' reports will concur with the observations made by the FL teacher (for instance, both teacher and student observe problems with spelling). Figure 10.2 describes the most commonly reported problems found by the authors in their studies.

Formal and Informal Testing

FL educators have not been trained to administer tests of native language skill and FL aptitude. Nevertheless, there are testing measures that are usually available in a school setting (that is, from the school psychologist or educational diagnostician), easily administered to one or more students at a time, and can greatly assist an FL teacher in determining if a student's FL learning problems are the result of native language learning difficulties. For the testing procedure, we use the "linguistic coding differences" model to determine if the student has problems with the phonological/orthographic (sound and sound/symbol), syntactic (grammar), and/or semantic (meaning) "codes" of language. Formal and informal testing measures can be administered in two areas: (1) native language; and (2) FL aptitude.

Figure 10.3 shows testing measures in each of the three "codes" of language. Most of these testing measures take less than 30–45 minutes to administer. Generally, students with FL learning problems do not exhibit problems with all three "codes" of language. Instead, they have problems with one (or two) of the codes. Research by Sparks and Ganschow has shown that the largest number of students with FL learning problems have difficulty with the phonological/orthographic "code" (see, for instance, Ganschow & Sparks 1995, 1996; Sparks 1995; Sparks & Ganschow 1993b, 1993c; Sparks et al. 1992a, 1992b). Thus, many students with FL learning problems encounter difficulties with "lower level" tasks such as reading, spelling, and pronouncing FL words. These students generally score below the 25th–35th percentile on measures of native language skill.

Although FL aptitude measures are not routinely administered by FL teachers, recent research shows that these measures are helpful in identifying

FIGURE 10.3. List of Test Instruments to Measure Native Language Skills and Foreign Language Aptitude

177

CHAPTER 10
Native Language
Skills, Foreign
Language Aptitude,
and Anxiety About
Foreign Language
Learning

Phonology/Orthography

Test of Written Spelling-3
Wide Range Achievement Test-Revised (WRAT-R): Spelling
Woodcock-Johnson-Revised (WJ-R), Forms A and B
    Letter-Word Identification Subtest
    Word Attack Subtest
Woodcock Reading Mastery Test-Revised (WRMT-R), Forms G and H:
    Word Identification Subtest
    Word Attack Subtest

Syntax

Informal Writing Sample
Test of Written Language-2 (TOWL-2), Forms A and B
WJ-R Broad Written Language Cluster, Forms A and B
    Dictation Subtest
    Writing Samples Subtest

Semantics

Peabody Picture Vocabulary Test-Revised (PPVT-R), Forms L and M
Woodcock-Johnson Psychoeducational Battery (WJPB):
    Antonyms-Synonyms Subtest
    Picture Vocabulary Subtest
    Analogies Subtest
Woodcock Reading Mastery Test-Revised (WRMT-R), Forms G and H:
    Word Comprehension Subtest
    Passage Comprehension Subtest
Test of Adolescent Language-3 (TOAL-3)

Foreign Language Aptitude

Modern Language Aptitude Test (MLAT): tests foreign language aptitude using a simulated format to provide an indication of probable degree of success in learning a foreign language; includes five subtests. The Long Form consists of all five subtests, and the Short Form consists of three subtests (III, IV, and V). The subtests are:

Part I (Number Learning): Student learns numbers of a made-up language, and then transcribes spoken number words into written digits on hearing them presented rapidly.

Part II (Phonetic Script): Student listens to a sequence of syllables (many with no meaning in English) while looking at their graphemic transcriptions and is asked to quickly learn how the sounds (phonemes) correspond to the letters (graphemes).

Part III (Spelling Clues): Student reads English words presented as abbreviated spelling (e.g., luv) and then chooses the one word (out of five) that corresponds most nearly in meaning (e.g., carry, exist, affection, wash, spy).

Part IV (Words in Sentences): Student reads a "key" sentence in which a word is underlined, reads another sentence in which five words and phrases are marked as possible choices, and chooses the word or phrase in the second sentence that has the same grammatical function as the marked word or phrase in the "key" sentence.

Part V (Paired Associates): Student studies a list of nonsense words with their assigned English meanings.

students with potential FL learning problems and are also predictive of grades in FL courses (see, e.g., Sparks, Ganschow, & Patton 1995). If a student has problems with native language learning, he or she will generally have difficulty with foreign language learning and will achieve a low score (below the 25th–35th percentile) on an FL aptitude test such as the *MLAT*. The *MLAT* takes only one hour to complete and can be administered both individually and in groups.

If the FL teacher chooses to administer measures of native language skill and FL aptitude, he or she can often be assisted in interpreting the tests by the school's psychologist or educational diagnostician. (In some cases, a student might be referred to these specialists after the FL teacher has completed the observation and personal interview.) When interpreting the test results, Sparks and Ganschow (1993d) have suggested that students with FL learning problems are likely to cluster into one of four "prototypes": (1) low phonology/ orthography, high or low syntax, high semantics; (2) high phonology/orthography, high or low syntax, low semantics; (3) low phonology/orthography, low syntax, low semantics; and (4) high phonology/orthography, high syntax, high semantics with affective intrusions (for example, high anxiety, low motivation). The first three prototypes have linguistic coding (that is, language) problems. The fourth prototype has no linguistic coding problems. Instead, Sparks and Ganschow found that this type of student generally does poorly not only in an FL course but also in all or most of his or her courses (Sparks & Ganschow 1993e).

The assessment process outlined here allows an FL teacher to distinguish between students whose sole problem is affective (for instance, anxiety) and students whose anxiety is likely to be secondary to his/her language difficulties. This distinction becomes important in deciding on intervention procedures to assist struggling FL learners. In the next section, we describe some of these interventions.

CLASSROOM INTERVENTIONS AND ACCOMMODATIONS

What can FL teachers do to help students who are experiencing FL learning difficulties? To those students for whom the FL skills themselves pose difficulty, anxiety is best dealt with by directly addressing the student's difficulties with the task of learning a FL. Language learning problems occur on a continuum, ranging from mild to severe. Likewise, interventions can be flexible, ranging from in-class accommodations to consideration of waiver/substitution of the FL requirement if the school offers this latter alternative. In this section, the authors describe classroom interventions and accommodations for students with FL learning problems that have not been, for the most part, already suggested in this volume.

Within-Class Accommodations

Most desirable from the student's point of view would be within-class accommodations and modest modifications by the instructor. There are a number of things an instructor might do to assist the struggling language student. In keeping with our hypothesis that poor language skills exacerbate a student's anxiety, anything the teacher can do to facilitate the student's learning of the FL is likely to reduce anxiety. The chapters in the previous section of this volume focused on pedagogical practices that could result in more effective language learning. A few additional suggestions are presented here.

179

CHAPTER 10
Native Language
Skills, Foreign
Language Aptitude,
and Anxiety About
Foreign Language
Learning

Recognition of those aspects of the language setting (listening to the language, reading text, writing and spelling) that pose the most difficulty for the struggling student can be the first step. The instructor can often pinpoint the problem by asking the student and/or by analyzing errors on quizzes and looking for "patterns" (that is, categories of the same types of linguistic problems). Given substantial findings that poor FL learners have difficulties not only with the written aspects of an FL but also with the oral aspects of the language (listening/speaking), the instructor might use one or more of these strategies: (1) insofar as possible, present the information both auditorily and visually (for example, on an overhead projector or the blackboard) so that the learner can both hear and see the information simultaneously; (2) speak slowly and distinctly (not excessively slow, however) so that the learner can process words and sounds within words; (3) break down tasks in steps to teach concepts in manageable chunks and activate previous material learned; and (4) provide consistent review of previously learned materials.

Often, the struggling student will need more time than others in the class to learn the materials. Providing extra time on quizzes and exams can be helpful to this student. Grouping for instruction and/or providing one-one or small group tutoring might provide the student with what he or she needs to be successful.

For the student with more severe language learning problems, it might be helpful for the FL instructor to consult with the school's learning specialist (for example, LD teacher) about ways to accommodate the struggling student. Some classroom accommodations that have been used with students who have been classified as LD include giving extra time on tests, allowing the student to tape record classes, providing notetaking assistance, and providing testing alternatives (for instance, oral only, written only, take-home) (Sparks, Ganschow, & Javorsky 1992).

The instructor should maintain documented records of the student's accommodations and his or her degree of success. Should these accommodations not work, the instructor may be obliged to refer the student for more substantive testing. (For a description of documentation and referral procedures, see Philips, Ganschow, & Anderson 1991.)

Separate Course Placement

Another option on the continuum is provision for a separate FL course for students who have shown through their participation in regular FL courses that they have significant difficulty meeting the demands of the traditional FL classroom, even with the accommodations described in the previous section. Separate course placement—that is, grouping students with FL learning difficulties for specialized instruction—may be an unrealistic option in many FL programs because of the expense incurred in developing a special class and

FIGURE 10.4. Portfolio on Instructional Materials:
A Multisensory Structured Language (MSL) Approach to FL Instruction—
Sound/Symbol Component

Develop Materials

- Prepare a card deck of letters and letter combinations in the FL (see, for example, Rome & Osman 1992); best to have a deck for an individual or a small group of students.
- For difficult-to-learn letter sounds, include an accompanying picture that is illustrative of a sound.
- Sequence the sounds/symbols from regular to irregular pronunciation/spellings, and from easy to difficult.

Plan Instruction

- Present 1–2 new letter sounds/symbols in one lesson.
- Spanish example: **i** = long *e* sound in English (sample word: **ito**); German example: **a** = short *o* sound in English (sample word: **lampe**).
- For each sound/symbol, do the following:
  —see and say symbol (student[s] sees symbol and says sound).
  —hear and write sound (student[s] hears instructor pronounce sound and student[s] repeats sounds; then, student[s] writes the letter[s] that represents the sound).
  —blend several symbols in simple letter combinations to form real or nonsense words in the language.
- Keep adding cards to the card deck in order of difficulty of the sound/symbol combinations; provide regular review of cards previously learned until the sounds/symbols are overlearned.

Locate References/Resources

- For samples of language tool kits in English and Spanish, contact Educators Publishing Service, 75 Moulton St., Cambridge, MA 02138-1104.
- For application of MSL method to Spanish, see Sparks et al. 1991; for German, see Ganschow, Sparks, and Schneider 1995.

the training it takes to educate a FL instructor to work with these learners. However, studies in the literature have shown success when this option has been exercised in both high school (Ganschow & Sparks 1995; Sparks et al. 1992; Sparks & Ganschow 1993b; Sparks et al. 1997) and college (Demuth & Smith 1987; Downey & Hill 1992) settings. The studies show that at-risk FL learners experience success in FL when the class is structured, paced to meet students' needs, and emphasizes multisensory teaching techniques (Sparks et al. in press). (See Sparks et al. 1991 for a description of specialized multisensory language techniques for teaching Spanish.) A sample portfolio that emphasizes the foundations of the phonetic and orthographic structure of the second language is outlined in Figure 10.4, "Portfolio on Instructional Materials." Sample classroom lessons that illustrate how to teach the phonological/orthographic system and morphological system of an FL, since this is a predominant problem area for weak FL learners, using multisensory techniques are illustrated in Figures 10.5 and 10.6. Self-reports of students enrolled in these

> # A
> (front of card)

> # Abend
> # Lampe
> (back of card)

Instructions to Teacher

This **A** in German sounds like /Ahh/ when it stands alone or is followed by a single consonant; when it is followed by more than one consonant, the length of the vowel is shorter, like the short vowel in the word *bottle*. Thus, this **A** card has two sounds: /Ahh/ and a clipped short /o/. Each sound could be taught separately; alternatively, the two sounds could be taught together. A key word such as **Abend** (*evening*) could be provided for the /Ahh/ sound and **Lampe** (*lamp*) for the /o/ sound, and the student could be provided with pictures of a night sky and a lamp.

The student should be shown that the /Ahh/ sound of **A** can appear in initial (**Abend**), middle (**sagen**), and final (**da**) positions. Likewise, the short /o/ sound of **A** can appear in initial (**Ast**) or middle (**Lampe**) positions.

Once the card has been taught, it goes into the student's card deck and is practiced regularly until mastered. (See Ganschow, Sparks, & Schneider 1995 and Sparks et al. 1991 for additional information on how to teach the sound/symbols.)

Thanks are extended to Elke Schneider for providing the sample card and instructions.

classes indicate that anxiety is reduced considerably when instruction is modified to meet their needs (Downey & Hill 1992).

Other Options

Anxiety levels are likely to be highest for students with severe language learning problems. The FL instructor can play an important role in the decision about whether a student should continue in the FL course and/or petition for waiver/substitution of the FL requirement, if this option is available.[4] Should there be options other than taking the FL course, the FL instructor can be helpful by: (1) helping the student document that he or she has put forth a reasonable, albeit unsuccessful, effort to fulfill the FL requirement; and (2) referring the student for formal evaluation. Not all students will need to be referred for formal testing. However, if the FL instructor has tried the suggestions

FIGURE 10.6. Sample from German Morphology Card Deck Along with Instructions to Teachers

-ig
(front of card)

die Luft—luftig
der Witz—witzig
die Sonne—sonnig
(back of card)

Instructions to Teachers

The **-ig** changes a noun to an adjective. (Some students will need an explanation and examples in English of the way in which nouns change into adjectives; examples might include *beauty* to *beautiful; mess* to *messy*). Students first are shown the card, given its pronunciation, and told how this bound morpheme changes some nouns into adjectives in German. Examples from German nouns the student already knows are provided. The student then practices seeing and saying the morpheme **-ig,** hearing **-ig,** and writing **-ig,** and then writing adjective forms of words with which he or she is familiar. Once the card has been taught, it goes into the student's card deck and is practiced regularly until mastered. (See Ganschow, Sparks, & Schneider 1995 for additional information on how to teach the sounds and symbols in German.)

Thanks are extended to Elke Schneider for providing the sample card and instructions.

described here and finds that the student is still struggling, he or she may refer the student to the school psychologist, educational diagnostician, or a private clinician. At the college level, the FL instructor could contact the school's LD coordinator, the coordinator for services for students with handicapping conditions, or the Learning Assistance program on campus to refer for evaluation.

Collaboration between the diagnostician and the FL teacher has the most potential for bringing about a successful solution for both. For the student, benefits include: (1) reduction of anxiety, because his/her problem is recognized and being addressed; and (2) a system for monitoring and feedback on learning the FL. For the instructor, benefits include: (1) dialogue with someone who has expertise on students with learning problems and who can provide ideas for classroom adaptations or advice on other alternatives; and (2) reduction of frustration because of lack of success in teaching at-risk FL learners.

CONCLUSION

183

CHAPTER 10
*Native Language
Skills, Foreign
Language Aptitude,
and Anxiety About
Foreign Language
Learning*

In this chapter the authors propose that a number of struggling FL learners are likely to have difficulties with language, generally, and that FL instructors could examine alternative methods for assessing and accommodating the language skills of these students. Language skill deficits and low aptitude for language must be considered before assuming that affective variables such as anxiety cause poor performance in the FL classroom. In sum, the authors draw the following conclusions about FL learning and its relationship to anxiety:

- One's native language skills directly affect one's aptitude for FL learning; the weaker the language skills, the harder it will be to learn an FL and the more anxious the student is likely to be.
- Weak FL learners show more anxiety than good FL learners, but the anxiety is likely to be a result of their weaker language skills.
- The FL instructor should attempt to differentiate anxiety associated with language proficiency from that which is not.
- The FL instructor could make modest but helpful in-class accommodations that may help to reduce anxiety for students with mild to moderate FL learning difficulties.
- The FL instructor could provide special instruction that focuses on a slower pace of learning, careful structuring and sequencing of lessons, and multisensory teaching techniques for FL learners with mild to moderate language learning problems.
- The FL instructor can refer students with severe language learning problems for formal evaluation to determine the nature of their FL learning difficulties.[5]

PORTFOLIO ASSIGNMENTS

1. a. Develop picture file cards (for students who experience FL learning difficulties) that correspond to the vocabulary or content of three chapters in the language textbook your school uses.
   b. Place your picture file card deck in your portfolio for use in the future.
2. a. Interview a learning disability (LD) specialist at your school for ideas on what FL teachers can do to help LD students in FL classes.
   b. Develop a flyer that summarizes the LD specialist's ideas (and yours) for language educators to share with their students who experience severe FL learning difficulties.
3. a. In Figure 10.4 on page 180, Sparks and Ganschow offer portfolio instructional materials that focus on a multisensory structured approach to FL instruction. Such materials attempt to reach a broad range of learners with a variety of language learning problems. Expand on one of their three categories (Develop Materials, Plan Instruction, and/or Locate References/Resources) by adding to their list of ideas.
   b. Write your ideas on the board or on a handout for your classmates to see. Is there much overlap in ideas that are suggested?

ACTION RESEARCH

1. a. Administer the FLSI, FLAPS (in this chapter), and the FLCAS (Appendix B, pp. 248–249) to a group of language learners to determine whether there are students in the group who express FL learning difficulties and also express high levels of language anxiety.
   b. Plan a course of action for these students.
   c. Write it up and turn it in to your instructor.
2. a. Research services and options your institution or school offers for learners who have difficulties learning a foreign language, such as specialized options, separate course placement, and referrals to specialists.
   b. Develop an information sheet that summarizes what you found.
   c. Share the information sheet with the class. Did everyone come up with the same services/options?
3. a. Tutor students who have difficulties in foreign language classes, and keep a journal of personal observations and notes.
   b. Write up your observations and insights, and either share them with your classmates or turn them in to your teacher.

NOTES

1. Recently, we have modified the title of our hypothesis from the Linguistic Coding *Deficit* Hypothesis to the Linguistic Coding *Differences* Hypothesis. We made this change for two reasons. First, we have found that poor (or unsuccessful, at-risk, and so on) FL learners in our studies generally do not have overt language deficits; however, they do exhibit subtle but significant language differences when compared to good (or successful, not-at-risk, and so forth) FL learners. Second, we believe that language learning occurs along a continumn of very good to very poor FL learners and that there is not a distinct entity such as "FL learning disability" (Sparks, Ganschow, & Javorsky 1993).
2. Students with LD are said to be those who exhibit a discrepancy between their potential learning ability (IQ) and their academic achievement in at least one of seven areas: basic reading skills, reading comprehension, written language, listening comprehension, oral expression, math calculation, and math computation. Heretofore, learning disabilities were thought to be due to "perceptual" problems of an "auditory" or "visual" nature. (See Sparks & Ganschow 1993e; Sparks, Ganschow, & Javorsky 1995; Sparks, Javorsky, & Ganschow 1995 for a discussion and clarification of the LD concept.) However, research has shown that most students classified as LD have *language* problems, particularly in reading, spelling, writing, and oral language (see Vellutino 1979; Wallach & Butler 1994).
3. "Phonological coding" refers to the sound-symbol code of language, sound discrimination, and memory for sounds. Phonological coding also refers to "phonemic awareness," or the recognition that spoken words are composed of sounds (phonemes), and the ability to segment phonemes within words. Phonemic awareness involves a "meta-awareness" of language (e.g., the knowledge that the word *blank* has five phonemes—b-l-a-n-k). Orthography refers to the "visual representation of a language and can be defined as the written patterns of a language and their mapping onto phonology and meaning" (Aaron & Baker 1991, p. 13).
4. Sparks, Philips, and Ganschow (1996) suggest that students classified as LD and other struggling FL learners not receive automatic waivers of or course substitu-

185

CHAPTER 10
Native Language
Skills, Foreign
Language Aptitude,
and Anxiety About
Foreign Language
Learning

tion for the FL requirement, even if these are available options. Likewise, a history of withdrawal from FL classes alone should not be sufficient to take advantage of a waiver/substitution policy. Instead, they propose that if students are being considered for an available course waiver/substitution, they should meet *all* the following criteria: (1) a verifiable history of native language learning problems; (2) a verifiable and recent standardized testing profile that shows weaknesses (i.e., below the 25th percentile) in both native language skills and FL aptitude (for example, on the MLAT); (3) a verifiable history of FL learning difficulties and failure in previous FL courses (that is, grades of F); (4) a verifiable record of formal tutoring in the FL; and (5) a verifiable record of receiving accommodations (if unsuccessful) in the FL classroom and/or enrollment (and failure) in a separate section of the FL for "at-risk" learners.
5. The authors contributed equally in the preparation of this chapter.

REFERENCES

Aaron, P. G., & Baker, C. (1991). *Reading disabilities in college and high school: Diagnosis and management.* Parkton, MD: York Press.

Carroll, J. (1962). The prediction of success in intensive foreign language training. In R. Glaser (Ed.), *Training and research in education.* Pittsburgh, PA: University of Pittsburgh Press, pp. 87–136.

Carroll, J. (1973). Implications of aptitude test research and psycholinguistic theory for foreign language teaching. *International Journal of Psycholinguistics, 2,* 5–14.

Carroll, J., & Sapon, S. (1959). *Modern language aptitude test (MLAT) manual.* San Antonio, TX: Psychological Corp.

Demuth, K., & Smith, N. (1987). The foreign language requirement: An alternative program. *Foreign Language Annals, 20,* 67–77.

Downey, D., & Hill, B. (1992, April). *Accommodating the foreign language learning disabled student.* Paper delivered at the Foreign Language Learning and Learning Disabilities Conference, American University, Washington, DC.

Dunn, L., & Dunn, L. (1981). *Peabody picture vocabulary test-revised.* Circle Pines, MN: American Guidance.

Gajar, A. (1987). Foreign language learning disabilities: The identification of predictive and diagnostic variables. *Journal of Learning Disabilities, 20,* 327–330.

Ganschow, L., & Sparks, R. (1986). Learning disabilities and foreign language learning difficulties: Deficit in listening skills? *Journal of Reading, Writing, and Learning Disabilities International, 2,* 305–319.

Ganschow, L., & Sparks, R. (1987). The foreign language requirement. *Learning Disabilities Focus, 2,* 116–123.

Ganschow, L., & Sparks, R. (1991). A screening instrument for the identification of foreign language learning problems. *Foreign Language Annals, 24,* 383–398.

Ganschow, L., & Sparks, R. (1993). "Foreign" language learning disabilities: Issues, research and teaching implications. In S. Vogel & P. Adelman (Eds.), *Success for college students with learning disabilities.* New York: Springer-Verlag, pp. 283–320.

Ganschow, L., & Sparks, R. (1995). Effects of direct instruction in Spanish phonology on the native language skills and foreign language aptitude of at-risk foreign language learners. *Journal of Learning Disabilities, 28,* 107–120.

Ganschow, L., & Sparks, R. (1996). Anxiety about foreign language learning among high school women. *Modern Language Journal, 80,* 199–212.

Ganschow, L., Sparks, R., Anderson, R., Javorsky, J., Skinner, S., & Patton, J. (1994). Differences in anxiety and language performance among high, average, and low anxious college foreign language learners. *Modern Language Journal, 78,* 41–55.

Ganschow, L., Sparks, R., & Javorsky, J. (1998). Foreign language learning problems: A decade of research. *Journal of Learning Disabilities, 31,* 248–258.

Ganschow, L., Sparks, R., Javorsky, J., Pohlman, J., & Bishop-Marbury, A. (1991). Identifying native language difficulties among foreign language learners in college: A "foreign" language learning disability? *Journal of Learning Disabilities, 24,* 530–541.

Ganschow, L., Sparks, R., & Schneider, E. (1995). Learning a foreign language: Challenges for students with language learning difficulties. *Dyslexia, 1,* 75–95.

Hammill, D., Brown, V., Larsen, S., & Wiederholt (1994). *Test of adolescent language-3.* Austin, TX: Pro-Ed.

Hammill, D., & Larsen, S. (1988). *Test of written language-2.* Austin, TX: Pro-Ed.

Horwitz, E., Horwitz, M., & Cope, J. (1986). Foreign language classroom anxiety. *Modern Language Journal, 70,* 125–132.

Javorsky, J., Sparks, R., & Ganschow, L. (1992). Perceptions of college students with and without learning disabilities about foreign language courses. *Learning Disabilities: Research and Practice, 7,* 31–44.

Larsen, S., & Hammill, D. (1994). *Test of written spelling-3.* Austin, TX: Pro-Ed.

Lerner, J. (1997). *Learning disabilities: Theories, diagnosis and teaching strategies.* Boston: Houghton Mifflin Co.

Philips, L., Ganschow, L., & Anderson, R. (1991). The college foreign language requirement: An action plan for alternatives. *NACADA (National Academic Advising Association) Journal, 11,* 51–56.

Pimsleur, P. (1966a). Testing foreign language learning. In A. Valdman (Ed.), *Trends in language teaching.* New York: McGraw-Hill, pp. 175–214.

Pimsleur, P. (1966b). *Language aptitude battery.* New York: Harcourt, Brace.

Pimsleur, P., Sundland, D., & McIntyre, R. (1964). Underachievement in foreign language learning. *International Review of Applied Linguistics, 2,* 113–150.

Rome, P., & Osman, J. (1992). *Spanish language tool kit.* Cambridge, MA: Educators Publishing.

Skehan, P. (1986a). Where does language aptitude come from? In P. Meara (Ed.), *Spoken language.* London: Centre for Information on Language Teaching, pp. 95–113.

Skehan, P. (1986b). The role of foreign language aptitude in a model of school learning. *Language Testing, 3,* 188–221.

Skehan, P. (1991). Individual differences in second language learning. *Studies in Second Language Acquisition, 13,* 275–298.

Sparks, R. (1995). Examining the linguistic coding deficit hypothesis to explain individual differences in foreign language learning. *Annals of Dyslexia, 45,* 187–219.

Sparks, R., Artzer, M., Patton, J., Ganschow, L., Miller, K., Hordubay, D., & Walsh, G. (in press). Benefits of multisensory language instruction for at-risk learners: A comparison study of high school Spanish students. *Annals of Dyslexia.*

Sparks, R., & Ganschow, L. (1991). Foreign language learning difficulties: Affective or native language aptitude differences? *Modern Language Journal, 75,* 3–16.

Sparks, R., & Ganschow, L. (1993a). Searching for the cognitive locus of foreign language learning difficulties: Linking first and second language learning. *Modern Language Journal, 77,* 289–302.

Sparks, R., & Ganschow, L. (1993b). The effects of a multisensory structured language approach on the native and foreign language aptitude of at-risk foreign language learners: A follow-up and replication study. *Annals of Dyslexia, 43,* 194–216.

Sparks, R., & Ganschow, L. (1993c). The impact of native language learning problems on foreign language learning: Case study illustrations of the linguistic coding deficit hypothesis. *Modern Language Journal, 77,* 58–74.

Sparks, R., & Ganschow, L. (1993d). Identifying and instructing at-risk foreign language learners in college. In D. Benseler (Ed.), *The dynamics of language program direction.* Boston: Heinle & Heinle, pp. 173–199.

187

CHAPTER 10
Native Language
Skills, Foreign
Language Aptitude,
and Anxiety About
Foreign Language
Learning

Sparks, R., & Ganschow, L. (1993e). Foreign language learning and the learning disabled/at-risk student: A review of recent research. *International Schools Journal, 25*, 47–54.

Sparks, R., & Ganschow, L. (1995a). A strong inference approach to causal factors in foreign language learning: A response to MacIntyre. *Modern Language Journal, 79*, 235–244.

Sparks, R., & Ganschow, L. (1995b). Parent perceptions in the screening for performance in foreign language courses. *Foreign Language Annals, 28*, 371–391.

Sparks, R., & Ganschow, L. (1996). Teachers' perceptions of students' foreign language academic skills and affective characteristics. *Journal of Educational Research, 89*, 172–185.

Sparks, R., & Ganschow, L. (1997). Word recognition as a predictor of foreign language proficiency. *Thalamus, 16*, 20–24.

Sparks, R., Ganschow, L., Artzer, M., & Patton, J. (1997). Foreign language proficiency of at-risk and not-at-risk learners over two years of foreign language instruction: A follow-up study. *Journal of Learning Disabilities, 30*, 92–98.

Sparks, R., Ganschow, L., Artzer, M., Siebenhar, D., & Plageman, M. (1997). Anxiety and proficiency in a foreign language. *Perception and Motor Skills, 85*, 559–562.

Sparks, R., Ganschow, L., & Javorsky, J. (1992). Diagnosing and accommodating the foreign language learning difficulties of college students with learning disabilities. *Learning Disabilities: Research and Practice, 7*, 150–160.

Sparks, R., Ganschow, L., & Javorsky, J. (1993). Perceptions of low and high risk students and students with learning disabilities about high school foreign language courses. *Foreign Language Annals, 26*, 491–510.

Sparks, R., Ganschow, L., & Javorsky, J. (1995). I know one when I see one (or I know one because I am one). *Foreign Language Annals, 28*, 479–487.

Sparks, R., Ganschow, L., Javorsky, J., Pohlman, J., & Patton, J. (1992a). Identifying native language deficits in high- and low-risk foreign language learners in high school. *Foreign Language Annals, 25*, 403–418.

Sparks, R., Ganschow, L., Javorsky, J., Pohlman, J., & Patton, J. (1992b). Test comparisons among students identified as high-risk, low-risk, and learning disabled in high school foreign language courses. *Modern Language Journal, 76*, 142–159.

Sparks, R., Ganschow, L., Kenneweg, S., & Miller, K. (1991). Use of an Orton-Gillingham approach to teach a foreign language to dyslexic/learning disabled students: Explicit teaching of phonology in a second language. *Annals of Dyslexia, 41*, 96–118.

Sparks, R., Ganschow, L., & Patton, J. (1995). Prediction of performance in first-year foreign language courses: Connections between native and foreign language learning. *Journal of Educational Psychology, 87*, 638–655.

Sparks, R., Ganschow, L., Patton, J., Artzer, M., Siebenhar, D., & Plageman, M. (in press). *Differences in native language skills, foreign language aptitude, and foreign language grades among high, average, and low proficiency foreign language learners: Two studies.* (Manuscript submitted for publication.) *Language Testing.*

Sparks, R., Ganschow, L., & Pohlman, J. (1989). Linguistic coding deficits in foreign language learners. *Annals of Dyslexia, 39*, 179–195.

Sparks, R., Ganschow, L., Pohlman, J., Skinner, S., & Artzer, M. (1992). The effects of a multisensory, structured language approach on the native and foreign language aptitude skills of at-risk foreign language learners. *Annals of Dyslexia, 42*, 25–53.

Sparks, R., Javorsky, J., & Ganschow, L. (1995). Satiating the appetite of the sociologic sponge. *Foreign Language Annals, 28*, 495–498.

Sparks, R., Philips, L., & Ganschow, L. (1996). Students classified as learning disabled and the foreign language requirement: A case study of one university. In J. Liskin-Gasparro (Ed.), *Patterns and Policies: The Changing Demographics of Foreign Language Instruction* (pp. 123–159). Boston, MA: Heinle and Heinle.

Spolsky, B. (1989). *Conditions for second language learning.* Oxford, England: Oxford University Press.

Vellutino, F. (1979). *Dyslexia: Theory and research.* Cambridge, MA: MIT Press.

Vogel, S., & Adelman, P. (Eds.) (1993). *Success for college students with learning disabilities.* New York: Springer-Verlag.

Wallach, G., & Butler, K. (1994). *Language learning disabilities in school-aged children.* Columbus, OH: Merrill.

Wells, L. (1985). *Language development in the pre-school years.* England: Cambridge Univ. Press.

Wilkinson, G. (1993). *Wide range achievement test-3.* Wilmington, DE: Jastak, Inc.

Woodcock, R. (1987). *Woodcock reading mastery test-revised.* Circle Pines, MN: American Guidance.

Woodcock, R., & Johnson, M. B. (1978). *Woodcock-Johnson psychoeducational battery.* Allen Park, TX: DLM Teaching Resources.

Woodcock, R., & Johnson, M. B. (1989). *Woodcock-Johnson-revised: Tests of achievement, tests of cognitive ability.* Allen Park, TX: DLM Teaching Resources.

APPENDIX A

The Foreign Language Screening Instrument for College (FLSI-C)

Foreign Language Learning

1. How easy has it been for you to learn a foreign language?
2. Estimate your overall grade in languages you have taken in high school and college.

Developmental History

3. Did you have articulation (speech) or language difficulties as a young child?
4. Were you early or late in learning to walk?
5. Were you early or late in learning to talk?
6. Do any of your biological brothers and/or sisters have a history of academic learning difficulties?
7. As a child, how easy was it for you to learn to tell time?
8. How easy was it for you to learn self-help skills (that is, tie shoes; button, zip, snap clothing).
9. How easy was it for you to distinguish right from left?

Learning History

10. How easy was it for you to learn to read?
11. How easy has spelling been for you?
12. How easy was phonics for you?
13. How easy was it for you to understand what you read?
14. How easy was it for you to learn basic arithmetic computation, such as multiplication tables?
15. How easy was school for you at the elementary and junior high levels?
16. Estimate your elementary school grades in reading.
17. Estimate your elementary school grades in spelling.
18. How easy were chemistry, biology, and/or physics in high school or college?

189

CHAPTER 10
*Native Language
Skills, Foreign
Language Aptitude,
and Anxiety About
Foreign Language
Learning*

19. How easy was English in high school or college?
20. How easy was algebra in high school or college?
21. How easy was geometry in high school or college?

Tests and Classroom Learning Characteristics

22. How easy are most college tests for you?
23. How easy is it for you to complete a test in class when a time constraint is imposed?
24. How easy is it for you to learn in a class in which the professor talks fast?
25. How easy is it for you to learn to recall specific facts (that is, names, dates, places, times)?
26. How easy is it for you to learn in a class in which the professor writes few or no notes on the board?
27. Which phrase best describes the time you spend and the degree of difficulty you have in studying for a test?
28. How easy is note-taking for you in a typical college class?
29. How easy is it for you to learn through the lecture method?

KEY

On yes/no questions (3–6), students are rated as High Risk if they answer *yes* to articulation problems (Q. 3), biological brothers/sisters with academic learning difficulties (Q. 6), and *late* on learning to walk and talk (Qs. 4–5). On the questions relating to grades (Qs. 2, 16, 17), students are rated High Risk if they indicate *D* or *F*. The remaining questions are on a 5-point scale (very easy to very difficult); students are rated High Risk if they indicate on the scale either a 4 (somewhat difficult) or a 5 (very difficult).

APPENDIX B

Foreign Language Learning Skills and Attitude Inventory (FL-LSA)

Instructions: This questionnaire is designed to gather information about your foreign language learning background, attitudes, and study skills. On the following pages you will find twenty-six questions. Please read each statement carefully. For questions 1 and 2 you will estimate your grade and state whether you have received tutoring. Question 3 asks for your opinion on how easy it has been for you to learn a foreign language. The remaining questions ask you to circle the response (A, B, C, D, or E) that *tells how much you agree or disagree with each statement* according to the following criteria:

☐ Strongly Agree
☐ Agree
☐ Neutral (Neither Agree nor Disagree)
☐ Disagree
☐ Strongly Disagree

I. *Foreign Language Background*

1. Estimate your overall grade in your foreign language course based on your report card grades.

   A   B   C   D   F

2. Have you received tutoring in your foreign language course?

   _____ Yes   _____ No

3. How easy has it been for you to learn a foreign language?
   (a) Very easy (b) Somewhat easy (c) Moderate
   (d) Somewhat difficult (e) Very difficult

II. *Foreign Language Learning Attitudes*

   a. strongly agree
   b. agree
   c. neutral
   d. disagree
   e. strongly disagree

4. I feel I have spent too much time studying for my foreign language course.
5. I feel I should study harder for my foreign language course.
6. I have not gotten tense and nervous when studying for my foreign language course.
7. I do not worry about my foreign language course.
8. I do not feel capable of studying for my foreign language course.
9. I am more easily distracted when I study for my foreign language course than my other courses.
10. I feel I fall asleep more easily in my foreign language course than in my other courses.
11. I feel my attention wanders more easily in my foreign language course than in my other courses.
12. I feel nervous and afraid about participating in class discussions during my foreign language course.
13. I feel that I am not in control of my grades in my foreign language course.
14. I feel anxious about foreign language exams.
15. I want to learn a foreign language.
16. I define being successful in my foreign language course as a(n). . .
    (a) A (b) B (c) C (d) D (e) Passing
17. I will never be successful in a foreign language course.

III. *Foreign Language Academic Perceptions*

18. I feel I learn the vocabulary of my foreign language course easily.
19. I feel I have difficulty with spelling words in my foreign language course.
20. I feel I learn the rules of grammar in my foreign language course easily.
21. I feel I have difficulty in conversing/speaking in a foreign language.
22. I feel I write in a foreign language easily.
23. I feel I have difficulty in translating a foreign language into English.
24. I feel I have difficulty in listening to and understanding a foreign language as it is spoken.
25. I feel I translate from English into a foreign language easily.
26. I feel I read in my foreign language course easily.

Language Anxiety in Men and Women: Dealing with Gender Difference in the Language Classroom

Christine M. Campbell
Defense Language Institute

Personal Reflections

a. Have you observed any differences between male language learners and female language learners in your classroom? What kind of differences have you observed? Was one of them anxiety level?
b. Do you believe a teacher should modify the curriculum to take gender difference into account? Why or why not?

Fundamental Concepts

Individual differences

LCDH

DLI

DLAB

T-test

Likert scale

SASFLC

Two-way repeated measures ANOVA

Are women more anxiety-ridden about learning a second language than men? Are men more apprehensive about speaking in the target language in a classroom setting than women? A recent study on the relationship between language anxiety and gender difference in second language learning conducted by the author and a colleague (Campbell & Shaw 1994) attempted to answer these and other questions. The results suggest that, after 60 hours of instruction, a considerable number of male postsecondary students in intensive language courses are significantly more anxiety-ridden about using the target language in the classroom than their female counterparts. The results further indicate that both male and female postsecondary students in intensive courses are more anxious about listening than they are about the other skills both before a course begins and after 60 hours of instruction. Since the learning context was a government institute rather than a university, and the course type was intensive rather than standard, the conclusions may not be applicable to all postsecondary language learners. Nevertheless, the study supports the proposition that individual differences, and the subset gender difference, play a critical role in classroom language learning. After exploring the notion that language anxiety is a construct, the author will provide a synopsis of the study[1] mentioned and suggest ways for dealing with gender difference in the language classroom based on her own and Aida's (1994) findings.

TOWARD IDENTIFYING LANGUAGE ANXIETY[2] AS A CONSTRUCT

Most second language teachers have noticed that a certain number of their students seem especially apprehensive in the classroom. Typically, the beginning learners are the most nervous. Over the past 50 years, researchers in the language learning field have attempted to understand more thoroughly whether these reactions are displays of anxiety *per se*. Traditionally, psychologists have used the term "anxiety" to describe an unpleasant emotional state or condition. In the early 1960s, Cattell (1966; Cattell & Scheier 1961, 1963) introduced the concepts of state and trait anxiety. Today, psychologists view the two types of anxiety as related, yet quite different, constructs. Spielberger (1983), creator of the widely used *State-Trait Anxiety Inventory*, defines the two constructs as follows:

> In contrast to the transitory nature of emotional states, personality traits can be conceptualized as relatively enduring differences among people in specifiable tendencies to perceive the world in a certain way and in dispositions to react or behave in a specified manner with predictable regularity. . . . Trait anxiety (T-Anxiety) refers to relatively stable individual differences in anxiety-proneness, that is, to differences between people in the tendency to perceive stressful situations as dangerous or threatening and to respond to such situations with elevations in the intensity of their state anxiety (S-Anxiety) reactions. . . . The stronger the anxiety trait, the more probable that the individual will experience more intense elevations in S-Anxiety in a threatening situation (p. 1).

193

CHAPTER 11
*Language Anxiety in
Men and Women:
Dealing with Gender
Difference in the
Language Classroom*

Test anxiety and math anxiety are well-known types of state anxiety. Is language anxiety, then, just another type of state anxiety? Language learning researchers are still investigating whether the nervousness and worry exhibited by some language learners is actually "language anxiety" or a manifestation of one or both of the two most common types of anxiety—trait anxiety and state anxiety. Also under investigation is the relationship of language anxiety to social evaluation anxiety. When discussing anxiety peculiar to language learning (whatever term might apply), all researchers agree, however, that the nature of the anxiety in question is debilitating, not facilitating; that is, it impedes rather than enhances learning.

Perhaps MacIntyre and Gardner (1988a, 1988b, 1989, 1991a, 1991b, 1991c; Gardner & MacIntyre 1993) have done the most research on the relationships between the different constructs and subconstructs identified with language anxiety. In their 1991 article, "Language Anxiety: Its Relationship to Other Anxieties and to Processing in Native and Second Languages," for example, they identified language or "situational" (p. 514) anxiety as one of three factors obtained in an analysis of a factor structure underlying twenty-three scales assessing language anxiety and other forms of anxiety. The other two factors obtained were state anxiety and social evaluation anxiety. While this study indicates that language anxiety and state anxiety are separate constructs, it is premature to conclude they are. Recently, the two researchers (1993) conducted a study focusing on four issues concerning aspects of the validity of the *Attitude/Motivation Test Battery* (*AMTB*) (Gardner 1985). One of the issues dealt with the relationship of the subtests in the *AMTB* to higher order constructs. A factor analysis offered empirical support for the higher order constructs of integrativeness, attitudes toward the learning situation, language anxiety, and motivation.

In 1992, Phillips published an article in which she divided 50 years of anxiety research related to language learning into three areas: trait anxiety, state anxiety, and language anxiety. She cites six references dealing with the first,[3] five dealing with the second,[4] and twenty-eight dealing with the third.[5]

Since Phillips' categorization of the anxiety research, scholars have continued to study the role of anxiety in language learning: Some have focused on language anxiety *per se*; others have touched on anxiety as part of a broader discussion on affective variables in general, language learning difficulties, and so on. A review of the literature in more than fifty journals associated with language learning for 1992, 1993, and 1994 yields seven articles. In 1992, Young compiled the perspectives of well-known language specialists on language anxiety, and Komiya Samimy and Tabuse explored the possible relationships between affective variables and performance in beginning students of Japanese. The latter used a five-item instrument adapted from one developed by Ely (1984, 1986), entitled *Language Classroom Discomfort*, to measure the anxiety, self-consciousness, or embarrassment felt by the second language learner while speaking in a classroom environment. They found that discomfort negatively affected risk taking in both the autumn and spring quarters. Also, the level of language class discomfort was significantly higher in the spring than in the preceding autumn quarter.

In 1993, as stated earlier, Gardner and MacIntyre's research indicated that integrativeness, attitudes toward the learning situation, language anxiety, and motivation are higher order constructs in language learning as measured by the *Attitude/Motivation Test Battery*. That same year, Kennedy Vande Berg (1993) suggested that small group activities helped both teacher and learner manage what she calls "learner anxiety" (p. 28) in literature courses, and Sparks and Ganschow (1993a, 1993b) proposed what they call "an alternative to affective explanations for FL learning problems"—the Linguistic Coding Deficit Hypothesis (LCDH) (1993b, p. 289). The LCDH holds that foreign language learning is enhanced or limited by the degree to which students have control over the phonological, syntactic, and semantic components of the linguistic code. A deficiency in one or more of the components is likely to affect the student's ability to learn a foreign language. In their second article published in 1993, they reiterate what they asserted in 1991: " . . . [L]ow motivation, poor attitude, or high levels of anxiety are, most likely, a manifestation of deficiencies in the efficient control of one's native language, though they are obviously correlated with difficulty in FL learning" (p. 10). They speculate that the code processing problem described, and not affective variables such as attitude and motivation, cause individual differences in language learning.

In 1994, Aida examined language anxiety among second-year learners of Japanese at a major university. *Using the Foreign Language Classroom Anxiety Scale (FLCAS)* developed by Horwitz (1983), Aida discovered that one-third or more subjects were anxiety-ridden on the first day of a second-semester course in Japanese. For six of the items in the scale, over one-half of the subjects indicated they were anxiety-ridden. The results of her findings on the interplay of anxiety and gender are described in the Discussion and Implications sections below.

A careful examination of five decades of research on the role of anxiety in language learning reveals inconsistent, and often contradictory, results.[6] The conflicting reports suggest that anxiety in language learning is a complex, multifaceted construct. Researchers are continually challenged to define the phenomenon in more exact terms and to determine more accurately the connection between language anxiety, state anxiety, and social evaluation anxiety. We hope that future research will answer these and other questions about the nature of language anxiety and its role in language learning. The study summarized below attempts to answer one of the questions: namely, whether a relationship between language anxiety and gender difference exists.

INVESTIGATING LANGUAGE ANXIETY AND GENDER DIFFERENCE: A SYNOPSIS OF A STUDY

As the above literature review indicates, considerable research on state, trait, and language anxiety in second language learning has been done. One aspect of language anxiety recently explored by both the author and Aida (1994) is the relationship between language anxiety and gender difference. Recognizing that individual or learner differences constitute a complex, multifaceted variable made up of variables such as gender difference, attitudes toward the

195

CHAPTER 11
*Language Anxiety in
Men and Women:
Dealing with Gender
Difference in the
Language Classroom*

target language and culture, learning style, and beliefs about language learning, the author and a colleague (Campbell & Shaw 1994) chose to focus on gender as one aspect of individual differences.

The study described below examined male and female postsecondary learners' anxiety about using the target language in a classroom setting. The authors did not attempt to delineate anxiety types—that is, determine whether the anxiety observed was a form of state anxiety or a separate construct. They assumed, along with many of the researchers cited earlier, that the anxiety they saw in learners was language anxiety, a phenomenon peculiar to language learning.

Using an instrument especially designed to measure anxiety about using the target language for speaking, understanding oral production, reading, and writing in a classroom setting—the *Survey of Attitudes Specific to the Foreign Language Classroom (SASFLC)* (Campbell & Ortiz 1986), the authors surveyed 177 students at two key points in their language program: Immediately before beginning a foreign language course and fourteen days or 60 hours of classroom instruction later. (See Appendix A for a copy of the scale.) They decided on 60 hours because they deem that students who are exposed to this number of contact hours—approximately the number of contact hours in a college semester course—can provide meaningful commentary about their language learning experience.

The authors wanted to determine:

1. Whether the level of language anxiety in male students in Survey 1 differed significantly from the level of language anxiety in female students in Survey 1.
2. Whether the level of language anxiety in male students in Survey 2 differed significantly from the level of language anxiety in female students in Survey 2.
3. Whether the level of language anxiety in male students in Survey 1 and Survey 2 differed significantly.
4. Whether the level of language anxiety in female students in Survey 1 and Survey 2 differed significantly.
5. Whether gender and time of survey administration interacted significantly.

Hypotheses three, four, and five were aimed at determining whether the levels of language anxiety in males and females, respectively, change over time.

METHOD

Subjects

All the subjects were military personnel who were students at the Defense Language Institute (DLI), San Francisco branch. The majority of the subjects were high-school graduates between 18 and 21 years of age who had enlisted in the service immediately after high school. One hundred seventy-seven students of four different languages participated in the study—21 Spanish, 63 German, 66 Russian, 27 Korean—from five consecutive inputs of students to

DLI, San Francisco branch. The four languages mentioned were the only languages taught at the site of the study.

Although these language courses differed in length—Spanish lasted 25 weeks; German, 34 weeks; Russian, 47 weeks; Korean, 47 weeks—all students had 30 hours of team-taught classroom instruction per week. The teams were made up of four or five male and female teachers in different combinations—three males and two females, one male and three females, and so on—who were native or near-native speakers of the target language. One team taught each course of twenty-five to thirty students. All teachers purportedly used a learner-centered, communicative approach to promote language proficiency.

To minimize the effect of possible confounding variables, the authors eliminated subjects who (a) were fluent in a foreign language and (b) had successfully completed one or more college semesters of foreign language, because the authors assumed that fluent speakers and subjects who had passed a college foreign language course would be relatively comfortable, and not anxiety-ridden, in the foreign language classroom. The authors also eliminated subjects who had not taken the *Defense Language Aptitude Battery* (1977) (*DLAB*), a standardized test of foreign language aptitude developed by DLI taken by all students a short time before coming to DLI. The distribution by language of the 163 subjects who were included in the final analyses was as follows: 20 Spanish; 58 German; 60 Russian; 25 Korean. (The author and her colleague will examine the role of language difference in a separate article.)

To determine whether the two groups of subjects—males and females—were homogeneous in terms of degree of aptitude for foreign language learning, the authors used the results of the *DLAB*. The results showed no significant differences at the .05 level between males and females ($t = -1.79$, $p = .076$). Although the differences were not significant, the females tended to score higher than the males.

Materials

The authors used the *SASFLC* to measure language anxiety about using the target language in a classroom setting among male and female students. In the *SASFLC*, subjects are asked to react to 16 statements using a 5-point Likert scale ranging from 1 = strongly agree to 5 = strongly disagree. Eleven statements in the *SASFLC* center on communication apprehension as it specifically applies to the four skills (for example, "I become anxious when I have to speak in a foreign language in a classroom setting"); five statements deal with commonly held beliefs about foreign language study (for instance, "It is necessary to have a special aptitude—that is, an inborn talent—in order to learn a foreign language well"). Although the statements in the *SASFLC* and in the *FLCAS* developed by Horwitz (1983) both deal with communication apprehension, they differ in emphasis. As described above, the *SASFLC* statements specifically focus on the four skills and, separately, on commonly held beliefs about foreign language study; the *FLCAS* statements refer to communication apprehension in general (for example, "In language class, I can get so nervous I forget things I know"), test anxiety, and fear of negative evaluation in the foreign language classroom. Horwitz later made five items from the *French Class Anxiety Scale* created by Gardner, Clément, Smythe, and Smythe (1979) generic and added them to the *FLCAS* item pool. Before constructing the *SASFLC*, Campbell and Ortiz studied instruments for measuring anxiety from other fields such as psychology, consulted with professionals in the foreign language field, and asked students to respond to questions about language anxiety. A panel of one statistician, one foreign language measurement expert, and one foreign language instructor well-versed in testing examined the *SASFLC* and concluded that it was a valid measure of language anxiety in the classroom setting. Work is underway to establish its construct validity. To date, over 500 postsecondary foreign language students have taken the *SASFLC*.

Using Cronbach's alpha coefficient, reliability analysis for internal consistency for the *SASFLC* is .89 for the eleven items in the survey that deal directly with foreign language anxiety.

Procedures

After arriving at DLI, San Francisco, students took Survey 1 immediately before starting the intensive course in Spanish, German, Russian, or Korean. Two weeks later, or after 60 hours of instruction, students took Survey 2, which was identical to Survey 1 except for item order.

RESULTS

The authors performed a two-way repeated measures Analysis of Variance (ANOVA) on the results of Surveys 1 and 2 with gender and time of survey administration as the two independent variables. The results follow:

1. The interaction between gender and time of survey administration is significant ($F = 4.81$, $p = .030$) (see Table 11.1).[7] (To enhance data readability, the Likert Scale values for the survey responses were converted. For example, whereas in the original Survey 1 = strongly agree [indicating high anxiety], after the conversion this value of 1 became 5.)

2. The results of Survey 1 and Survey 2 are moderately correlated (see Table 11.2). Specifically, the correlation between the two surveys for males and females is .5181. The correlation between the two surveys for males is .5039; the correlation between the two surveys for females is .5796. One major trend is observable across genders: those subjects with high levels of language anxiety in Survey 1 had higher levels in Survey 2; those with low levels of language anxiety in Survey 1 had low levels in Survey 2.

TABLE 11.1. Repeated Measures Analysis of Variance

Source of Variation	SS	DF	MS	F	p
Within cells	19180.24	161	119.13		
Gender	222.90	1	222.90	1.87	.173
Within cells	6041.98	161	37.53		
Time of survey	5.43	1	5.43	.14	.704
Gender by time of survey	180.38	1	180.38	4.81	.030

TABLE 11.2. Correlations of Anxiety Scores Between Survey 1 and Survey 2

Subjects	N	r	p
Male and female	163	.5181	0.000
Male	119	.5039	0.000
Female	44	.5796	0.000

3. The results of Survey 1, which was administered to subjects the first day of the course, *before* the students entered class, revealed no significant differences in the level of language anxiety between male and female students ($t = .13$, $p = .899$) (see Tables 11.3 and 11.4).

4. The results of Survey 2, which was administered to the subjects on the fourteenth day of the course, after 60 hours of instruction, showed significant differences in the level of language anxiety between male and female students ($t = 2.15$, $p = .033$) (see Tables 11.3 and 11.4).

5. The results of a *t*-test comparing levels of language anxiety in male students in Survey 1 and Survey 2 revealed significant differences ($t = -2.42$, $p = .017$) (see Tables 11.3 and 11.4).

6. The results of a *t*-test comparing levels of language anxiety in female students in Survey 1 and Survey 2 did not show significant differences ($t = 1.13$, $p = .264$) (see Tables 11.3 and 11.4).

7. Table 11.5 shows the number of subjects who responded "Strongly Agree" and those who responded "Agree" to statements in the *SASFLC*. Although the *SASFLC* has sixteen items, Table 11.5 contains only those statements in the survey that deal specifically with language anxiety. Information regarding a particular skill can be obtained by pooling and averaging the

TABLE 11.3. Descriptive Statistics of Survey Administrations

		Survey 1		Survey 2	
Gender	N	Mean	SD	Mean	SD
Male	119	27.90	8.41	29.87	9.29
Female	44	27.71	8.25	26.33	9.34

TABLE 11.4. *T*-Tests for Selected Comparisons

	Anxiety Level Difference	t	p
Male vs. female			
Survey 1	0.19	0.13	0.899
Survey 2	3.54	2.15	0.033
Survey 1 vs. Survey 2			
Male	−1.97	−2.42	0.017
Female	1.38	1.13	0.264

199

CHAPTER 11
Language Anxiety in
Men and Women:
Dealing with Gender
Difference in the
Language Classroom

TABLE 11.5. Percentages of Strongly Agree and Agree by Sex

	Survey 1 (Course beginning)		Survey 2 (Two weeks later)	
	Male n/N* (%)	Female n/N* (%)	Male n/N* (%)	Female n/N* (%)
3. I fear making a mistake when I speak in an FL in a classroom setting.	28/119 (24%)	11/44 (25%)	45/119 (38%)	10/44 (23%)
4. I become anxious when I am being spoken to in an FL in a classroom setting.	25/119 (21%)	11/43 (25%)	51/119 (43%)	16/44 (36%)
5. I fear failing this course.	49/119 (41%)	20/44 (46%)	68/119 (57%)	22/44 (50%)
7. I become anxious when I am asked to write in an FL in a classroom setting.	15/119 (13%)	6/44 (14%)	22/119 (19%)	6/44 (14%)
9. I fear making a mistake in writing in an FL in a classroom setting.	17/119 (14%)	6/44 (14%)	26/119 (22%)	5/44 (11%)
10. I fear making a mistake in reading in an FL in a classroom setting.	19/119 (16%)	7/44 (16%)	25/119 (21%)	3/43 (7%)
11. I become anxious when I have to speak in an FL in a classroom setting.	31/119 (26%)	12/43 (27%)	58/119 (49%)	17/43 (40%)
12. I fear receiving a low final grade (D or below) in this course.	49/119 (41%)	22/44 (50%)	66/119 (56%)	18/43 (42%)
14. I fear not understanding what the teacher is saying in an FL when I am in an FL classroom.	48/119 (40%)	16/44 (36%)	49/119 (41%)	19/43 (44%)
15. I feel silly when I have to speak an FL in a classroom setting.	10/119 (8%)	5/43 (11%)	11/119 (9%)	2/43 (5%)
16. I become anxious when I have to read in an FL in a classroom setting.	15/119 (13%)	7/44 (16%)	31/119 (26%)	5/43 (12%)

Note: Table 11.5 includes only those statements in the *SASFLC* that deal with language anxiety.
*n = Number of students who responded "Strongly Agree" or "Agree" to the statement.
N = Total number of students who responded to the statement.

data for statements in the survey referring to that skill. Survey 1, for example, revealed that language anxiety afflicts approximately 19% of the male students and 22% of the female students when speaking, 31% of the males and 31% of the females when listening, 14% of the males and 16% of the females when reading, and 13% of the males and 14% of the females when writing.

Survey 2 revealed that language anxiety afflicts 32% of the male students and 22% of the female students when speaking, 42% of the males and 40% of the females when listening, 24% of the males and 9% of the females when reading, and 20% of the males and 13% of the females when writing.

DISCUSSION

Results of the Present Study

The data from the present study reveals a significant interaction between gender and time of survey administration with opposite trends in levels of language anxiety in male and female students over a two-week period. From the administration of Survey 1, before the course began, until the administration of Survey 2, two weeks after the start of the course, or after 60 hours of classroom instruction, the level of language anxiety in male students rose significantly while the level of language anxiety in female students slightly dropped (see Tables 11.3 and 11.4). As stated earlier, moderate correlations exist between the results of Survey 1 and Survey 2. The results reveal one major tendency across genders: Those subjects with high levels of language anxiety in Survey 1 had higher levels in Survey 2; those with low levels of language anxiety in Survey 1 had low levels in Survey 2.

The authors can only speculate about the reasons for the opposite trends. Although it is clear that gender interacted with time of survey administration, it is not clear exactly why it did. Most likely, the rise is due to the interaction of different combinations of variables such as teaching methodology, testing practices, individual or learner differences (with the subsets gender difference, attitudes toward the target language and culture, learning style, and beliefs about language learning), and teacher differences. Detecting the effect of one specific variable on the subjects would require further research. In this paper, the authors will refrain from speculating about the reasons for the rise in the level of language anxiety in male students in Survey 2 and, instead, will summarize the data results and suggest ways to deal with gender difference in the classroom.

A review of the data in Table 11.5 reveals gender-related difference as it pertains to the four language skills. Approximately the same percentage of male and female students felt anxious about speaking in the target language before the course began; two weeks later, however, a greater percentage of males felt anxious about speaking than females. The same held true for reading and writing. For speaking, the percentage of females in Survey 2 who felt anxious rose less than 1%, while the percentage of males who felt anxious rose almost 13%. For reading and writing, the percentage of anxious females fell by approximately 7% and 1%, respectively, while the percentage of anxious males rose approximately 9% and 7%. In the case of listening, approximately the same percentage of males and females felt anxious before the course began; 2 weeks later, the percentage difference between males and females was slight (less than 2%) while the percentage hike from Survey 1 to Survey 2 for both groups was considerable (almost 12% for males; 9% for females). Overall, both males and females felt more anxious about listening than the other three skills both before the course began and two weeks later.

Why are both genders especially anxiety-ridden about listening? Perhaps listening is inherently more threatening than the other skills because of the inability of the listener to control what the other party might say. Speaking, one could argue, is to some degree under the control of the speaker; one can choose to say much or little, or even to bluff. (Undoubtedly, the reader knows someone who can spout off several phrases in the target language perfectly, but whose knowledge stops there.) Listening, in contrast, is more elusive. The degree of predictability from one discourse experience to another can vary considerably. For example, the listener at the lower proficiency levels can predict and understand routine, conventional questions such as "How is your family doing?"; he cannot, however, control for a sudden digression into another topic at a higher level of proficiency, a humorous twist with a heavy cultural load, and other deviations in discourse.

A second reason for the higher levels of anxiety for listening might be connected with the students' career goals: The majority are aware that they should have particularly strong listening skills to succeed in their future work. Because this realization alone could explain the apprehension about listening, research should be conducted using prototypic university students to determine whether nervousness about listening in particular is generalizable to all postsecondary students.

The data in Table 11.5 also provides some insight into gender-related difference. A slightly greater percentage of female students—5%—feared failing the course before the course began (see question 5); two weeks later, the percentage of females fearing failure rose only 4% while the percentage of males rose 16%. Likewise, a greater percentage of female students—9%—feared receiving a low final grade in the course before the course began (see question 12); two weeks later, the percentage of females fearing receiving a low final grade in the course dropped by 8% while the percentage of males rose 15%.

The results of this study, *grosso modo*, suggest the following about male and female postsecondary students learning the target language in an intensive course:

1. After 60 hours of instruction, a considerable number of males are significantly more anxiety-ridden in the classroom than their female counterparts. This anxiety among the males, it seems, is directly connected to (a) language activities requiring the student to listen, speak, read, and write in the target language and to (b) a fear of academic failure.
2. Overall, both males and females are more anxious about listening than they are about the other skills both before a course begins and two weeks later.

Results of the Present Study Compared with Those of Other Studies

The result about listening previously mentioned is consistent with findings in the study by Campbell and Ortiz (1988) in which approximately one-third of the DLI students surveyed with the *SASFLC* immediately *before* starting language instruction at the Institute experienced anxiety when listening; *after* 60 hours of language instruction at the Institute, approximately one-half did. Regarding gender difference and levels of anxiety, neither Campbell and Shaw (1994) nor Aida (1994) found significant gender difference in the first anxiety survey. In the latter study, anxiety levels in males and females did not differ significantly ($t = .41$, $p = .69$).

The results of the two studies differ in other ways as well. Aida concentrated on the relationship between language anxiety and performance as measured through final course grade, not gender difference and changes in levels of language anxiety over time. A two by two ANOVA performed by Aida with anxiety (high versus low level, with subjects placed in one or the other group) and gender as the independent variables and final course grade as the dependent variable showed significant main effects for both anxiety ($F = 7.35$, $p = .008$) and gender ($F = 4.74$, $p = .032$). In the former case, the high anxiety group received significantly lower grades ($\overline{X} = 85.6$) than the low anxiety group ($\overline{X} = 89.8$); in the latter case, the females scored higher than males ($\overline{X} = 89.7$ and $\overline{X} = 86.1$, respectively). There was no significant anxiety-gender interaction effect on final course grade ($F = 3.20$, $p > .05$). In both male and female groups, students with high levels of anxiety were more likely to receive low grades than students with low levels of anxiety.

The student type in the two studies is also different: In the former, learners were beginning their first postsecondary language course; in the latter, they were starting the second semester of a one-year beginning language course sequence.

Limitations on the Conclusions

The authors recognize that in learning research, certain factors inevitably limit the generalizability of the conclusions. Of particular interest in this study are factors of context, student type, role of the language course in the student's career, and course type. Concerning the first two factors, one could argue that the military context is somehow more stressful than the academic context and that more demands are made of DLI students than of most college students because they are both students and soldiers, among other pressures. The authors suggest that DLI students suffer as much academic and emotional stress as today's college students who have to take part-time jobs to offset tuition and room and board costs. DLI students, it must be remembered, have free room and board and receive a monthly salary. The third factor more clearly distinguishes DLI students from college students: Undoubtedly, DLI students feel greater pressure to succeed in a language course than college students who are not majoring in a language or a language-related discipline because, as was mentioned earlier, the course is critical for their career. The fourth factor limiting the generalizability of the conclusion is course type. Intensive courses, regardless of discipline, are considered inherently more stressful than regular courses.

Given the factors limiting the generalizability of the conclusions, what are the implications of the results for the language classroom?

IMPLICATIONS OF THE RESULTS FOR THE LANGUAGE CLASSROOM: SUGGESTIONS FOR DEALING WITH GENDER DIFFERENCE

203

CHAPTER *11*
*Language Anxiety in
Men and Women:
Dealing with Gender
Difference in the
Language Classroom*

As stated earlier, Campbell and Shaw's (1994) findings on the relationship between gender difference and language anxiety differ from Aida's in several ways. First, the former examined differences in levels of language anxiety in males and females over time—that is, immediately before the start of the students' first postsecondary language course and after 60 hours of instruction. Aida analyzed these differences at one specific point in the language learner's experience—the first day of a second-semester course in beginning Japanese, after 50 hours (at 3 hours of class per week by 16 weeks or 4 months) of instruction. Neither found significant differences in the level of language anxiety between male and female students. After 60 hours of instruction, however, Campbell and Shaw did discover significant differences in the level of language anxiety between male and female students, with males more anxious than females. More specifically, gender significantly interacted with time of survey administration: Two weeks into the course, the level of language anxiety in males rose significantly while it slightly dropped in females.

According to Aida's further investigation of language anxiety and gender effect on final course grade, anxiety significantly affected final course grade. In her study, the higher the anxiety, the lower the grade. Her study also showed significant differences in final course grades between females and males, with females scoring higher. Furthermore, there was no significant anxiety-gender interaction; that is, anxiety was independent of gender in terms of performance as measured by final course grade.

Campbell and Shaw's study suggests the following about male and female language learners at a postsecondary level: (1) Males feel more anxiety-ridden than females after 60 hours of instruction, and (2) both males and females are more anxious about listening than they are about the other skills, both before a course begins and after 60 hours of instruction.

Given these results, what should the teacher's *modus operandi* be for dealing with gender difference in the classroom? Should the teacher covertly discriminate—for example, have the females model new structures and activities before the males do or ask the females to do oral reports before the males do? Surely, most teachers would balk at the idea and rightly so. Students of both genders would quickly become aware of the discriminatory practices. While some females might flaunt their edge, some would resent the performance burden. The males' pride, no doubt, would be hurt. While segregating students by learner styles for small-group activity and pair work apparently enhances learning (Oxford 1990a; Oxford & Lavine 1992), treating male students differently from female students in the language classroom could actually impede it.

While teachers should not give preferential treatment to one gender versus the other in the classroom, they could carefully monitor the males for signs of anxiety. This anxiety can manifest itself in a variety of ways: Blanking when asked to contribute in class, shyness, general sullenness, and even hostility toward the teacher and peers. The sensitive teacher should identify students, irrespective of gender, who are exhibiting these signs and systematically work with each one during office hours. First, the teacher can administer an anxiety instrument such as the *FLCAS* or the *SASFLC* for diagnostic purposes if this was not done on the first day of class. Next, the teacher can set up an anxiety-reduction program consisting of a series of 20-minute sessions once a week for three weeks during which the students work through materials especially designed to help them become successful language learners by lowering their debilitating anxiety. Teachers can create their own materials or use those prepared by Horwitz, Horwitz, and Cope (1986) and Campbell and Ortiz (1991a, 1991b).[8] At the sessions, the students can discuss the material they have been given by the teacher.

While the special attention afforded to overly anxious males during office hours will no doubt help them, how should teachers deal with both the males and females who, as the results of this study indicate, are especially apprehensive about listening in the classroom? They should ease students into listening comprehension activities. Although engaging students in both listening and speaking activities within a real-life context early on is one of the principles of proficiency-oriented instruction, research (Campbell & Ortiz 1988; Campbell & Shaw 1994) indicates that learners are especially anxious about using these two skills. In contrast, their research reveals moderate levels of anxiety for reading and writing. Given these findings, the teacher might consider gradually introducing listening and speaking activities during the first three weeks of class. Some strategies for doing so are listed next.

1. Because the Natural Approach (NA) stresses development of the receptive skills before communicative speaking activities, pick a textbook having an underlying NA philosophy. A recent study by Young and Oxford (1993) of student reactions to two well-known communicatively oriented Spanish textbooks revealed that the NA textbook appeared to create less anxiety than the proficiency-oriented textbook.

2. On the first day of class, before starting instruction in the target language, discuss with students the importance of using language learning strategies such as deducing meaning from context, listening for and using cognates, taking risks, learning to deal with uncertainty, or understanding the gist of what is heard or read. Oxford's (1990b) *Language Learning Strategies: What Every Teacher Should Know* is an excellent reference for this purpose.

3. During the critical first two weeks of the course, provide students with extremely easy listening comprehension and speaking activities designed to build up their confidence.

4. Throughout the course, make an effort to devise listening comprehension and speaking activities involving group and pair work as research indicates most language students tend to feel less intimidated working with partners (for example, Bejarano 1987; Chang & Smith 1991; Gunderson & Johnson 1980; McGroarty 1989). Refer to Milleret (1992) for examples of cooperative learning tasks for the language classroom. (Also see Lee, Vogely, and Phillips, in this volume.)

205

CHAPTER *11*
*Language Anxiety in
Men and Women:
Dealing with Gender
Difference in the
Language Classroom*

5. Postpone testing of listening and speaking until the third week of the course.
6. Have students do more reading and writing activities during the first two weeks of class.

Aside from working individually with anxiety-ridden male students and gradually introducing both male and female students to listening and speaking activities, what are the other implications of the research results? Campbell and Shaw (1994) results show that the language anxiety levels of males and females do not differ significantly immediately *before* starting language instruction at a postsecondary level for the first time. Although Campbell and Shaw did not observe significant gender differences at this point, they did detect high levels of anxiety: Approximately 31%[9] of the students felt anxious about listening, 20% about speaking, 15% about reading, and 13.5% about writing in the target language in the classroom. *After* 60 hours of instruction, approximately 41% of the students were nervous about listening, 27% about speaking, 16.5% about reading, and 16.5% about writing.

These results support those of Horwitz, Horwitz, and Cope (1986) and Campbell and Ortiz (1988). The former reported that a third or more of the students surveyed during the third week of a first-semester language course indicated they felt anxious about their language learning experience in nineteen of thirty-three items; in seven of thirty-three items, more than half indicated the same. Campbell and Ortiz discovered high anxiety levels both immediately before and after two weeks or 60 hours of intensive instruction. Before instruction, approximately one-third suffered from anxiety about listening, one-fourth about speaking, one-sixth about reading, and one-sixth about writing. Two weeks later, approximately one-half felt anxiety about listening, one-third to one-half about speaking, one-fifth about reading, and one-fifth about writing.

Given these results, an anxiety-reduction program like those referred to earlier, conducted during the first phase of language learning, might benefit both males and females. Horwitz, Horwitz, and Cope (1986) and Campbell and Ortiz's (1988) experience in devising and conducting special programs of this nature has convinced them of their merit. These programs, in which the teacher acts as a facilitator of group discussion, provide students with a forum in which they can talk about their previous language learning experiences and their expectations about the upcoming course, discuss commonly held negative beliefs about language learning, hear about strategies for language learning, and more.

The format of the program can vary based on factors such as student need and administrative constraints. Horwitz, Horwitz, and Cope's original program consisted of a series of one-hour group sessions over a five-week period that students volunteered to attend outside of class for no credit; Campbell and Ortiz's was a four-hour workshop conducted for groups of students right before language courses began.

Ideally, the program should be set up before the course begins so that the student can start the course better equipped to be a successful language learner. However, because it is not administratively feasible to organize programs outside class or office hours, the best alternative would be to hold them during the first three days of the course. Teachers who worry about spending valuable classroom hours in this way should read the literature on these programs and talk with colleagues who have organized them. The benefits most definitely outweigh the disadvantages. As one university professor (T. Critchfield, personal communication, September 4, 1988) who conducted a four-hour workshop using Campbell and Ortiz's materials describes:

> [As a result of the workshop, there is] good humor and trust among members of the class as well as the [sic] lack of formal distance between students and instructor. Such is not unusual in my classes but [this] is a very, very early phenomenon, and one that I believe will result in a lower level of classroom frustration and consequent higher rate of student survival in the class.

For an outstanding list of other approaches for reducing language anxiety, consult Young's 1991 article, "Creating a Low-Anxiety Classroom Environment: What Does Language Anxiety Research Suggest?" In this publication, Young cites strategies gleaned from the research for use by both teacher and student. Teachers, for example, can use less threatening error-correction techniques such as modeling, incorporate meaningful games emphasizing problem solving into lesson plans, and have students use an anxiety graph to monitor their feelings. Students can join a language club, do relaxation exercises, practice positive self-talk, and/or keep a journal in which they write about their reactions to language learning. For more detailed work on anxiety-reduction strategies, refer to the germinal text *Language Anxiety* (1991) edited by Horwitz and Young.

CONCLUSION

While researchers such as Sparks and Ganschow (1991, 1993a, 1993b) submit that cognitive, rather than affective, variables cause individual differences in language learning, most likely both variable types, in combination with external variables such as learning conditions, determine whether an individual succeeds in learning a language. This chapter has examined a subset of individual differences—gender difference—and their relationship to language anxiety in postsecondary students. While the results of the study by Campbell and Shaw (1994) suggest that male students after 60 hours of language instruction are significantly more anxiety-ridden about language learning than females, the author concludes that overt preferential treatment of any sort would be pedagogically detrimental. Of course, teachers are encouraged to monitor the progress of the males versus the females during the critical first few weeks of class and give special attention during office hours to those students having difficulties.

The results also indicate that both males and females are especially apprehensive about listening. Several strategies for helping students become more comfortable with listening were proposed.

If, as research by Campbell and Ortiz (1988), Campbell and Shaw (1994), and Horwitz, Horwitz, and Cope (1986) suggests, between 20% and 50% of postsecondary students (whether male or female) in the first stages of a language program (whether conventional or intensive) suffer from what appears to be language anxiety, then teachers should feel compelled to help those students become successful language learners. If, as Krashen (1982) has hypothesized, a low-stress language learning environment encourages acquisition, then teachers should search out ways to challenge, but not threaten, learners in the classroom. The teacher who makes the effort to combat language anxiety will improve the learning environment and ultimately curb attrition.

PORTFOLIO ASSIGNMENTS

1. a. Prepare a handout that summarizes one of the following articles. The focus of these articles is on reducing language anxiety in language learners, males and females alike.

   Campbell, Christine M., & Ortiz, José (1991). Helping students overcome foreign language anxiety: A foreign language anxiety workshop. In E. Horwitz & D. Young (Eds.), *Language anxiety: From theory and research to classroom implications.* Upper Saddle River, NJ: Prentice Hall, pp. 3–14.

   Cope Powell, Jo Ann (1991). Foreign language classroom anxiety: Institutional responses. In E. Horwitz & D. Young (Eds.), *Language anxiety: From theory and research to classroom implications.* Upper Saddle River, NJ: Prentice Hall.

   Crookall, David, & Oxford, Rebecca (1991). Dealing with anxiety: Some practical activities for language learners and teacher trainees. In E. Horwitz & D. Young (Eds.), *Language anxiety: From theory and research to classroom implications.* Upper Saddle River, NJ: Prentice Hall.

   Foss, Karen A., & Reitzel, Armeda C. (1991). A relational model for managing second language anxiety. In E. Horwitz & D. Young (Eds.), *Language anxiety: From theory and research to classroom implications.* Upper Saddle River, NJ: Prentice Hall, pp. 129–140.

   b. Share your summary with your class. Remember to place all handouts in your portfolio.

2. a. Develop a list of classroom practices that you can refer to when you teach that briefly enumerates ways you can alleviate language anxiety in all learners (males and females).

   b. Share your list with two other classmates. What practices do all three of you agree on?

ACTION RESEARCH

1. a. Just as learners have myths about what they think reading in an SL is, or what they believe grammar instruction in the SL should look like, learners also hold myths related to gender difference. Interview three males and three females for their myths about language learning based on gender.

   b. You may write your own questions to ask in the interview or base it on the following questions.

   • Is there a difference in how males and females learn a foreign language? If yes, what are those differences?

- Do males or females do better in language learning?
- Do you think males use different strategies to study foreign languages than females? If so, what are they?
- Does one gender experience more language anxiety than the other?

   c. Look for common responses in the interviews and summarize your findings in writing.

   d. Share your findings orally or in writing with the class. Are there general patterns you can identify based on the results?

2. a. Investigate whether the anxiety levels of men and women in an FL or SL class differ using the following anxiety thermometer. Be sure to give the anxiety thermometer to an equal number of males and females.

Language Anxiety Thermometer
How anxious do you feel in your foreign language class?

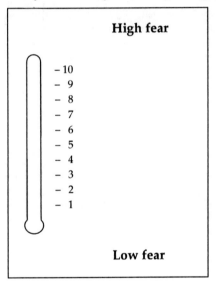

   b. Share your findings with the rest of the class to ascertain whether men and women's anxiety levels were very different.

NOTES

1. For an in-depth description of the study, see the article by C. Campbell & V. Shaw (1994) entitled "Language Anxiety and Gender Differences in Adult Second Language Learners: Exploring the Relationship" in *Faces in a Crowd: Individual Learners in Multisection Programs,* edited by C. Klee and published by Heinle & Heinle Publishers, Inc., Boston, Mass.

2. The author will use the term *language anxiety* throughout the article to refer to the anxiety some students experience in learning in a language.

3. Bartz (1975); Brewster (1971); Dunkel (1947); Pimsleur, Sundland, & McIntyre (1964); Swain & Burnaby (1976); Wescott (1973).

4. Chastain (1975); Scott (1986); Steinberg (1982); Wittenborn, Larsen, & Mogil (1945); Young (1986).

209

CHAPTER 11
*Language Anxiety in
Men and Women:
Dealing with Gender
Difference in the
Language Classroom*

5. Backman (1976); Bailey (1983); Campbell & Ortiz (1991a); Cope Powell (1991); Crookall & Oxford (1991); Daly (1991); Ely (1986); Ehrman & Oxford (1990); Foss & Reitzel (1988); Gardner et al. (1976); Horwitz (1986); Horwitz, Horwitz, & Cope (1986); Horwitz & Sadow (1992); Horwitz & Young (1991); Koch & Terrell (1991); Lavine & Oxford (1990); Loughrin-Sacco (1990); MacIntyre & Gardner (1989); Madsen, Brown, & Jones (1991); Mejías, Applbaum, Applbaum, & Trotter II (1991); Phillips (1990a); Phillips (1990b); Price (1991); Scott (1986); Scovel (1978); Tucker, Hamayan, & Genesee (1976); Young (1986); Young (1990).

Phillips did not include in the listing the following two articles published in 1991, undoubtedly because her article was at press when the other two appeared: Sparks, R., & Ganschow, L. (1991) and Young, D. (1991).

6. Scovel (1978) cites studies by Swain and Burnaby (1976); Tucker, Hamayan, and Genesee (1976); Backman (1976); and Chastain (1975; 1980) to illustrate to what degree the research results are inconsistent and frequently contradictory.

7. For those readers concerned about the differing Ns in the t-tests performed on the *DLAB* scores and survey results in this study, the authors provide the following information: According to the bulk of the literature in educational statistics, the difference in the Ns is taken into account in the process to determine t values. Guilford and Fruchter, two psychologists renowned for their expertise in educational statistics, refer to differing Ns when using t tests in their germinal text *Fundamental Statistics in Psychology and Education* (1956). In the last line of the section entitled "When t Tests Do Not Apply," Guilford and Fruchter state "On the whole, t is not markedly affected except by rather strong violations [of the assumptions of the t tests, such as the one establishing that Ns should be as similar as possible], unless N is very small" (p. 162). The differing Ns in the present study do not constitute a "strong violation" because the variances of the two groups are not significantly different ($F = 1.20$, $p = .439$). A strong violation, according to Guilford and Fruchter, would be differing variances. They posit: "The reader should also be warned that if the two samples have markedly differing variances, the t test is questionable" (p. 161).

8. Readers interested in program materials by Horwitz, Horwitz, and Cope and by Campbell and Ortiz can contact the authors at the following addresses, respectively: The University of Texas, Austin; The Defense Language Institute, ATFL-ES-T (Dr. Campbell), Presidio of Monterey, CA 93944-5006. A complete set of Campbell and Ortiz materials and a description about how to use them can be found in *Language and Anxiety* (1991), edited by E. Horwitz and D. Young and published by Prentice Hall.

9. The percentages for males and females are averaged.

REFERENCES

Aida, Y. (1994). Examination of Horwitz, Horwitz, and Cope's construct of foreign language anxiety: The case of students of Japanese. *The Modern Language Journal, 78,* 155–168.

Backman, N. (1976). Two measures of affective factors as they relate to progress in adult second-language learning. *Working Papers in Bilingualism, 10,* 100–122.

Bailey, K. (1983). Competitiveness and anxiety in adult second language learning: Looking at and through the diary studies. In H. Seliger & M. Long (Eds.), *Classroom oriented research in second language acquisition.* Rowley, MA: Newbury House, pp. 67–102.

Bartz, W. (1975). A study of the relationship of certain learner factors with the ability to communicate in a second language (German) for the development of measures of communicative competence. *Dissertation Abstracts International, 35,* 4852A.

Bejarano, Y. (1987). A cooperative small-group methodology in the language classroom. *TESOL Quarterly, 21,* 483–501.

Brewster, E. (1971). Personality factors relevant to intensive audio-lingual foreign language learning. *Dissertation Abstracts International, 33,* 68A.

Campbell, C., & Ortiz, J. (1986). *Survey of attitudes specific to the foreign language classroom.* Presidio of Monterey, CA: The Defense Language Institute.

Campbell, C., & Ortiz, J. (1988). Dispelling students' fears and misconceptions about foreign language study: The foreign language anxiety workshop at the Defense Language Institute. In T. Fryer and F. Medley, Jr. (Eds.), *New challenges and opportunities: Dimension—Languages '87.* Columbia, SC: Southern Conference on Language Teaching, pp. 29–40.

Campbell, C., & Ortiz, J. (1991a). Helping students overcome foreign language anxiety: A foreign language anxiety workshop. In E. Horwitz and D. Young (Eds.), *Language anxiety: From theory and research to classroom implications.* Upper Saddle River, NJ: Prentice Hall, pp. 153–168.

Campbell, C., & Ortiz, J. (1991b). Towards a more thorough understanding of foreign language anxiety. In L. Strasheim (Ed.), *Focus on the foreign language learner: Priorities and strategies.* Lincolnwood, NJ: National Textbook Company, pp. 12–24.

Campbell, C., & Shaw, V. (1994). Language anxiety and gender differences in adult second language learners: Exploring the relationship. In C. Klee (Ed.), *Faces in a crowd: The individual learner in multisection courses.* Boston: Heinle & Heinle.

Cattell, R. (1966). *Handbook of multivariate experimental psychology.* Chicago: Rand McNally.

Cattell, R., & Scheier, I. (1961). *The meaning and measurement of neuroticism and anxiety.* New York: Ronald Press.

Cattell, R., & Scheier, I. (1963). *Handbook for the IPAT anxiety scale* (2d ed.). Champaign, IL: Institute for Personality and Ability Testing.

Chang, K., & Smith, W. (1991). Cooperative learning and CALL/IVD in beginning Spanish: An experiment. *The Modern Language Journal, 75,* 205–211.

Chastain, K. (1975). Affective and ability factors in second language acquisition. *Language Learning, 25,* 153–161.

Chastain, K. (1980). *A philosophy of second language learning and teaching.* Boston: Heinle & Heinle.

Cope Powell, J. (1991). Foreign language classroom anxiety: Institutional responses. In E. Horwitz & D. Young (Eds.), *Language anxiety: From theory and research to classroom implications.* Upper Saddle River, NJ: Prentice Hall, pp. 169–176.

Crookall, D., & Oxford, R. (1991). Dealing with anxiety: Some practical activities for language learners and teacher trainees. In E. Horwitz & D. Young (Eds.), *Language anxiety: From theory and research to classroom implications.* Upper Saddle River, NJ: Prentice Hall, pp. 141–150.

Daly, J. (1991). Understanding communication apprehension: An introduction for language educators. In E. Horwitz & D. Young (Eds.), *Language anxiety: From theory and research to classroom implications.* Upper Saddle River, NJ: Prentice Hall, pp. 3–14.

Defense language aptitude battery. (1977). Defense Language Institute, Presidio of Monterey, California.

Dunkel, H. (1947). The effect of personality on language achievement. *Journal of Educational Psychology, 38,* 177–182.

Ehrman, M., & Oxford, R. (1990). Adult language learning styles and strategies in an intensive training setting. *The Modern Language Journal, 73,* 311–327.

211

CHAPTER 11
*Language Anxiety in
Men and Women:
Dealing with Gender
Difference in the
Language Classroom*

Ely, C. (1984). *A causal analysis of the affective, behavioral and aptitude antecedents of foreign language proficiency.* Unpublished doctoral dissertation, Stanford University, Palo Alto, California.

Ely, C. (1986). An analysis of discomfort, risktaking, sociability, and motivation in the L2 classroom. *Language Learning, 36,* 1–25.

Foss, K., & Reizel, A. (1988). A relational model for managing second language anxiety. *TESOL Quarterly, 22,* 427–454.

Gardner, R. (1985). *Social psychology and second language learning: The role of attitudes and motivation.* London: Edward Arnold Publishers.

Gardner, R., Clément, C., Smythe, P. C., and Smythe, C. C. (1979). *Attitudes and motivation test battery, revised manual* (Research Bulletin No. 15). London, Ontario: University of Western Ontario.

Gardner, R., & MacIntyre, P. (1993). On the measurement of affective variables in second language learning. *Language Learning, 43,* 157–194.

Gardner, R., Smythe, P. C., Clément, C., & Gliksman, L. (1976). Second language learning: A social-psychological perspective. *Canadian Modern Language Review, 32,* 198–213.

Guilford, J. P., & Fruchter, B. (1956). *Fundamental statistics in psychology and education.* New York: McGraw-Hill.

Gunderson, B., & Johnson, D. (1980). Building positive attitudes by using cooperative learning groups. *Foreign Language Annals, 13,* 39–43.

Horwitz, E. (1983). *Foreign language classroom anxiety scale.* Unpublished manuscript. Reprinted with permission.

Horwitz, E. (1986). Preliminary evidence for the reliability and validity of a foreign language anxiety scale. *TESOL Quarterly, 20,* 559–562.

Horwitz, E., Horwitz, M., & Cope, J. (1986). Foreign language classroom anxiety. *The Modern Language Journal, 70,* 125–132.

Horwitz, E., & Sadow, S. (1992). A preliminary exploration of the relationship between learner beliefs about language learning and foreign language anxiety. Manuscript submitted for publication.

Horwitz, E., & Young, D. (Eds.) (1991). *Language anxiety: From theory and research to classroom implications.* Upper Saddle River, NJ: Prentice Hall.

Kennedy Vande Berg, C. (1993). Managing learner anxiety in literature courses. *The French Review, 67,* 27–36.

Koch, A., & Terrell, T. (1991). Affective reactions of foreign language students to natural approach activities and teaching techniques. In E. Horwitz & D. Young (Eds.), *Language anxiety: From theory and research to classroom implications.* Upper Saddle River, NJ: Prentice Hall, pp. 37–40.

Krashen, S. (1982). *Principles and practice in second language acquisition.* New York: Pergamon.

Lavine, R., & Oxford, R. (1990). *Dealing with affective issues in the foreign- or second-language classroom.* Paper presented at the annual meeting of the Modern Language Association, Chicago.

Loughrin-Sacco, S. (1990). Inside the "black box" revisited: The integration of naturalistic inquiry in classroom research on foreign language learning. *Polylingua, 1,* 22–26.

MacIntyre, P., & Gardner, R. (1988a). *Anxiety factors in language learning* (Research Bulletin No. 677). London, Ontario: The University of Western Ontario, Department of Psychology.

MacIntyre, P., & Gardner, R. (1988b). *The measurement of anxiety and applications to second language learning: An annotated bibliography* (Research Bulletin No. 672). London, Ontario: The University of Western Ontario, Department of Psychology. (ERIC Document Reproduction Service No. FL 017 649.)

MacIntyre, P., & Gardner, R. (1989). Anxiety and second-language learning: A theoretical clarification. *Language Learning, 32,* 251–275.

MacIntyre, P., & Gardner, R. (1991a). Language anxiety: Its relationship to other anxieties and to processing in native and second languages. *Language Learning, 41,* 513–534.

MacIntyre, P., & Gardner, R. (1991b). Methods and results in the study of foreign language anxiety: A review of the literature. *Language Learning, 41,* 85–117.

MacIntyre, P., & Gardner, R. (1991c). Investigating language class anxiety using the focused essay technique. *The Modern Language Journal, 75,* 296–304.

Madsen, H., Brown, B., & Jones, R. (1991). Evaluating student attitudes toward second-language tests. In E. Horwitz & D. Young (Eds.), *Language anxiety: From theory and research to classroom implications.* Upper Saddle River, NJ: Prentice Hall, pp. 65–86.

McGroarty, M. (1989). The benefits of cooperative learning arrangements in second language instruction. *NABE, 13,* 127–143.

Mejías, H., Applbaum, R., Applbaum, S., & Trotter II, R. (1991). Oral communication apprehension and Hispanics: An exploration of oral communication apprehension among Mexican American students in Texas. In E. Horwitz & D. Young (Eds.), *Language anxiety: From theory and research to classroom implications.* Upper Saddle River, NJ: Prentice Hall, pp. 87–97.

Milleret, M. (1992). Cooperative learning in the Portuguese-for-Spanish-speakers classroom. *Foreign Language Annals, 25,* 435–440.

Oller, J. (1979). *Research on the measurement of affective variables: Some remaining questions.* Paper presented at the Colloquium on Second Language Acquisition and Use Under Different Circumstances, 1979 TESOL Convention. Boston, MA.

Oxford, R. (1990a). Language learning strategies and beyond: A look at strategies in the context of styles. In S. Magnan (Ed.), *Shifting the instructional focus to the learner.* Middlebury, VT: Northeast Conference Reports, pp. 35–55.

Oxford, R. (1990b). *Language learning strategies: What every teacher should know.* New York: Newbury House Publishers.

Oxford, R., & Lavine, R. (1992). Teacher-student style wars in the language classroom: Research insights and suggestions. *ADFL Bulletin, 23,* 38–45.

Pimsleur, P., Sundland, D., & McIntyre, R. (1964). Under-achievement in foreign language learning. *International Review of Applied Linguistics in Language Teaching, 2,* 113–150.

Phillips, E. (1990a). The effects of anxiety on performance and achievement in an oral test of French. *Dissertation Abstracts International, 51,* 1941A.

Phillips, E. (1990b). *Anxiety and oral proficiency tests.* Paper presented at Modern Language Association Annual Meeting. Chicago.

Phillips, E. (1992). The effects of language anxiety on students' oral test performance and attitudes. *The Modern Language Journal, 76,* 15–26.

Price, M. (1991). The subjective experiences of foreign language anxiety: Interviews with anxious students. In E. Horwitz & D. Young (Eds.), *Language anxiety: From theory and research to classroom implications.* Upper Saddle River, NJ: Prentice Hall, pp. 101–108.

Samimy, K., and Tabuse, M. (1992). Affective variables and a less commonly taught language: A study in beginning Japanese classes. *Language Learning, 42,* 377–398.

Scott, M. (1986). The effect of affect: A review of the anxiety literature. *Language Testing, 3,* 99–118.

Scovel, T. (1978). The effect of affect on foreign language learning: A review of the anxiety research. *Language Learning, 28,* 129–142.

Sparks, R., & Ganschow, L. (1991). Foreign language learning differences: Affective or native language aptitude differences? *The Modern Language Journal, 75,* 3–16.

213

CHAPTER 11
*Language Anxiety in
Men and Women:
Dealing with Gender
Difference in the
Language Classroom*

Sparks, R., & Ganschow, L. (1993a). The impact of native language learning problems on foreign language learning: Case study illustrations of the linguistic coding deficit hypothesis. *The Modern Language Journal, 77*, 58–74.

Sparks, R., & Ganschow, L. (1993b). Searching for the cognitive locus of foreign language learning difficulties: Linking first and second language learning. *The Modern Language Journal, 77*, 289–302.

Speilberger, C. (1983). *Manual for the State-Trait Anxiety Inventory.* Palo Alto, CA: Consulting Psychologists Press.

Steinberg, F. (1982). *The relationship between anxiety and oral performance in a foreign language.* Unpublished Master's Thesis, University of Texas, Austin, Texas.

Swain, M., & Burnaby, B. (1976). Personality characteristics and second language learning in young children: A pilot study. *Working Papers in Bilingualism, 11*, 115–128.

Tucker, R., Hamayan, E., & Genesee, F. (1976). Affective, cognitive, and social factors in second language acquisition. *The Canadian Modern Language Review, 32*, 214–226.

Westcott, D. (1973). Personality factors affecting high school students learning a second language. *Dissertation Abstracts International, 34*, 2183A.

Wittenborn, J., Larsen, R., & Mogil, R. (1945). An empirical evaluation of study habits for college courses in French and Spanish. *Journal of Educational Psychology, 36*, 449–474.

Young, D. (1986). The relationship between anxiety and foreign language oral proficiency ratings. *Foreign Language Annals, 19*, 439–445.

Young, D. (1990). An investigation of students' perspectives on anxiety and speaking. *Foreign Language Annals, 23*, 539–553.

Young, D. (1991). Creating a low-anxiety classroom environment: What does language anxiety research suggest? *The Modern Language Journal, 75*, 426–439.

Young, D. (1992). Language Anxiety from the Foreign Language Specialist's Perspective: Interviews with Krashen, Omaggio Hadley, Terrell, and Rardin. *Foreign Language Annals, 25*, 157–172.

Young, D., & Oxford, R. (1993). Attending to learner reactions to introductory Spanish textbooks. *Hispania, 76*, 593–605.

APPENDIX A

[For office use: WS__Y/N]

Course # _____ Survey # _____ Date _____ SS# _____ Age _____

Location _____

SURVEY OF ATTITUDES SPECIFIC TO THE FOREIGN LANGUAGE CLASSROOM (SASFLC)

Please answer parts I and II below honestly and carefully. Because the results will be used to better the current foreign language curriculum, it is very important that you spend time thinking about each answer. Your answers are anonymous.

I. Experience with the foreign language

1. Were any of your immediate family members (father, mother, brothers, or sisters) born in a foreign country?

_____

Which one(s)?   Where?

_____   _____

_____   _____

_____   _____

_____   _____

2. Were you born in a foreign country?_____
   Where? _____

3. Do any of your immediate family members speak a foreign language *fluently* (not *slightly*)?

   _____

   Which family member(s)?   Which language(s)?

   _____   _____

   _____   _____

   _____   _____

   _____   _____

4. Do you speak a foreign language *fluently* (not *slightly*)?

   _____

   Which one(s)?   Did you learn it at home or in school?

   _____   _____

   _____   _____

   _____   _____

5. Below, fill in the number of years that you studied the foreign language(s) at school. First, identify the language; then, place the number of years.

	First foreign language (FL)	Second FL	Third FL
elementary school (grades 1–6)	_____	_____	_____
junior high school (grades 7–9)	_____	_____	_____
high school (grades 10–12)	_____	_____	_____
college	Number of semesters of the first FL	Second FL	Third FL
	_____	_____	_____

II. Attitudes Specific to the Foreign Language Classroom

215

CHAPTER 11
Language Anxiety in
Men and Women:
Dealing with Gender
Difference in the
Language Classroom

Please respond to the statements below using the following scale:

1. strongly agree
2. agree
3. undecided
4. disagree
5. strongly disagree

Once again, please answer honestly and carefully. Spend time thinking about each answer. Your answers are anonymous.

1. It is necessary to have a special aptitude (that is, an inborn talent) in order to learn a foreign language well.
2. It is necessary to have a special intelligence (that is, a higher I.Q.) in order to learn a foreign language well.
3. It is necessary to have a special "ear" in order to learn a foreign language well.
4. I become anxious when I have to speak in a foreign language in a classroom setting.
5. I feel silly when I have to speak in a foreign language in a classroom setting.
6. I become anxious when I am being spoken to in a foreign language in a classroom setting.
7. I become anxious when I am asked to write in a foreign language in a classroom setting.
8. I become anxious when I have to read in a foreign language in a classroom setting.
9. I fear failing this course.
10. I fear receiving a low final grade (D or below) in this course.
11. I fear making a mistake when I speak in a foreign language in a classroom setting.
12. I fear not understanding what the teacher is saying in a foreign language when I am in a foreign language classroom.
13. I fear making a mistake in writing in a foreign language in a classroom setting.
14. I fear making a mistake in reading in a foreign language in a classroom setting.

Answer No. 15 only if you are a high school graduate:

15. I think that the standard foreign language high school course is more difficult than the standard "verbally oriented" high school course such as History.

Answer No. 16 only if you are a high school graduate:

16. I think that the standard foreign language high school course is more difficult than the standard "numerically oriented" high school course such as Algebra I.

"Style Wars" as a Source of Anxiety in Language Classrooms

Rebecca L. Oxford
The University of Alabama

Personal Reflections

1. Do you believe anxiety can have positive side effects? For example, do you recall ever experiencing anxiety that seemed to heighten your learning or improve your performance in some event? If so, describe the situation.

2. What perceptions do you have about how you learn best? In other words, do you learn better when you hear information or see it in writing? Do you have to touch, hold, or do something with material to learn it? Do you like to learn things sequentially, step by step, or globally and spontaneously? Do you prefer assignments that offer structure, or do you feel more comfortable with assignments that leave room for interpretation? Based on your answers to these questions, how aware of your own learning styles are you?

3. Have you ever experienced feelings of frustration or anxiety toward a specific teacher? If so, describe in detail your conflict with this teacher.

217

CHAPTER 12
*"Style Wars" as a
Source of Anxiety in
Language Classrooms*

Fundamental Concepts

Language anxiety

Facilitating anxiety

Debilitating anxiety

Learning/teaching style

Style conflict (style war)

Self-esteem

Tolerance of ambiguity

Risk-taking ability

Competitiveness/cooperation

Introversion/extroversion

Intuitive-random/concrete-sequential

Thinking/feeling

Sensory preferences

Analytic/global

Language anxiety is defined as a specialized anxiety related to language use situations or language learning circumstances, rather than just a reflection of generalized anxiety (Gardner & MacIntyre 1993; Horwitz, Horwitz, & Cope 1986; Horwitz & Young 1991). Language anxiety is the fear or apprehension learners sometimes feel when they are expected to perform in a target language in which they are not proficient (Gardner & MacIntyre 1993). Numerous indicators or manifestations of language anxiety have been mentioned throughout this volume and reference to its debilitating effects posited. This chapter introduces a potential source of anxiety that has not been discussed up to now. Anxiety can be heightened in foreign language learning when the classroom has an additional burden of a "style conflict" or "style war"—that is, a clash between the style of a particular language learner and the style of a given language teacher (Oxford & Ehrman 1993; Reid 1995).

Style refers to the individual's general, most favored approach for dealing with the environment, situations, or problems (Cornett 1983; Oxford 1990). A person's learning style is his or her favored approach for learning, while an individual's teaching style is his or her preferred approach when instructing others. That simple statement becomes important for understanding the data presented later in this chapter. No separate systems of teaching styles and learning styles are included here, because styles of teachers and learners can typically be described using the same systematic terminology (see Reid 1995 for examples).

Moreover, this chapter does not distinguish between an individual teacher's learning style and that same person's teaching style. A person's learning style and his or her teaching style are usually similar. Most teachers, unless they have had specific training about styles and unless they intentionally alter their behavior in the classroom, tend to teach the way they learn. (See examples of styles characterizing both learners and teachers in Myers & McCaulley 1985; Oxford, Ehrman, & Lavine 1991.) Conflicts between the styles of a given learner and a particular teacher can generate or exacerbate anxiety in the language classroom, as shown by Ehrman (1996), Reid (1995), and Oxford, Ehrman, and Lavine (1991).

STYLES AND LANGUAGE ANXIETY: AN OVERVIEW

Styles can have a direct relationship with language anxiety. This section defines various style dimensions, at the same time suggesting how anxiety relates to these dimensions.

Style Dimensions

Some important aspects of style are shown in Table 12.1. These are also echoed in the Style Analysis Survey in the appendix, pp. 230–237. In each dimension most people have some elements of both poles; therefore, each dimension is a continuum indicating general preferences.

Introverted Versus Extroverted

Introverted students or teachers are energized by their own ideas, feelings, and thoughts (Reid 1995). They prefer to work alone or with others whom they know well, and they are often uninspired by typical kinds of group work. They can, in certain circumstances, become extremely anxious if put into a situation in which they feel the need to perform or communicate, particularly with strangers (Leary 1983; McCroskey 1984), because they dislike evaluation by other people in social settings. Yet some introverted individuals can become good at hiding their introversion so that others don't notice their discomfort with crowds. In contrast, *extroverted* students or teachers receive most of their

TABLE 12.1. Selected Dimensions of Style

Title	Focus of This Dimension
Introverted vs. extroverted	How the individual is energized or stimulated
Intuitive-random vs. concrete-sequential	Whether the individual wants to have flexibility or structure
Analytic vs. global	How the individual wants to receive and process information
Closure-oriented vs. open	Whether the individual needs a rapid decision
Sensory preferences (visual vs. auditory vs. hands-on)	Which sensory mode the individual prefers for processing information

energy from people and events outside themselves. They are usually eager to engage in conversation and work in groups. Social situations ordinarily do not cause extroverted people to become anxious; they might become anxious when they have to work alone (Oxford, Ehrman, & Lavine 1991).

219

CHAPTER 12
"Style Wars" as a
Source of Anxiety in
Language Classrooms

Intuitive-Random Versus Concrete-Sequential

As discussed in Reid (1995), students and teachers whose style is *intuitive-random* think in abstract, large-scaled, nonsequential ways and can distill the main principles of the language rather easily. They are often made anxious or bored by concrete, step-by-step processes and would rather take daring intellectual leaps. In contrast, *concrete-sequential* students and teachers focus on concrete facts in an organized, step-by-step fashion. Abstract principles of language systems are not important to these learners and teachers, who prefer to concentrate on one task at a time. Frequently slow and steady, they move at their own rate. As students or teachers, concrete-sequential individuals can achieve goals that are made clear to them by authority figures, and they become anxious about randomness and lack of consistency in planning.

Closure-Oriented Versus Open

"Closure-oriented" is associated with the Jungian "judging" style, while "open" is related to the Jungian "perceiving" style (Reid 1995). A *closure* orientation signifies that the individual is serious, concerned about finishing tasks, goal-directed, intolerant of ambiguity, and desirous of rapid decision-making (closure). Anxiety emerges for closure-oriented people who are forced to deal with open-ended situations in which decisions are not made; or for closure-oriented individuals whose workload is so overwhelming that they do not get a sense of closure on most tasks. An *open* style indicates that the person is lighthearted, is not concerned with finishing tasks, can easily be distracted from goals, tolerates ambiguity, and prefers to put off decisions so that more data can be gathered. Anxiety is most common for open-style people when they are forced to make decisions quickly, face many deadlines, and are not allowed to have much free time to relax or play.

Analytic Versus Global

Wallace and Oxford (1992) described the analytic and global components of style. This dimension deals with how people prefer to receive and process information: through logical analysis or through a global overview. Students or teachers with an *analytic* style prefer logical thinking, complexity, multiple details, precision, and objectivity. They apply their impersonal problem-solving techniques to many aspects of their lives, including work, relationships, and self. They like dealing with grammatical rules, making contrastive analyses, and dissecting words and sentences. Analytic learners and teachers often become anxious when forced to deal with spontaneous-communication situations, because their preferred emphasis is on accuracy. In contrast, *global* students and teachers look for the "big picture," try to avoid the minor details in favor of the main idea, simplify and synthesize rather than analyze data, employ subjective or personal thinking modes, and use interactive communication techniques. Global students or teachers are concerned more with fluency than with accuracy in the language classroom. They are typically more sensitive and feeling-oriented than analytic students. They frequently display anxiety over activities that involve remembering or presenting many small points of information.

Sensory Preferences (Visual Versus Auditory Versus Hands-on)

The sensory preferences of language learners and teachers are the physical, perceptual learning channels with which they most easily process information (Oxford, Ehrman, & Lavine 1991). *Visual* students and teachers enjoy reading and need extensive visual stimulation: pictures, video, computers, bulletin boards, and photos; they dislike purely auditory lectures, conversations, and oral directions. *Auditory* students and teachers, unlike visual individuals, are comfortable without much visual input and therefore enjoy lectures, conversations, and oral directions. They are excited by classroom interactions in role plays and similar activities but sometimes experience anxiety with tasks that are totally visual, without any auditory input. *Hands-on* students and teachers like considerable movement and enjoy working with models, collages, flashcards, and objects. Uncomfortable and anxious when sitting at a desk for long, they prefer frequent breaks and moving around the room. Many hands-on students and teachers would rather sit on the floor, the table, or the couch than in the traditional straight-backed, knees-bent academic posture.

Teacher-Learner Interactions

Many researchers relate language anxiety to instructor-learner interactions (Horwitz, Horwitz, & Cope 1986; Koch & Terrell 1991; Price 1991; Scarcella & Oxford 1992; Young 1990, 1991). An aspect of teacher-learner interactions that has been emphasized in recent years is that of style conflicts (Oxford, Ehrman, & Lavine 1991). In one study (Wallace & Oxford 1992), the ESL students were significantly more extroverted and feeling-oriented than their American teachers, who were more introverted and thinking-oriented. These differences suggested greater outgoingness and personal subjectivity on the part of the students, as contrasted with more internal self-direction and impersonal objectivity on the part of the teachers. In writing, reading, and grammar (but not in speaking), these major style contrasts consistently and negatively affected student grades. This means that students suffered grade-wise because of the style clashes in three out of four skill areas examined.

EVIDENCE ABOUT STYLE CONFLICTS AND ANXIETY IN NARRATIVES

This section presents the methodology of this study and its results.

Methodology

Participants

For 5 years the present author, with a colleague at a large east coast university in the United States and with occasional others, has been gathering

221

CHAPTER 12
"Style Wars" as a
Source of Anxiety in
Language Classrooms

students' written narratives, with names altered for confidentiality, about their experiences with teacher/student style conflicts. Approximately 300–350 participants have been involved to date in the ongoing study. Because of space restrictions, only a small number of participants' narratives can be included in this paper.

Group A was from an east coast university in the United States, and Group B was from a large state university in the southeastern United States. See Table 12.2 for characteristics.

Participants in Groups A and B were involved in some way with languages, and all had experienced some exposure to information on styles. In these two groups, each individual had either taken a style inventory or had engaged in a class discussion of styles. Thus, although they were in all other respects typical, they had the advantage of knowing something about styles.

Data Collection Procedures

The participants in Groups A and B were asked to respond in writing to the following question: "Have you ever had a conflict of style with a teacher? *If so*, describe your teacher, tell what happened, and explain what you felt in the situation. *If not*, select a situation in which you were compatible with a teacher, then describe the teacher, tell what happened, and explain what you felt in the situation." In most cases, participants in Groups A and B were able to identify a style conflict right away, though a few participants could identify only harmonious teacher/student circumstances. In some classes, Group A or B participants were asked to do this assignment at home, whereas in other classes, the writing took place during the class period. There were no differences in the quality or length of the essays based on when or where the narratives were written.

Data Analysis and Interpretation Procedures

Data analysis followed the principles of content analysis, in which main themes emerge from the data and are not predetermined. Interpretation of the results occurred in iterations, with two researchers coding the data for the

TABLE 12.2. Types of Participants in the Study

	Groups	
	A	B
Students enrolled in undergraduate (required) language courses	x	x
Students enrolled in advanced (elective) language courses	x	x
Undergraduate students in Foreign Language Education (FLED) preparing to become teachers of foreign languages	x	x
Graduate students in FLED		x
Undergraduate or graduate foreign language student teachers in the public schools	x	
Graduate foreign language teaching assistants	x	x
Doctoral candidates in Curriculum and Instruction with an emphasis on FLED		x

themes and periodically checking the interpretations for coding reliability (see Stempel 1989). Note that in the study, we were listening as directly as possible to the voices of students as expressed in their narratives (for justification, see Bailey & Nunan 1996). Our interpretations of classroom dynamics, including style conflicts, were based on a close reading of what the students themselves said and how they said it (including emotional responses and connotations). Interpretation of results from qualitative research typically involves this process.

Results

In some cases, the style conflicts are multidimensional; that is, they involve more than one aspect of style on the part of both teacher and student. The most frequently occurring style conflicts found so far in the data fall into four categories, as indicated in Table 12.3. In each of these kinds of clashes, anxiety emerged.

Conflict Type 1: Students Who Disliked Ambiguity and Whose Closure Needs Were Ignored

Libby, a master's degree candidate, described her university language teacher.

> One of my college courses was very difficult for me until I got used to the teacher's teaching style. She would assign a project but would not assign a due date. She never gave details, you would never know exactly what she wanted. You would never know if you were doing your work right until she graded it.

Interpretation: Libby needed much more structure in course assignments than she was getting from her language professor. She was unhappy and anxious because of the ambiguity of the situation. Libby was typical of many students who felt their teacher did not provide enough clarity and closure about assignments.

Dorothy, a master's degree candidate in teaching English as a second language, wrote about her language professor's delegation of authority.

> The conflict centered on methodology—no textbook, no syllabus, no expectations explained, no grading procedures detailed, no structure whatsoever, very, very laissez-faire and open. I am myself quite open, but this was too much even for me. At first it seemed good. We choose the topics to discuss and we create the "book" or "text" as we go along. I was at the beginning of the semester excited by this freedom,

TABLE 12.3. Types of Style Conflicts Appearing Most Often in the Data

1. Students who disliked ambiguity and whose closure needs were ignored
2. Introverted students coping with extroverted teachers who "entertained" the class
3. Global, intuitive-random students dealing with analytic, concrete-sequential details provided by the teacher
4. Students whose sensory preferences were thwarted

but then it seemed to get harder and harder to continue talking like this. I did not ultimately feel "open" enough to disclose myself to the teacher . . . I clammed up and wilted emotionally. The time in class seemed interminable to me—time and space were transformed to an endless eternity.

223

CHAPTER 12
"Style Wars" as a
Source of Anxiety in
Language Classrooms

Intuition: Dorothy initially welcomed the freedom of this class, but the ambiguity became overwhelming, and she "wilted emotionally," turning silent. She ended up intensely disliking the lack of structure of her extraordinarily open teacher. Her own style was open, but the teacher's openness verged on anarchy, and Dorothy could not deal with it; even she needed some closure and clarity.

Conflict Type 2: Introverted Students Coping with Extroverted Teachers Who Liked to "Entertain" the Class

Young, a Korean doctoral candidate describing a graduate course in English communications, wrote:

I once had a style conflict with one of my professors at a California university, when I took an elementary communication class in English. The professor was a strong haptic [hands-on] person who always wanted his students to demonstrate certain kinds of motions and actions in class. The professor himself liked to act, dance, mime, and move around in the classroom. He rarely wrote down his lecture points on the chalkboard. I have no doubt that many of the activities that the professor developed were excellent for the course. Personally, however, I had difficulties adapting to such activities because I am an introvert, and I am not a haptic learner. I often skipped the required group activities. Frankly, I did not enjoy the course at all. In the classroom I had often been anxious because I didn't want to be called to be a demonstrator in front of the whole class. Outside the classroom, I had always been nervous about being with a group of extroverted American students; I was the only foreign and introverted student in the group.

Interpretation: Young, a female doctoral candidate in the field of Curriculum and Instruction, came from Korea. In her first American educational experience, she encountered a communications professor whose style was very different from her own. This professor provided entertainment and dramatic action, but, to introverted Young, this type of teaching was anxiety-producing. It is likely that cultural influences played a part in the discomfort experienced by this student. In Korea, instructors would typically not have performed in the fashion of her American teacher, and students would not have been asked to perform similarly.

Mickey, an adult student learning Spanish, disliked his extroverted, entertaining professor.

I learned very little in the class. It was more of an atmosphere of fun and games. She [the professor] was the star performer. The students were an audience. We often felt it was time to get down to work, but it never quite came.

The outgoing, dramatic teacher of a Spanish course made things seem like fun, but Mickey was there primarily to work hard at learning. He did not believe he was in a serious educational situation because of the teacher's "star performance." Her extroversion was possibly intended to dazzle and engage the students, but according to Mickey, this behavior distracted students from their main purpose of being in the classroom: to learn.

Conflict Type 3: Global, Intuitive Students Dealing with Analytic, Concrete-Sequential Details from the Teacher

Melissa, an undergraduate describing difficulties in a language course, stated:

> There's one professor I've had in Spanish where there was some overlap in styles but also some conflict. I'm not quite sure in what areas, but I think she was reflective and analytical whereas I am impulsive and global. Her tests asked for exactness, not only on definition questions but also on theories and ideas. When I learned these, I learned the main idea and translated it into my own words and expressions. She expected exact wording or expression. This difference really hurt me on theoretical or essay questions.

Interpretation: Melissa was anxious and disturbed because she was asked to present analytic, step-by-step, perfectionist details, even on theoretical or essay-type tests. Her comments suggest that she was a more global, intuitive student who liked theories and major ideas rather than small details. She preferred to speak in her own voice, using "my own words and expressions" rather than the teacher's. Her learning preferences clearly harmed her performance on this teacher's examinations and created significant anxiety for the student.

Allen, a master's candidate, was very unhappy with his former Russian and Latin teachers.

> I took Russian in my sophomore year. In the first two weeks we covered the alphabet, and then we hit grammar. I immediately got lost. I wanted to go back to the alphabet. I wanted personal attention and guidance [but did not get it]. I got out of Russian by dropping the course. . . . The next semester I got a teacher of Latin. The second Latin teacher was very analytical, expecting you to know grammatical patterns, declensions, conjugations, and so on. I got a C and two Ds from that professor [low grades for this student] and felt very anxious and frustrated.

Interpretation: Allen was anxious about grammar and other analytic aspects of the Russian language. Like many other global learners faced with a welter of grammatical rules, patterns, and paradigms, Allen felt the situation was too confusing and impersonal. In vain he sought personal attention and supportive guidance from the Russian teacher. Finally he concluded that the only way to deal with his anxiety was to drop the course. Then he entered a Latin class that was just as grammar-centered and analytic as the Russian class had been. He stuck with it but again became very anxious, and his language performance was poor.

Conflict Type 4: Students Whose Sensory Preferences Were Thwarted

225

CHAPTER 12
*"Style Wars" as a
Source of Anxiety in
Language Classrooms*

Michael, a master's candidate, complained about a language and culture teacher who paid no attention to students' sensory preferences.

> I presently have a professor who does not fulfill my stylistic needs. I am a very visual learner. This teacher almost never writes on the board, which is, in my opinion, a vital practice to the study of phonetic structure. He does not provide the class with adequate visual examples of the art about which we are studying. I have learned much more about art from one of my classmates than from my professor because he [my classmate] provides the class with books containing pictures of art. Although my professor thrives on names, dates, and the smallest of details, he does not actually break down large amounts of material into smaller, tolerable amounts. He does not know how to make wordy definitions more concise or make memory charts or teach key words. He does not teach analytically; but he tests analytically.

Interpretation: According to the narrative, Michael was a highly visually oriented student but at the time of the study was receiving mostly auditory input from the teacher. Moreover, this student appeared to need a great deal of structure, which was not provided by the teacher whom he mentioned. The teacher focused on many small details but did not organize the material so that students could distinguish the more important issues from the less important. An additional clash arose from the discrepancy between the instructional techniques and evaluation methods of the teacher. Though Michael's list of problems sounded superficially calm, the length and complexity of the list indicated serious discomfort on his part.

Louise, a bilingual student born in Southeast Asia who was focusing on English studies as an undergraduate, had trouble with her college teachers because of a conflict in sensory preferences. She was diagnosed by a psychologist as having two general kinds of auditory problems: low auditory processing ability and poor auditory memory. Therefore,

> I sat dumbfounded in lecture halls from all the information that was being thrown at me. . . . I was barely able to keep my head over water. . . . I was unable to take notes, since it was difficult for me to remember facts [from lectures] long enough to write them down. This also affected any oral questions that may have been directed towards me. My auditory problems, along with my high anxiety level, made the processing of information take a lot longer. Classes that were more discussion-oriented [were] smaller in size, based more on papers, which was beneficial to me, but higher in stress level, since attention would increase and there would be more time to call upon students. If such were the case, I usually picked a seat in the last row, directly behind another classmate, and hardly uttered a sound.

Interpretation: Louise could not deal effectively with professors who lectured, thus conflicting with her favored sense: visual. Her auditory difficulties made note-taking in lectures almost impossible and created style conflicts with her auditory-style teachers. Even smaller, discussion-centered classes were difficult, because Louise feared she would be called on to answer. Thus, Louise's sensory style preferences were influenced by her own neurological difficulties. These problems, when encountered in a highly auditory college learning situation, generated anxiety, which caused her to try to avoid attention at all costs.

In addition to the clashes shown previously, the narratives also revealed two general kinds of situations in which style conflicts did not happen, as seen in Table 12.4. Anxiety did not arise in these two situations.

TABLE 12.4. Nonconflict Situations

- A potential style conflict did not develop into a real conflict
- No potential conflict was ever present

Nonconflict Type 1: Student Teacher Describing Differences That Did Not Develop into a Real Conflict

Leila, a student teacher of Romance languages, commented on her experience with a supervising teacher.

> There is one example that I have of "style conflict" where it was not a conflict. During one of my student teaching experiences, I was placed with a Spanish teacher who was analytical. She was not an extreme case, which may be the reason for no conflict. She used the visual sense almost exclusively with very little auditory stimulus. Each of her days was planned in detail and written in outline form. Rather than clashing, we complemented each other very well. She gave me the opportunity to teach several lessons and encouraged me to proceed in my own style. Rather than book work, the students participated in learning family vocabulary, dressing up in clothes that specify a certain member of the family and asking questions of each other. For Spanish culture week, I brought in several moments of my trip to Spain and answered any questions that they had. She told me later that some of the students that spoke up had never voluntarily spoken before. They must have been the global learners. The teacher and I liked each other very much. We wished that we had some of each other's style. She would have liked some of my spontaneity, and I would have liked some of her organization.

Interpretation: Leila was a student teacher whose style was generally auditory, global, and spontaneous. She was placed with a supervisor who was more visual, analytic, and organized. Instead of having an overt style conflict, their styles complemented each other. Students in the classroom benefited by having experience with both styles.

Nonconflict Type 2: Student Who Recognized Style Compatibility

LeAnne, an undergraduate, described her Spanish teacher in glowing terms.

> I'm a transfer student and had Ms. _____ for 301 and now again for 302. I think she tries to do a little of everything—written homework,

reading Spanish stories in class and discussing them, speaking Spanish aloud, discussing analytical and controversial (emotional) topics, and we write out answers to questions on the board. I personally feel this is the best and most well rounded way of teaching a class, because it touches all parts of the senses (except smell and taste) while making us use both sides of the brain. 301 seemed more analytic than 302 because in 301 there were so many rules to memorize, and so many processes of writing to learn. In 302, especially with the diaries and letters to classmates, Ms. _____ is making us think and reflect more.

227

CHAPTER 12
*"Style Wars" as a
Source of Anxiety in
Language Classrooms*

I don't ever have a problem with a teacher's style of teaching because I find a little bit of every style in me. I have no set pattern of studying, but I do center around working with people. I prefer to study in groups, because I feel if you can talk about what you learned with another person, you can learn even more by sharing information and getting feedback. But sometimes I like going on a computer and typing out notes. I don't like to read but I like to summarize things I read.

Interpretation: LeAnne appreciates her Spanish teacher, who provides a wide array of creative stimulation and input—"a little of everything." LeAnne is a self-aware learner who says "I find a little bit of every style in me" and who has "no set pattern of studying." Her academic flexibility does not appear to be harmful or confusing with regard to her own Spanish language performance. LeAnne also points out that her teacher's approach to the material changes depending on the nature of the material and the level of the class.

These students' narratives have shown a range of common classroom style conflicts, including students whose needs for closure were disregarded, introverted students clashing with extroverted teachers, global and intuitive-random students encountering analytic and concrete-sequential instruction, students whose sensory needs were not met, and analytic students coping with global teachers. Two narratives have displayed situations in which style conflicts did not emerge. All these narratives, taken together, have offered a personal understanding of "style wars." Now let's turn to the implications.

IMPLICATIONS FOR REDUCING ANXIETY

Language teachers can take action to reduce anxiety, depending on students' needs and cultural background. Among the most important actions is assessing style preferences. Language teachers should assess their own learning and teaching styles and the styles of their students (most easily done through style inventories like the Style Analysis Survey, Oxford 1995, a short form of which is included in the appendix, pp. 230–237). Such assessment helps teachers identify any style differences between them and their students (or among the students themselves) before these differences grow into anxiety-provoking clashes.

Applying this important style assessment information, teachers can effectively tailor their instructional strategies. For example, teachers can become more effective by following the suggestions in Table 12.5.

TABLE 12.5. Suggestions for Reducing Anxiety in the Language Classroom

- Offer clear, detailed, precise instructions to help concrete-sequential and analytic learners, but still allow the needed flexibility and freedom for intuitive and global learners.
- Show empathetic concern for all students (but especially those students who are personally sensitive or for whom a style conflict appears to be present).
- Give analytic learners the time they need to answer, but permit others to have the spontaneous activities that they require.
- Offer some cooperative learning tasks as well as some individual and/or competitive tasks to benefit the full range of learners.
- Provide a multitude of multisensory language learning tasks to meet the needs of visual, auditory, and hands-on students.

CONCLUSION

How can the preceding all be achieved? It can be done through the principled use of *variety* in classroom activities—variety that takes into account learners' stylistic preferences and enables them to learn most easily. The recommendation to use variety certainly does not mean that teachers have to become slaves to every aspect of each student's style; nor does it mean that the teacher is responsible for offering totally individualized instruction. Using variety simply means that teachers must pay attention to how individual students learn and must provide instruction that touches each student's preferred style *sometime* during every lesson. In doing this, teachers are not only offering activities that match a given student's style, but they are also providing tasks that stretch the student's style, thus enhancing learning flexibility.

If language teachers know their students' styles and adapt instruction (through variety in activities) to those styles, then anxiety will become a much smaller issue in the language classroom. It is clear that style clashes are a source of anxiety, and that anxiety can have many negative repercussions for language learners. Reducing style clashes through sensitive, intelligent instructional planning and delivery can lower anxiety for language learners and increase the probability of attaining success.

PORTFOLIO ASSIGNMENTS

1. a. Take the Style Analysis Inventory developed by Oxford (see the appendix, pp. 230–237). This is a relatively simple questionnaire that is also easy to score.
   b. What do the results of the SAI indicate? Describe your learning style.
   c. Based on the results in **b**, write a checklist of your potential style conflicts so you can refer to it when you teach. This checklist may help you diagnose sources of frustration and anxiety stemming from style conflicts between you and a language learner.
2. a. The first step in reducing language anxiety stemming from teacher/student style conflicts is to identify the various learning styles. Design a

229

CHAPTER 12
*"Style Wars" as a
Source of Anxiety in
Language Classrooms*

handout for your language students that gives a brief overview of learning styles, which you can summarize from this chapter. Be sure to preface the handout by explaining how style clashes could be a potential source of anxiety for some language learners.

b. Exchange your handout with another classmate. Are all learning styles listed? Are the descriptions appropriate? Is the link between anxiety and learning styles clear?

c. Place your handout in your portfolio for use when you teach.

ACTION RESEARCH

1. a. Write about a problem you had with a teacher in the past, one that made you feel particularly anxious.

   b. With a classmate, analyze the problem you wrote about in **a** to determine whether it could be explained in terms of style clashes.

   c. Share your findings with the rest of the class. Out of the total number of students in your class, how many of the teacher conflicts involved some degree of clash in learning styles?

2. a. Interview an FL or SL learner who has been identified by the teacher as appearing to experience a lot of frustration and anxiety, or is simply "problematic." In your interview, attempt to ascertain whether the student's anxiety involves a clash in learning styles between the teacher and the student.

   b. Share your findings with the class. Out of the total number of students interviewed, how many appeared to experience some degree of teacher/student style clash?

REFERENCES

Bailey, K. M., & Nunan, D. (Eds.) (1996). *Voices from the language classroom.* Cambridge, UK: Cambridge University Press.

Cornett, C. E. (1983). *What you should know about teaching and learning styles.* Bloomington, IN: Phi Delta Kappa Educational Foundation.

Ehrman, M. E. (1996). *Understanding second language learning difficulties.* London: Sage Publications.

Gardner, R. C., & MacIntyre, P. D. (1993). On the measurement of affective variables in second language learning. *Language Learning 43,* 157–194.

Horwitz, E. K., Horwitz, M. B., & Cope, J. (1986). Foreign language classroom anxiety. *Modern Language Journal 70,* 125–132.

Horwitz, E. K., & Young, D. J. (1991). *Language anxiety: From theory and research to classroom implications.* Upper Saddle River, NJ: Prentice Hall.

Koch, A., & Terrell, T. (1991). Affective reactions of foreign language students to Natural Approach activities and teaching techniques. In E. K. Horwitz & D. J. Young (Eds.), *Language anxiety: From theory and research to classroom implications.* Upper Saddle River, NJ: Prentice Hall, pp. 109–126.

Leary, M. (1983). *Understanding social anxiety: Social, personality, and clinical perspectives.* Beverly Hills: Sage.

McCroskey, J. C. (1984). The communication apprehension perspective. In J. A. Daly & J. C. McCroskey (Eds.), *Avoiding communication: Shyness, reticence, and communication apprehension.* Beverly Hills: Sage, pp. 13–38.

Myers, I. B., & McCaulley, M. H. (1985). *A guide to the development and use of the Myers-Briggs Type Indicator.* Manual. Palo Alto, CA: Consulting Psychologists Press.

Oxford, R. L. (1990). Language learning strategies and beyond: A look at strategies in the context of styles. In S. S. Magnan (Ed.), *Shifting the instructional focus to the learner.* Middlebury, VT: Northeast Conference on the Teaching of Foreign Languages, pp. 35–55.

Oxford, R. L. (1995). *Style Analysis Survey (SAS).* In J. Reid (Ed.), *Learning styles in the ESL/EFL classroom.* Boston: Heinle & Heinle, pp. 208–215.

Oxford, R. L., & Ehrman, M. E. (1993). Second language research on individual differences. In W. Grabe (Ed.), *Annual Review of Applied Linguistics.* Cambridge: Cambridge University Press, pp. 188–205.

Oxford, R. L., Ehrman, M. E., & Lavine, R. L. (1991). Style wars: Teacher-student style conflicts in the language classroom. In S. S. Magnan (Ed.), *Challenges in the 1990s for college foreign language programs.* Boston: Heinle & Heinle, pp. 1–25.

Price, M. L. (1991). The subjective experience of foreign language anxiety interviews with high-anxious students. In E. K. Horwitz & D. J. Young (Eds.), *Language anxiety: From theory and research to classroom implications.* Upper Saddle River, NJ: Prentice Hall, pp. 101–108.

Reid, J. (Ed.). (1995). *Learning styles in the ESL/EFL classroom.* Boston: Heinle & Heinle.

Scarcella, R. L., & Oxford, R. L. (1992). *The tapestry of language learning: The individual in the communicative classroom.* Boston: Heinle & Heinle.

Stempel III, G. H. (1989). Content Analysis. In Stempel III, G. H., & Westley, R. H. (Eds.), *Research Methods in Mass Communication,* 2nd edition. Englewood Cliffs, NJ: Prentice Hall, pp. 124–136.

Wallace, W., & Oxford, R. L. (1992). Disparity in learning styles and teaching styles in the ESL classroom: Does this mean war? *AMTESOL Journal 1,* 45–68.

Young, D. J. (1990). An investigation of students' perspectives on anxiety and speaking. *Foreign Language Annals 23,* 539–553.

Young, D. J. (1991). Creating a low-anxiety classroom environment: What does language anxiety research suggest? *Modern Language Journal 75,* 426–437.

APPENDIX A

STYLE ANALYSIS SURVEY

Your *learning and working style* is defined as the overall pattern that gives general direction to your behavior. Such styles are related partly to a person's inherited, genetic characteristics. However, they are also strongly influenced by the person's family and culture.

Take the time—probably 30–45 minutes—to discover your own learning and working styles right now. To do so, complete the *Style Analysis Survey (SAS).* YOUR ANSWERS DO NOT AFFECT THE GRADES YOU WILL RECEIVE IN ANY CLASSES OR YOUR EVALUATIONS ON THE JOB. ALL RESPONSES ARE CONFIDENTIAL.

FOR EVERYONE:

NAME OR I.D. # _____

AGE (Circle one)   Below 18   18–22   23–30   31–40   41–50   50+

GENDER (Circle one)   Female   Male

FOR LANGUAGE LEARNERS ONLY:

LANGUAGE YOU ARE CURRENTLY STUDYING _____

CURRENT LANGUAGE COURSE NUMBER _____

REASON WHY YOU ARE STUDYING THE LANGUAGE
(Circle most important reason)

    To fulfill a language requirement

    To get to know another culture

    To communicate in the language

    To travel internationally

    To improve career possibilities

    To enhance world peace

    Other: _____

Part A: How You Use Your Physical Senses for Study and Work
For each item, circle the response that best describes what you do: 0 = never,
1 = sometimes, 2 = very often, 3 = always.

1. I remember something better if I write it down.   0 1 2 3
2. I take lots of notes.   0 1 2 3
3. I visualize pictures, numbers, or words in my head.   0 1 2 3
4. I prefer to learn with video or TV more than with   0 1 2 3
    other media.
5. I underline or highlight the important parts as I read.   0 1 2 3
6. I use color-coding to help me as I learn or work.   0 1 2 3
7. I need written directions for tasks.   0 1 2 3
8. I get distracted by background noises.   0 1 2 3
9. I have to look at people to understand what they say.   0 1 2 3
10. I am more comfortable when the walls have posters   0 1 2 3
    or pictures.

ADD UP YOUR SCORE FOR ITEMS 1–10 AND WRITE IT HERE: _____.
THIS REPRESENTS THE <u>VISUAL</u> LEARNING AND WORKING STYLE.

11. I remember things better if I discuss them out loud.   0 1 2 3
12. I prefer to learn by listening to a lecture or a tape,   0 1 2 3
    rather than by reading.
13. I need oral directions for tasks.   0 1 2 3
14. Background sounds help me think.   0 1 2 3
15. I like to listen to music when I study or work.   0 1 2 3

231

CHAPTER 12
"Style Wars" as a
Source of Anxiety in
Language Classrooms

16. I can easily understand what people say even if I cannot see their faces.   0 1 2 3
17. I remember better what people say than what they look like.   0 1 2 3
18. I easily remember jokes I hear.   0 1 2 3
19. I can identify people by hearing their voices.   0 1 2 3
20. When I turn on the TV, I listen to the sound more than watching the screen.   0 1 2 3

**ADD UP YOUR SCORE FOR ITEMS 11–20 AND WRITE IT HERE: _____.
THIS REPRESENTS THE <u>AUDITORY</u> LEARNING AND WORKING STYLE.**

21. I'd rather just start doing things than pay attention to directions.   0 1 2 3
22. I need frequent breaks when I work or study.   0 1 2 3
23. I move my lips when I read silently.   0 1 2 3
24. I avoid sitting at a desk when I don't have to.   0 1 2 3
25. I get nervous when I sit still too long.   0 1 2 3
26. I think better when I can move around.   0 1 2 3
27. Moving and touching objects helps me remember.   0 1 2 3
28. I enjoy building and making things.   0 1 2 3
29. I like a lot of physical activity.   0 1 2 3
30. I enjoy collecting cards, stamps, coins, or other things.   0 1 2 3

**ADD UP YOUR SCORE FROM ITEMS 21–30 AND WRITE IT HERE: _____.
THIS REPRESENTS THE <u>HANDS-ON</u> LEARNING AND WORKING STYLE.**

Now, circle the score that is the largest. If two of the scores are within two points of each other, circle both of them. If all three scores are within two points of each other, circle all three. The circle shows your preferred sense(s) for learning and working.

Interpretation of Part A
If you are a visual person, you rely on the sense of sight, and you learn best through visual means (books, video, graphics). If you are an auditory person, you prefer listening and speaking activities (discussions, debates, audiotapes, role-plays, lectures, meetings). If you are a hands-on person, you benefit from doing projects, conducting experiments, playing active games, building models, working with objects, and moving around the room. If two or all three of these senses are strong, you enjoy a wide variety of activities.

Part B: How You Deal with Other People
For each item, circle the response that best describes what you do: 0 = never, 1 = sometimes, 2 = very often, 3 = always.

31. I prefer to work or study with others.   0 1 2 3
32. I make new friends easily.   0 1 2 3
33. I like to be in groups of people.   0 1 2 3

233

CHAPTER 12
"Style Wars" as a
Source of Anxiety in
Language Classrooms

34. It is easy for me to talk to strangers.	0 1 2 3
35. I keep up with personal news about other people.	0 1 2 3
36. I like to stay late at parties.	0 1 2 3
37. Interactions with new people give me energy.	0 1 2 3
38. I remember people's names easily.	0 1 2 3
39. I have many friends and acquaintances.	0 1 2 3
40. Wherever I go, I develop personal contacts.	0 1 2 3

ADD UP YOUR SCORE FOR ITEMS 31–40 AND WRITE IT HERE: _____.
THIS REPRESENTS THE <u>EXTROVERTED</u> LEARNING AND WORKING STYLE.

41. I prefer to work or study alone.	0 1 2 3
42. I am rather shy.	0 1 2 3
43. I prefer hobbies or sports that I can do by myself.	0 1 2 3
44. It is hard for most people to get to know me.	0 1 2 3
45. People view me as more detached than sociable.	0 1 2 3
46. In a large group, I tend to keep silent.	0 1 2 3
47. Gatherings with lots of people tend to stress me.	0 1 2 3
48. I get nervous when dealing with new people.	0 1 2 3
49. I avoid parties if I can.	0 1 2 3
50. Remembering names is difficult for me.	0 1 2 3

ADD UP YOUR SCORE FOR ITEMS 41–50 AND WRITE IT HERE: _____.
THIS REPRESENTS THE <u>INTROVERTED</u> LEARNING AND WORKING STYLE.

Circle the larger score of the two. If the two scores are within two points of each other, circle them both. The circle represents your preferred way of dealing with people.

Interpretation of Part B
If you are extroverted, you enjoy a wide range of social, interactive learning tasks (games, conversations, discussions, debates, role-plays, simulations, meetings, teamwork). If you are introverted, you like to do more independent learning or working (studying or reading by yourself or working with the computer), or you enjoy working with one other person you know well. If your scores are close, you are able to learn alone and with others very easily.

Part C: How You Handle Possibilities
For each item, circle the response that best describes what you do: 0 = never, 1 = sometimes, 2 = very often, 3 = always.

51. I have a vivid imagination.	0 1 2 3
52. I like to think of lots of new ideas.	0 1 2 3
53. I can think of many different solutions to a problem.	0 1 2 3
54. I like multiple possibilities and options.	0 1 2 3
55. I enjoy considering future events.	0 1 2 3
56. Following a step-by-step procedure bores me.	0 1 2 3

57. I like to discover things rather than having   0 1 2 3
everything explained.
58. I consider myself original.   0 1 2 3
59. I am an ingenious person.   0 1 2 3
60. It feels fine if the teacher or boss changes the plan.   0 1 2 3

**ADD UP YOUR SCORE FOR ITEMS 51–60 AND WRITE IT HERE: _____ .
THIS REPRESENTS THE <u>INTUITIVE-RANDOM</u> LEARNING AND
WORKING STYLE.**

61. I am proud of being practical.   0 1 2 3
62. I behave in a down-to-earth way.   0 1 2 3
63. I like to be around sensible people.   0 1 2 3
64. I prefer realism instead of new, untested ideas.   0 1 2 3
65. I prefer things presented in a step-by-step way.   0 1 2 3
66. I want a class or work session to follow a clear plan.   0 1 2 3
67. I like concrete facts, not speculation.   0 1 2 3
68. Finding hidden meanings is frustrating and   0 1 2 3
irrelevant to me.
69. I prefer to avoid too many options.   0 1 2 3
70. I feel it is useless for me to think a lot about the future.   0 1 2 3

**ADD UP YOUR SCORE FOR ITEMS 61–70 AND WRITE IT HERE: _____ .
THIS REPRESENTS THE <u>CONCRETE-SEQUENTIAL</u> LEARNING AND
WORKING STYLE.**

Circle the larger score. If the two scores are within two points of each
other, circle them both. The circle represents your preferred way of handling
possibilities.

Interpretation of Part C
If you are intuitive-random, you are future-oriented, able to find the major
principles of the topic, like to speculate about possibilities, enjoy abstract
thinking, and avoid step-by-step instruction. If your preference is concrete-
sequential, you are oriented to the present, prefer one-step-at-a-time learning
activities, and want to know where you are going in your learning at every moment. If your scores are similar, then you have the flexibility to learn in either an
intuitive-random way or a concrete-sequential fashion at any given time.

Part D: How You Approach Tasks
For each item, circle the response that best describes what you do: 0 = never,
1 = sometimes, 2 = very often, 3 = always.

71. I reach decisions quickly.   0 1 2 3
72. I am an organized person.   0 1 2 3
73. I make lists of things I need to do.   0 1 2 3
74. I consult my lists to get things done.   0 1 2 3
75. Messy, unorganized environments make me nervous   0 1 2 3
or unhappy.

235

CHAPTER 12
*"Style Wars" as a
Source of Anxiety in
Language Classrooms*

76. I start tasks on time or early.   0 1 2 3
77. Deadlines help me organize my work.   0 1 2 3
78. I get places on time.   0 1 2 3
79. I enjoy having a lot of structure.   0 1 2 3
80. I follow through with what I have planned.   0 1 2 3

ADD UP YOUR SCORE FOR ITEMS 71–80 AND WRITE IT HERE: _____.
THIS REPRESENTS THE <u>CLOSURE-ORIENTED</u> LEARNING AND
WORKING STYLE.

81. I am a spontaneous person.   0 1 2 3
82. I like to just let things happen, not plan them.   0 1 2 3
83. I feel uncomfortable with a lot of structure.   0 1 2 3
84. I put off decisions as long as I can.   0 1 2 3
85. I have a messy desk or room.   0 1 2 3
86. I believe that deadlines are artificial or useless.   0 1 2 3
87. I keep an open mind about things.   0 1 2 3
88. I believe that enjoying myself is the most important thing.   0 1 2 3
89. Lists of tasks make me feel tired or upset.   0 1 2 3
90. I feel OK when I have to change my mind.   0 1 2 3

ADD UP YOUR SCORE FOR ITEMS 81–90 AND WRITE IT HERE: _____.
THIS REPRESENTS THE <u>OPEN</u> LEARNING AND WORKING STYLE.

Circle the larger score of the two. If the two scores are within two points of each other, circle them both. The circle represents your preferred way of approaching tasks.

Interpretation of Part D
If your score is higher for closure, you focus carefully on all tasks, meet deadlines, plan ahead, prefer neatness and structure, and want rapid decisions. If openness has a higher score, you enjoy discovery learning (in which you pick up information in an unstructured way), accept messiness, put off decisions, and prefer to learn or work without deadlines or rules.

Part E: How You Deal with Ideas
For each item, circle the response that best describes what you do: 0 = never, 1 = sometimes, 2 = very often, 3 = always.

91. I prefer simple answers, not a lot of explanation.   0 1 2 3
92. Too many details tend to confuse me.   0 1 2 3
93. I ignore details that do not seem relevant.   0 1 2 3
94. It is easy for me to see the overall plan or big picture.   0 1 2 3
95. I see the main point very quickly.   0 1 2 3
96. It is easy for me to paraphrase what other people say.   0 1 2 3
97. I can summarize information rather easily.   0 1 2 3
98. I am satisfied with knowing the major ideas without knowing details.   0 1 2 3

99. I can pull together (synthesize) things easily.   0 1 2 3
100. When I make an outline, I write down only the   0 1 2 3
key points.

**ADD UP YOUR SCORE FOR ITEMS 91–100 AND WRITE IT HERE: _____.
THIS REPRESENTS THE <u>GLOBAL</u> LEARNING AND WORKING STYLE.**

101. I prefer detailed answers instead of short answers.   0 1 2 3
102. It is difficult for me to summarize detailed information.   0 1 2 3
103. I focus on specific facts or information.   0 1 2 3
104. I enjoy breaking general ideas down into smaller pieces.   0 1 2 3
105. I prefer looking for differences rather than similarities.   0 1 2 3
106. I use logical analysis to solve problems.   0 1 2 3
107. My written outlines contain many details.   0 1 2 3
108. I get nervous when only the main ideas are presented.   0 1 2 3
109. I focus on the details rather than the big picture.   0 1 2 3
110. When I tell a story or explain something, it takes   0 1 2 3
a long time.

**ADD UP YOUR SCORE FOR ITEMS 101–110 AND WRITE IT HERE: _____.
THIS REPRESENTS THE <u>ANALYTIC</u> LEARNING AND WORKING STYLE.**

Circle the larger score. If the two scores are within two points of each
other, circle them both. The circle represents your preferred way to deal with
ideas.

Interpretation of Part E
If you are global, you enjoy getting the main idea, guessing meanings, pre-
dicting what will come next in a story or in an activity, and communicating
even if you don't know all the words or concepts. You prefer to avoid breaking ideas and themes down into parts and dislike specific rules. If you are analytic, you focus more on details, logical analysis, and contrasts while you are
learning. You like to break broad concepts into units and prefer to have specific rules. If your scores are close, then you can easily use both the global and
the analytic way of learning.

You have now completed the *Style Analysis Survey* and have learned about
your learning and working styles. Next you will discover what to do with this
information. You will gain new tips about learning and working styles on the
next page.

TIPS ON LEARNING AND WORKING STYLES

Each style preference offers significant benefits for learning and working.
There are great advantages in each one! Recognize your strengths and apply
them often. Your "comfort zone" is your favorite style. It is the style range
where you feel most relaxed and least challenged. For instance, if you are a
global person, your comfort zone is found in tasks for learning and working
that do not require you to use analysis (breaking ideas down); you are much
more at ease when you can bring lots of ideas together into a single whole.

However, you can enhance your learning and working power by being aware of the style areas that you do not use very much and by developing those areas. Doing activities that do not seem quite as suited to your style preferences can often help you stretch beyond your ordinary "comfort zone." For instance, if you are concrete-sequential, try doing tasks that require you to think of multiple possibilities and that make you think in terms of the future. If you are intuitive, try something that makes you go step-by-step through a series of activities.

If you are a highly global person, you might need to learn to use analysis and logic in order to work and learn more effectively. If you are an extremely analytic person, you might be missing out on some useful global features, like getting the main idea quickly. Occasionally break out of your comfort zone and try new behaviors.

You can develop new style qualities through practice. Even though these new features might not be comfortable at first, they might be very helpful. You won't lose your basic strengths by trying something new. You will simply develop another side of yourself.

If you are not sure how to attempt new behaviors that go beyond your favorite styles, then as your colleagues, friends, or teachers to give you a hand. Talk with someone who has a different style from yours, and see how that person operates. Improve your learning and working abilities by stretching your style a little bit, even though your basic preferences are likely to remain the same.

In addition, your style can develop slowly and naturally throughout your lifespan, without any conscious attempt to stretch it. Some people start out as introverts, then become extroverted through their college and working years, and later become introverted again. Some are always concrete-sequential, but others develop their intuitive capabilities during a period of their lives. Do not be surprised if some of your style aspects change a little (or even a lot) during your lifetime. This can happen through your experiences and through changes in your desires and needs.s

237

CHAPTER 12
"Style Wars" as a
Source of Anxiety in
Language Classrooms

PART V

Conclusion

CHAPTER 13

Giving Priority to the Language Learner First

Dolly J. Young
The University of Tennessee

In their seminal article, Horwitz, Horwitz, and Cope (1986) state:

> In general, educators have two options when dealing with anxious students: (1) they can help them learn to cope with the existing anxiety-provoking situation; or (2) they can make the learning context less stressful (p. 131).

In the first volume on language anxiety, *Language Anxiety: From Theory and Research to Classroom Implications* (Horwitz & Young 1991), researchers established the concept of anxiety particular to the FL/SL class, identified several sources of language anxiety, and suggested ways to help learners cope with anxiety, Horwitz's et al. option (1). The following is a summary of their findings (see Young 1991 for details).

SOURCES OF LANGUAGE ANXIETY

Personal factors stemming from:

  a. low self-esteem
  b. competitiveness
  c. self-perceived low ability levels
  d. communication apprehension
  e. lack of FL/SL group membership
  f. learners' beliefs about language learning
  g. learners' fears of being incorrect in front of their peers

Role-related beliefs about language teaching:

  a. that a little student intimidation is necessary
  b. that the instructor's role is to correct students constantly
  c. that the instructor cannot have students working in pairs because the class may get out of control

d. that the instructor should be doing most of the talking and teaching in class

e. that the instructor's role is parallel to a drill sergeant

Classroom procedures:

a. having students speak in the target language in front of the class
b. giving frequent oral quizzes (listening comprehension, in particular)
c. calling on students to respond orally and exclusively in the FL or SL

Aspects of language testing:

a. certain test formats evoke more anxiety than others (for example, listening comprehension, translation from SL to native language)
b. over-studying for hours only to find the tests assess different material
c. unfamiliar test tasks

The following is a summary of suggestions for coping with or reducing language anxiety that were gleaned from the chapters in this first volume on language anxiety. Some of the recommendations were made directly by the authors, and others were made by simply responding rationally to the sources of the anxieties.

SUGGESTIONS FOR COPING WITH OR REDUCING LANGUAGE ANXIETY

For anxiety stemming from personal factors:

a. Have students recognize their irrational beliefs or fears through group work activities and games designed specifically for this.
b. Suggest that highly anxious students participate in some form of supplemental instruction, such as a support group, individual tutoring, or a language club.
c. Suggest students do relaxation exercises and practice self-talk.

For anxiety stemming from role-related beliefs about teaching:

a. Discuss periodically with students reasonable commitments for successful language learning.
b. Adopt a role of facilitator instead of drill sergeant.
c. Complete the Beliefs About Language Learning Inventory designed to target misconceptions about language learning (Horwitz 1988).
d. Participate in language teaching workshops and action research designed to promote state-of-the-art teaching practices and pedagogical approaches.
e. Assess error-correcting approach as well as attitudes toward learners and learn to
—give students more positive feedback.
—help them develop more realistic expectations.
—adopt an attitude that mistakes are part of language learning and will be made by everyone.
—be more friendly, relaxed and patient.

—develop a sense of humor.

—offer learners correct linguistic feedback through modeling, rather than harsh overt correction.

—emphasize the importance of conveying meaning as much as grammatical accuracy.

f. Since instructor beliefs about language learning are often reflected in teacher behaviors, videotaping or reciprocal class visits might facilitate the identification and discussion of teacher assumptions about language learning.

For anxiety stemming from classroom procedures:

a. Do more small group and pair work.
b. Personalize language instruction.
c. Tailor activities to the affective needs of the learners, such as having students practice their role-plays in groups before presenting them to the class.

For anxiety stemming from aspects of language testing:

a. Test what you teach in the context of how you teach it.
b. Provide pretest practice of test item-types.
c. Designate points on a test for conveyance of meaning and not just grammar.

In this second volume on language anxiety, we focus on Horwitz's et al. option (2), making the learning context less stressful. Experts in FL or SL teacher training and language acquisition explore potential sources of in-class practices that can create unnecessarily negative experiences for language learners, and they suggest specific techniques that provide learners with the cognitive, linguistic, and emotional support they need to be successful language learners. The following is a sampling of the sources of language anxiety they posit and ways to make the learning context less stressful, discussed in much more detail throughout this book.

PEDAGOGICAL AND INSTRUCTIONAL SOURCES OF LANGUAGE ANXIETY

Anxiety derived from the following learner misconceptions:

a. that reading successfully means answering comprehension questions
b. that reading is a private act
c. that comprehending in reading or listening is an absolute
d. that speaking in the FL or SL should be grammatically perfect
e. that pronunciation must sound native
f. that studying four semesters of a FL makes fluent speakers
g. that listening to the FL entails understanding every word

Anxiety rooted in such ineffective pedagogical practices as:

a. teaching too much grammatical material or avoiding grammar altogether
b. teaching writing by focusing on product rather than process

   c. practicing listening comprehension without enough time for processing chunks of a text
   d. practicing listening activities without a clear purpose
   e. practicing listening exercises without the repetition and redundancies in natural language
   f. practicing listening activities that do not include instruction in how to listen strategically
   g. practicing listening instruction that does not make use of extra-linguistic strategies for comprehension
   h. using listening tasks that rely on speech too fast to be understood by non-native speakers
   i. using speaking activities that put the learner "on the spot" in front of peers without allowing prior preparation

Anxiety stemming from such individual differences in language learners as:

   a. learners with poor native language skills
   b. learners whose cognitive style may clash with the instructor's cognitive style

Anxiety evoked by instructor qualities, such as one who:

   a. does not see learners in class as part of a social community
   b. makes no distinction between learner competence and performance or recognition and production

SUGGESTIONS FOR MAKING THE LEARNING CONTEXT LESS STRESSFUL

Dispel misconceptions about FL or SL learning

Provide learners with discussions about the process of learning an FL or SL through consciousness-raising activities that focus on dispelling myths about language learning so that learners understand that:

   a. they will make mistakes
   b. mistakes are a natural part of language learning
   c. they will be able to understand much more than they will be able to speak
   d. their pronunciation will not be expected to be perfect
   e. reading comprehension is more than merely answering questions about a text
   f. reading can be a social act whereby learners can help one another construct meaning from a text
   g. reading is not a linear process but one where students scan, skim, read, and re-read, skim, read, re-read again, and so on
   h. reading comprehension and listening comprehension are not absolutes; learners do not have to understand every word to get meaning from what they read or hear

Provide effective and engaging language instruction:

   a. Focus on processing language before requiring complete language production.

b. Engage learners in prereading, listening, and writing activities.

c. Focus on techniques to develop writing skills, such as looping, cubing, outlining, or engaging learners in structural input tasks to effectively prepare learners for writing tasks, thereby increasing their chances of being successful.

d. Offer structured input as well as structured output practice.

e. Enhance learner comprehension by providing paralinguistic support in listening tasks.

f. Encourage learners to teach each other.

g. Engage learners in collaborative tasks, such as information gap activities, surveys, role-plays, and peer evaluations.

h. Focus on learners' exchange of information and not merely on the "practice" of the FL or SL.

i. Enable learners to achieve small successes.

j. Make effective use of learner's background knowledge.

Improve instructor qualities:

a. Build a community of learners within the language class.

b. Acknowledge the distinction between learner competence and performance, and recognition and production.

Recognize individual differences:

a. Identify poor language learners and accommodate them as much as possible.

b. Acknowledge the variety of learning styles in the language class.

c. Assess your own learning style.

d. Be sensitive to potential gender-related differences in the language class.

The preceding list is, in essence, a summary of the ideas generated in the essays in this book. From these, though, several fundamental pedagogical premises or principles can be inferred. First and foremost is the notion that we can make the language-learning context less stressful by designing in-class instruction and developing language learning materials that give priority to the learner first, not to external factors, such as the material (for example, the vocabulary or grammar in a textbook), the curriculum (for instance, the textbook), or a test (for example, the Advanced Placement Test), and so on.

Instead of continuing in-class practices that are driven by textbooks with exercises that insist learners can internalize each linguistic feature of an FL and immediately produce it, giving priority to the language learner would mean offering learners the skills they need to experience success in language learning. In-class practices would focus on process-oriented, communicative and collaborative, prereading, writing, listening, and speaking tasks before requiring learners to "perform." This is not to say learners should not be expected to produce in an FL or SL classroom; rather, we should provide instruction that will increase their chances of success once they do have to produce.

By giving priority to the language learner, in-class practices and instructional materials would also emphasize what learners can accomplish, as opposed to what they cannot accomplish, in a context that promotes realistic language use. In addition, giving priority to language learners in the language-learning process would mean informing learners about why we do what we do in class, dispelling misconceptions about language learning, offering them a sense of empowerment, and above all encouraging them not only to cooperate but to collaborate.

Lastly, by placing the language learner before all other factors in the language-learning process, we would be forced to rethink the natural forces in academia that persist in viewing language learners almost exclusively as potential literary scholars and instead would try to meet their linguistic, cognitive, and affective needs first.

If the objective of the foreign language profession is to encourage the learning of foreign languages, then learners must continue their language study even after their language requirements are met. To encourage language learning, even within the required sequence of FL courses, we must make our number one priority the language learner. We need to recognize that there are variables that can influence emotions, attitudes, and personal goals, even without an individual's awareness (see LeDoux 1996). We must support research, such as Sparks and Ganschow's, Cambell's, and Oxford's, that advances our understanding of the relationship between affect, cognition, and behavior. Most importantly, however, success in the language classroom depends on changing our perceptions of what we believe language learning is about.

Collectively, the contributors to this volume help advance the field of language acquisition by acknowledging the interdisciplinary nature of language learning and the interdependent role that linguistics, cognition, and affect play in FL and SL learning. Individually, contributors to this volume share with teachers concrete, practical tools to face the challenges of language teaching today and in the next millennium.

REFERENCES

Horwitz, Elaine K. (1988). The beliefs about language learning of beginning university foreign language students. *Modern Language Journal, 70,* 283–293.

Horwitz, E., Horwitz, M. B., & Cope, J. (1986). Foreign language classroom anxiety. *Modern Language Journal, 70,* 125–132.

Horwitz, E., & Young, D. J. (1991). *Language anxiety: From theory and research to classroom implications.* Upper Saddle River, NJ: Prentice Hall.

LeDoux, Joseph (1996). *The emotional brain.* New York: Simon and Schuster.

Young, D. J. (1991). Creating a low-anxiety classroom environment: What does the anxiety research suggest? *Modern Language Journal, 75,* 426–439.

Appendix A

French Class Anxiety Scale

Agree   1   2   3   4   5   6   Disagree

(+)   1. It embarrasses me to volunteer answers in our French class.
(+)   2. I never feel quite sure of myself when I am speaking in our French class.
(+)   3. I always feel that the other students speak French better than I do.
(+)   4. I get nervous and confused when I am speaking in my French class.
(+)   5. I am afraid the other students will laugh at me when I speak French.

Gardner, R. C. (1985). *Social psychology and second language learning: The role of attitudes and motivation*. London: Edward Arnold.

Appendix B

Foreign Language Classroom Anxiety Scale (FLCAS)

| Strongly Agree | Agree | Neither Agree Nor Disagree | Disagree | Strongly Disagree |

(+) 1. I never feel quite sure of myself when I am speaking in my foreign language class.

(–) 2. I don't worry about making mistakes in language class.

(+) 3. I tremble when I know that I'm going to be called on in language class.

(+) 4. It frightens me when I don't understand what the teacher is saying in the foreign language.

(–) 5. It wouldn't bother me at all to take more foreign language classes.

(+) 6. During language class, I find myself thinking about things that have nothing to do with the course.

(+) 7. I keep thinking that the other students are better at languages than I am.

(–) 8. I am usually at ease during tests in my language class.

(+) 9. I start to panic when I have to speak without preparation in language class.

(+) 10. I worry about the consequences of failing my foreign language class.

(–) 11. I don't understand why some people get so upset over foreign language classes.

(+) 12. In language class, I can get so nervous I forget things I know.

(+) 13. It embarrasses me to volunteer answers in my language class.

(–) 14. I would not be nervous speaking the foreign language with native speakers.

(+) 15. I get upset when I don't understand what the teacher is correcting.

(+) 16. Even if I am well prepared for language class, I feel anxious about it.

(+) 17. I often feel like not going to my language class.

(–) 18. I feel confident when I speak in the foreign language class.

(+) 19. I am afraid that my language teacher is ready to correct every mistake I made.

(+) 20. I can feel my heart pounding when I'm going to be called on in language class.
(+) 21. The more I study for a language test, the more confused I get.
(−) 22. I don't feel pressure to prepare very well for language class.
(+) 23. I always feel that the other students speak the foreign language better than I do.
(+) 24. I feel very self-conscious about speaking the foreign language in front of other students.
(+) 25. Language class moves so quickly I worry about getting left behind.
(+) 26. I feel more tense and nervous in my language class than in my other classes.
(+) 27. I get nervous and confused when I am speaking in my language class.
(−) 28. When I'm on my way to language class, I feel very sure and relaxed.
(+) 29. I get nervous when I don't understand every word the language teacher says.
(+) 30. I feel overwhelmed by the number of rules you have to learn to speak a foreign language.
(+) 31. I am afraid that the other students will laugh at me when I speak the foreign language.
(−) 32. I would probably feel comfortable around native speakers of the foreign language.
(+) 33. I get nervous when the language teacher asks questions that I haven't prepared in advance.

Horwitz, E. K., Horwitz, M. B., & Cope, J. (1986). Foreign language classroom anxiety. *Modern Language Journal, 70*, 125–132.

Appendix C

French Classroom Anxiety Scale—Revised
(R. C. Gardner)

(–) 1. When I was taking it, I didn't usually get anxious when I had to respond to a question in French class.

(+) 2. I was always afraid that the other students would laugh at me if I spoke up in French class.

(+) 3. I always felt that the other students were more at ease than I was in French class.

(–) 4. When I took it, I was never embarrassed to volunteer answers in French class.

(+) 5. I was generally tense whenever participating in French class.

(–) 6. I never understood why other students were so nervous in French class.

(–) 7. I usually felt relaxed and confident when active participation took place in French class.

(+) 8. Whenever I had to answer a question, out loud, I would get nervous and confused in French class.

Editor's note: This scale may be adapted for use with other classroom courses such as Mathematics or English. MacIntyre (1988) used the following format:

I was generally tense whenever participating in . . .

French class	agree	1 ☐	2 ☐	3 ☐	4 ☐	5 ☐	6 ☐	disagree
Math class	agree	1 ☐	2 ☐	3 ☐	4 ☐	5 ☐	6 ☐	disagree
English class	agree	1 ☐	2 ☐	3 ☐	4 ☐	5 ☐	6 ☐	disagree

MacIntyre, P. D. (1988). *The effects of anxiety on foreign language learning and production.* Unpublished Master's thesis, The University of Western Ontario.

Appendix D

Input Anxiety Scale

- 1. I am not bothered by someone speaking quickly in French.
- 2. It does not bother me if my French notes are disorganized before I study them.
- 3. I enjoy just listening to someone speaking French.
+ 4. I get flustered unless French is spoken very slowly and deliberately.
+ 5. I get upset when I read in French because I must read things again and again.
+ 6. I get upset when French is spoken too quickly.

Processing Anxiety Scale

- 1. Learning new French vocabulary does not worry me; I can acquire it in no time.
+ 2. I am anxious with French because, no matter how hard I try, I have trouble understanding it.
+ 3. The only time that I feel comfortable during French tests is when I have had a lot of time to study.
+ 4. I feel anxious if French class seems disorganized.
- 5. I am self-confident in my ability to appreciate the meaning of French dialogue.
- 6. I do not worry when I hear new or unfamiliar words; I am confident that I can understand them.

Output Anxiety Scale

- 1. I never feel tense when I have to speak in French.
- 2. I feel confident that I can easily use the French vocabulary that I know in a conversation.
+ 3. I may know the proper French expression, but when I am nervous it just won't come out.
+ 4. I get upset when I know how to communicate something in French but I just cannot verbalize it.

− 5. I never get nervous when writing something for my French class.

+ 6. When I become anxious during a French test, I cannot remember anything I studied.

Note: Each section above includes three positively worded items and three negatively worded items.

MacIntyre, P. D., & Gardner, R. C. (1994). The subtle effects of language anxiety on cognitive processing in the second language. *Language Learning*, 44, 283–305.

Appendix E

Anxiety Measures—References

Affect adjective checklist

Zuckerman, M. (1960). The development of an affect adjective check list for the measurement of anxiety. *Journal of Consulting Psychology, 24,* 457–462.

Attitude toward the language class

Ely, C. M. (1986). An analysis of discomfort, risktaking, sociability, and motivation in the L2 classroom. *Language Learning, 36,* 1–25.

Classroom anxiety scale, revised by MacIntyre

MacIntyre, P. D. (1988). *The effects of anxiety on foreign language learning and production.* Master's thesis, The University of Western Ontario.

Concern for grade

Ely, C. M. (1986). An analysis of discomfort, risktaking, sociability, and motivation in the L2 classroom. *Language Learning, 36,* 1–25.

Debilitating anxiety scale

Alpert, R., & Haber, R. N. (1960). Anxiety in academic achievement situations. *Journal of Abnormal and Social Psychology, 61,* 207–215.

Facilitating anxiety scale

Alpert, R., & Haber, R. N. (1960). Anxiety in academic achievement situations. *Journal of Abnormal and Social Psychology, 61,* 207–215.

Fear of negative evaluation

Watson, D., & Friend, R. (1969). Measurement of social-evaluative anxiety. *Journal of Consulting and Clinical Psychology, 33,* 448–457.

The fear thermometer

Walk, R. D. (1956). Self ratings of fear in a fear-invoking situation. *Journal of Abnormal and Social Psychology, 52,* 171–178.

French Class Anxiety Scale

Gardner, R. C. (1985). *Social psychology and second language learning: The role of attitudes and motivation.* London: Edward Arnold.

French Use Anxiety Scale (R. C. Gardner)

Gliksman, L. (1981). *Improving the prediction of behaviours associated with second language acquisition.* Ph.D. diss., The University of Western Ontario.

Foreign Language Classroom Anxiety Scale

Horwitz, E. K., Horwitz, M. B., & Cope, J. (1986). Foreign language classroom anxiety. *Modern Language Journal, 70,* 125–132.

Language class discomfort

Ely, C. M. (1986). An analysis of discomfort, risktaking, sociability, and motivation in the L2 classroom. *Language Learning, 36,* 1–25.

Language class risk-taking

Ely, C. M. (1986). An analysis of discomfort, risktaking, sociability, and motivation in the L2 classroom. *Language Learning, 36,* 1–25.

Language class sociability

Ely, C. M. (1986). An analysis of discomfort, risktaking, sociability, and motivation in the L2 classroom. *Language Learning, 36,* 1–25.

Personal Report of Communication Apprehension (PRCA)–College

McCroskey, J. C. (1970). Measures of communication-bound anxiety. *Speech Monographs, 37,* 269–277.

PRCA–Ten (grade 10 students), PRCA–Seven (grade 7 students)

McCroskey, J. C. (1970). Measures of communication-bound anxiety. *Speech Monographs, 37,* 269–277.

PRPSA

McCroskey, J. C. (1970). Measures of communication-bound anxiety. *Speech Monographs, 37,* 269–277.

PRCA–Long Form, PRCA–Short Form

McCroskey, J. C. (1978). Validity of the PRCA as an index of oral communication apprehension. *Communication Monographs, 45,* 192–203.

Social Avoidance and Distress Scale

Watson, D., & Friend, R. (1969). Measurement of social-evaluative anxiety. *Journal of Consulting and Clinical Psychology, 33,* 448–457.

Speech A/Trait Scale (sample items)

Lamb, D. H. (1972). Speech anxiety: Towards a theoretical conceptualization and preliminary scale development. *Speech Monographs, 39,* 62–67.

Speech A/State Scale (sample items)

Lamb, D. H. (1972). Speech anxiety: Towards a theoretical conceptualization and preliminary scale development. *Speech Monographs, 39,* 62–67.

The S-R Inventory of General Trait Anxiousness

Endler, N. S., & Okada, M. (1975). A multidimensional measure of trait anxiety: The S-R Inventory of general trait anxiousness. *Journal of Consulting and Clinical Psychology, 43,* 319–329.

Strength of motivation

Ely, C. M. (1986). An analysis of discomfort, risktaking, sociability, and motivation in the L2 classroom. *Language Learning, 36,* 1–25.

Suinn Test Anxiety Behavior Scale

Suinn, R. M. (1969). The STABBS, a measure of test anxiety for behavior therapy: Normative data. *Behaviour Research and Therapy, 7,* 335–339.

Taylor Manifest Anxiety Scale

Taylor, J. A. (1953). A personality scale of manifest anxiety. *Journal of Abnormal and Social Psychology, 48,* 285–290.

Test Anxiety Scale

Sarason, I. G., & Ganzer, V. J. (1962). Anxiety, reinforcement, and experimental instructions in a free verbalization situation. *Journal of Abnormal and Social Psychology, 65,* 300–307.

Writing Apprehension Measure

Daly, J. A., & Miller, M. C. (1975). The empirical development of an instrument to measure writing apprehension. *Research in the Teaching of English, 9,* 242–249.

Reference list is from Peter D. MacIntyre and Robert Gardner (1988). The measurement of anxiety and applications to second language learning: An annotated bibliography. *Research Bulletin* No. 672. The University of Western Ontario, London, Canada.

Appendix F

Reading Anxiety Scale (RAS)

Directions: Please indicate the degree to which each statement describes you, on a scale from 1 to 5.

1—Never true of me
2—Almost never true of me
3—Somewhat true of me
4—Almost always true of me
5—Always true of me

− _____ 1. I am usually at ease reading in Spanish.
− _____ 2. I don't mind being assigned homework that consists of reading in Spanish.
+ _____ 3. I don't know enough Spanish to read well.
+ _____ 4. I need help in reading Spanish.
+ _____ 5. I do not enjoy reading in any language, Spanish or English.
− _____ 6. Reading helps me discover life's secrets.
− _____ 7. I read to know more about the world.
+ _____ 8. No matter how hard I try, I just can't real well.
− _____ 9. I like reading about new ideas.
+ _____ 10. I get frustrated reading when I read in Spanish.
+ _____ 11. When I read in Spanish, I understand the words; I just can't put them together to get meaning.
− _____ 12. I enjoy reading in Spanish even though I may not understand everything I read.
+ _____ 13. I can read Spanish, but I don't feel like it.
− _____ 14. I read to know more about the world.
+ _____ 15. I start to panic when I have to read silently in class.

Appendix G

Writing Apprehension

Directions: Below are a series of statements about writing. There are no right or wrong answers to these statements. Please indicate the degree to which each statement applies to you by writing the number that reflects your opinion: whether you (1) strongly agree, (2) agree, (3) are uncertain, (4) disagree, or (5) strongly disagree with the statement. While some of these statements may seem repetitious, take your time and try to be as honest as possible. Thank you for your cooperation in this matter.

_____ (+) 1. I avoid writing.

_____ (–) 2. I have no fear of my writing being evaluated.

_____ (–) 3. I look forward to writing down my ideas.

_____ (+) 4. I am afraid of writing essays when I know they will be evaluated.

_____ (+) 5. Taking a composition course is a very frightening experience.

_____ (–) 6. Handing in a composition course is a very frightening experience.

_____ (+) 7. My mind seems to go blank when I start to work on a compositon.

_____ (+) 8. Expressing ideas through writing seems to be a waste of time.

_____ (–) 9. I would enjoy submitting my writing to magazines for evaluation and publication.

_____ (–) 10. I like to write my ideas down.

_____ (–) 11. I feel confident in my ability to clearly express my ideas in writing.

_____ (–) 12. I like to have my friends read what I have written.

_____ (+) 13. I'm nervous about writing.

_____ (–) 14. People seem to enjoy what I write.

_____ (–) 15. I enjoy writing.

_____ (+) 16. I never seem to enjoy what I write.

_____ (–) 17. Writing is a lot of fun.

_____ (+) 18. I expect to do poorly in composition classes even before I enter them.

_____ (–) 19. I like seeing my thoughts on paper.

_____ (–) 20. Discussing my writing with others is an enjoyable experience.

_____ (+) 21. I have a terrible time organizing my ideas in a composition course.

_____ (+) 22. When I hand in a compositon, I know I'm going to do poorly.

_____ (–) 23. It's easy for me to write good compositions.

_____ (+) 24. I don't think I write as well as most other people.

_____ (+) 25. I don't like my compositions to be evaluated.

_____ (+) 26. I'm no good at writing.

The formula for scoring the twenty-six item instrument is:

writing apprehension = 78 + positive scores – negative scores

If one desires to use this instrument outside the classroom, items that specifiy class activity should be omitted. Items 4, 5, 6, 18, 21, and 22 would be omitted and the scoring formula would be:

writing apprehension = 48 + positive scores - negative scores

Daly, J. A., & Miller, M. C. (1975). The empirical development of an instrument to measure writing apprehension. *Research in the Teaching of English, 9,* 242–249.

Appendix H

PRCA–Long Form

Directions: This instrument is composed of twenty-five statements concerning your communication with other people. Please indicate the degree to which each statement applies to you by marking whether you (1) Strongly Agree, (2) Agree, (3) Are Undecided, (4) Disagree, or (5) Strongly Disagree with each statement. There are no right or wrong answers. Work quickly, just record your first impression.

1. While participating in a conversation with a new acquaintance, I feel very nervous.
2. I have no fear of facing an audience.
3. I talk less because I'm shy.
4. I look forward to expressing my opinions at meetings.
5. I am afraid to express myself in a group.
6. I look forward to an opportunity to speak in public.
7. I find the prospect of speaking mildly pleasant.
8. When communicating, my posture feels strained and unnatural.
9. I am tense and nervous while participating in a group discussion.
10. Although I talk fluently with friends, I am at a loss for words on the platform.
11. I have no fear about expressing myself in a group.
12. My hands tremble when I try to handle objects on the platform.
13. I always avoid speaking in public if possible.
14. I feel that I am more fluent when talking to people than most other people are.
15. I am fearful and tense all the while I am speaking before a group of people.
16. My thoughts become confused and jumbled when I speak before an audience.
17. I like to get involved in group discussions.
18. Although I am nervous just before getting up, I soon forget my fears and enjoy the experience.

19. Conversing with people who hold positions of authority causes me to be fearful and tense.
20. I dislike to use my body and voice expressively.
21. I feel relaxed and comfortable while speaking.
22. I feel self-conscious when I am called on to answer a question or give an opinion in class.
23. I face the prospect of making a speech with complete confidence.
24. I'm afraid to speak up in conversations.
25. I would enjoy presenting a speech on a local television show.

To compute the PRCA score, follow these three steps:

1. Add the scores for items 1, 3, 5, 8, 9, 10, 12, 13, 15, 16, 19, 20, 22, and 24.
2. Add the scores for items 2, 4, 6, 7, 11, 14, 17, 18, 21, 23, 25.
3. Complete the following formula:

PRCA = 84 - (total from step 1) + (total from step 2)

PRCA–Short Form

Directions: This instrument is composed of ten statements concerning your communication with other people. Please indicate the degree to which each statement applies to you by marking whether you (1) Strongly Agree, (2) Agree, (3) Are Undecided, (4) Disagree, or (5) Strongly Disagree with each statement. There are no right or wrong answers. Work quickly, just record your first impression.

1. I look forward to expressing myself at meetings.
2. I am afraid to express myself in a group.
3. I look forward to an opportunity to speak in public.
4. Although I talk fluently with friends, I am at a loss of words on the platform.
5. I always avoid speaking in public if possible.
6. I feel that I am more fluent when talking to people than most other people are.
7. I like to get involved in group discussion.
8. I dislike to use my body and voice expressively.
9. I'm afraid to speak up in conversations.
10. I would enjoy presenting a speech on a local television show.

To compute the PRCA score, follow these three steps:

1. Add the scores for items 2, 4, 5, 8, 9.
2. Add the scores for items 1, 3, 6, 7, 10.
3. Complete the following formula:

PRCA + 36 - (total from step 1) + (total from step 2)

McCroskey, J. C. (1978). Validity of the PRCA as an index of oral communication apprehension. *Communication Monographs, 45,* 192–203.

(T)   1. While taking an important examination, I perspire a great deal.
(T)   2. I get to feel very panicky when I have to take a surprise exam.
(T)   3. During tests, I find myself thinking of the consequences of failing.
(T)   4. After important tests I am frequently so tense that my stomach gets upset.
(T)   5. While taking an important exam I find myself thinking of how much brighter the other students are than I am.
(T)   6. I freeze up on things like intelligence tests and final exams.
(T)   7. If I were to take an intelligence test I would worry a great deal before taking it.
(T)   8. During course examinations, I find myself thinking of things unrelated to the actual course material.
(T)   9. During a course examination, I frequently get so nervous that I forget the facts I really know.
(F) 10. If I knew I was going to take an intelligence test, I would feel confident and relaxed beforehand.
(T) 11. I usually get depressed after taking a test.
(T) 12. I have an uneasy, upset feeling before taking a final examination.
(F) 13. When taking a test, my emotional feelings do not interfere with my performance.
(T) 14. Getting a good grade on one test doesn't seem to increase my confidence on the second.
(T) 15. After taking a test I always feel I could have done better than I actually did.
(T) 16. I sometimes feel my heart beating very fast during important tests.

Sarason, I. G., & Ganzer, V. J. (1962). Anxiety, reinforcement, and experimental instructions in a free verbalization situation. *Journal of Abnormal and Social Psychology, 65,* 300–307.

About the Contributors

The articles and essays that constitue this volume were prepared specifically for this book. The contributors represent a broad spectrum of professional expertise in foreign language and second language learning.

Margaret Healy Beauvois (Ph.D., The University of Texas) is currently Coordinator/Supervisor of the French Language Program at the University of Tennessee. Her area of research is computer-assisted classroom discussions using networked computers. She also does teacher training in cooperative learning, computer-assisted language learning, use of writing programs (Systéme D and the Daedalus Integrated Writing Environment), and integration of video into the foreign language curriculum in such programs as the semi-immersion method, *French in Action*. She has published articles on these topics in *Foreign Language Annals*, *The Canadian Modern Language Review*, *Computers in the Humanities*, and *CALICO*.

Christine M. Campbell (Ph.D., Purdue University) is Test Project Director in the Directorate of Evaluation and Standardization at the Defense Language Institute, Monterey, California. Her primary duty is to supervise an international team of test developers who write proficiency tests in a variety of foreign languages. She has published on language anxiety, motivation in language learning, and testing. She is Immediate Past Chair of the International Language and Culture Foundation and is Director of Test Development of the *National Spanish Examination*. In 1994 she was named distinguished Education Alumna by Purdue University.

Leonore Ganschow (Ed.D., University of Cincinnati) is Professor of Educational Psychology at Miami University, Oxford, Ohio, where she teaches undergraduate and graduate courses in learning disabilities and gifted education. Her research interests are in acquisition and development of literacy skills, oral and written language disabilities, and foreign language learning in at-risk populations. She has published numerous chapters in books and articles in journals. She is currently a member of the National Board of the Orton Dyslexia Society.

William R. Glass (Ph.D., The University of Illinois at Urbana-Champaign) is Senior Sponsoring Editor for Foreign Languages with the McGraw-Hill Higher Education Division in San Francisco. He formerly taught at The Pennsylvania State University, where he is currently Adjunct Assistant Professor of Spanish. His areas of research include reading in a second language and learners' processing of aural and written input. He is also co-editor, with Dr. Ana Teresa Pérez-Leroux, of *Contemporary Perspectives on the Acquisition of Spanish* (Volumes 1 and 2).

Elaine K. Horwitz (Ph.D., The University of Illinois at Urbana-Champaign) is Associate Professor of Curriculum and Instruction and Convener of Multilingual Studies at the University of Texas at Austin. She is known for her work on individual differences in second language acquisition, including learning styles, learner belief systems, and, particularly, foreign language anxiety. She co-edited *Language Anxiety: From Theory and Research to Classroom Implications* with Dr. Dolly J. Young.

James F. Lee (Ph.D., The University of Texas) is Associate Professor of Language Instruction in the Department of Spanish and Portuguese at Indiana University. He is a leading researcher of second language reading comprehension and second language teaching, having published many articles and chapters in these areas. With Dr. Bill VanPatten, he authored *Making Communicative Language Teaching Happen;* he also serves as series co-editor for the McGraw-Hill Second Language Professional Series.

Ilona Leki (Ph.D., The University of Illinois) is Professor of English and Director of ESL at the University of Tennessee. She edits *Journal of Second Language Writing* (with Tony Silva), is author of *Academic Writing: Exploring Processes and Strategies* (St. Martin's Press) and *Understanding ESL Writers: A Guide for Teachers* (Boynton/Cook), and is co-editor (with Joan Carson) of *Reading in the Composition Classroom: Second Language Perspectives* (Newbury House). Her research focuses on second language writing and reading.

Peter D. MacIntyre (Ph.D., The University of Western Ontario) is an Assistant Professor of Psychology at the University College of Cape Breton. He completed a post-doctoral fellowship at the University of Ottawa before moving to Cape Breton. His main research interests and areas of extensive publications include individual differences in communication and language learning, particularly the cognitive effects of anxiety.

Rebecca L. Oxford (Ph.D., The University of North Carolina) holds, in addition to her Ph.D. in Education Psychology, an Ed.M. in the same area from Boston University and two additional degrees in Russian (Yale and Vanderbilt Universities). She is currently Associate Dean for the College of Education at the University of Alabama, Tuscaloosa. She specializes in affective variables such as anxiety, learning styles and strategies, testing, and language teaching methodology. She is the author or co-editor of a number of books for language teachers and learners, the latest of which is *Patterns of Cultural Identity*. Her book *Language Learning Strategies: What Every Teacher Should Know* has been translated into Japanese and Arabic.

Elaine M. Phillips (Ph.D., The University of Texas) specializes in foreign language education and is the Field Specialist at the LOTE Center for Educator Development at the Southwest Educational Development Laboratory. She has published articles on language anxiety and the teaching of polite requests in the *Modern Language Journal, French Review,* and *Foreign Language Annals*. She is co-author (with Chantal Thompson) of the first-year, college-level French textbook *Mais Oui*, published by D.C. Heath/Houghton Mifflin.

Richard L. Sparks (Ed.D., University of Cincinnati) is Associate Professor of Education at the College of Mount St. Joseph in Cincinnati, Ohio, where he teaches undergraduate and graduate courses in learning disabilities, reading, diagnostic educational assessment, and testing. He also has a private practice as an educational consultant in which he conducts psychoeducational evaluations. He is the author of numerous publications in the areas of foreign language learning and oral and written language learning difficulties. His other research interests are in reading disabilities, the psychology of reading, and cognitive development.

Bill VanPatten (Ph.D., The University of Texas at Austin) is Full Professor of Spanish at the University of Illinois, where he is also Director of Graduate Studies in Spanish, Italian, and Portuguese, as well as Advisor for the Undergraduate Program in Spanish Teacher Education. He has published widely in the fields of second language acquisition and language teaching and is co-author, with Dr. James F. Lee, of the book *Making Communicative Language Teaching Happen*. He is also the designer and principal author of the highly acclaimed PBS telecourse *Destinos* and is the principal author of the innovative content- and task-based Spanish textbook *¿Sabías que... ?*

Anita Vogely (Ph.D., The University of Texas) is an Assistant Professor at The State University of New York, Binghamton. She is Director of the Master of Arts in Teaching Program for the School of Education and Human Development. Her interests include the psychology of human learning, brain-based learning, and alternative approaches to classroom instruction, as well as foreign language teaching methods. She has published in these areas in *Hispania, The Modern Language Journal,* and *Foreign Language Annals*. She regularly presents pedagogical workshops throughout the state of New York to current and aspiring language instructors.

Dolly J. Young (Ph.D., The University of Texas) is Associate Professor of Spanish in the Department of Romance Languages at the University of Tennessee. She supervises the first- and second-year Spanish programs and provides teacher training for graduate students. She has published widely in the areas of language anxiety and foreign language reading. She co-edited the first language anxiety volume *Language Anxiety: From Theory and Research to Classroom Implications*, with Dr. Elaine K. Horwitz, co-wrote a supplementary Spanish reader, *Esquemas*, with the late Darlene F. Wolf, and co-wrote the second-year Spanish textbook *¿Qué te parece?* with Dr. James F. Lee, Darlene Wolf, and Paul Chandler.

Index

accents, 31, 126, 241
accommodation, in the
    classroom, 178–183
acculturation model, 19
acquisition
  link between input and, 95
  relationship between low-
    stress language learning
    and, 207
acquisition orders, 95, 97
acquisitional sequences, strength
    of, in instructional settings,
    97
adjustments, linguistic and
    conversational, with non-
    native speakers, 110–111
advance organizers, 16–17
Advanced Placement Test, 245
adverbs of time, 100
affect
  adjective checklist, 253
  juxtaposed with cognition,
    19
  primacy over cognition, 18
"affective filter," 20, 35
Affective Filter Hypothesis, 20
affective variables, in second
    language acquisition, 3, 7,
    13–14, 19–20, 24. *See also*
    language anxiety
affiliation with the second
    language community, 33,
    37, 241
alterations in learning style
    behaviors, 236–237

ambiguity, tolerance for, 127,
    222–223
American Sign Language (ASL),
    145–146
Analysis of Variance (ANOVA),
    197, 202
analytic versus global approach,
    218–220, 222, 224, 228,
    236–237
anthropological linguistics, 13
anxiety arousal, 29, 31, 35, 37
anxiety, defined, 28, 192, 217. *See
    also* language anxiety
Anxiety Measures-References,
    253–255
anxiety-reduction program,
    204–205, 227–228, 242,
    244–246
"anxiety transfer" approach, 26
aptitude. *See* foreign language
    aptitude
artichoke analogy, for reading,
    53, 61
assessment. *See also* test(s);
    evaluation
  classroom observations, 174,
    176
  formal and informal testing,
    175–178
  personal interview, 175–176
  review of foreign language
    learning history, 175
  of students with foreign
    language learning problems,
    174–178

assimilation activity, 55–56
attentional capacity, 59–60
attitude(s), 3–6, 19–20, 125, 127,
    172
  toward the language class, 253
Attitude/Motivation Test Battery
    (AMTB), 193–194
audience anxiety, 29
Audiolingual Method (ALM),
    14–15
auditory preference, 218, 220, 232
Ausubel, David, 15
awareness-raising activities, 108,
    114–117, 204, 206, 245–246
avoidance, 32, 39, 65–66

background knowledge,
    activating, 109, 245
behaviorism, 14–15
beliefs about language learning,
    125–128, 241, 243–244
*Beliefs About Language Learning
    Inventory* (BALLI), 126–128,
    242
brain activities, tendency to
    compartmentalize, 20–21
brainstorming, 54, 69–70,
    147–148, 158
branching and clustering, 72
Bristol Language Project, 171

capable students, 30–31
career goals and language
    anxiety, 201–202
cartoon stories, 136–137

error(s), *continued*
    responding to, 138–139
    sociolinguistic, 94–95
evaluation
    fear of negative, 27, 118–119
    of input before output, 101
    oral evaluations, 139–140
event probabilities, 98
expectations
    of failure, 32, 35
    and language learning. *See*
        beliefs about language
        learning
explicit grammar instruction, 93,
    102
extra effort, 36–37, 51
extroverted personality, 31,
    218–219, 222–224, 233

facilitating (facilitative) anxiety,
    78, 253
factor analysis, 29
fear(s)
    of failure, 118–119
    of loss of ethnic identity, 32
    of loss of identity, 32
    of loss of native language, 32,
        38
    of miscomprehension, 35, 108
    of negative evaluation, 27,
        66–68, 92, 139, 253
    of speaking, 33, 241
    talking about, 127
    "thermometer," 254
feeling versus thinking, 218–219,
    222, 224
female versus male students,
    and language anxiety, 200,
        203, 206
"first noun strategy," 98
"flaming," in computer-
    mediated communication,
        159
focused repetition, 108, 114
foreign language aptitude, 8–9,
    127, 170, 172–178
    and grammatical sensitivity,
        171
    and inductive language
        learning ability, 171
    and phonetic coding, 171
    and rote memory, 171

*Foreign Language Classroom
    Anxiety Scale* (FLCAS), 90,
    128, 145, 173, 175, 194, 196,
    204, 248–249, 254
foreign language learning
    difficulties
    assessment for students with,
        174–178
    classroom interventions and
        accommodations for
        students with, 178–183
*Foreign Language Learning Skills
    and Attitude Inventory*
    (FLLSA), 175, 189–190
foreign language requirement,
    3–4, 181–182, 185
*Foreign Language Screening
    Instrument* (FLSI), 175,
    188–189
foreign language / second
    language instruction, since
    the mid-twentieth century,
    7
form/meaning connections,
    98–99
frames (schemata or scripts), 17,
    110
freewriting, 71
French
    classroom anxiety, 30, 247–250,
        254
    test anxiety, 30, 193,
        242–243
    use anxiety, 30, 254
French Class Anxiety Scale, 196,
    247, 250, 254
frequency of language use,
    38

gambits, 129–131, 139
gender-based difference, 9,
    191–192, 194–207, 244–245
generative linguistics, 15–16
global versus analytic approach,
    218–220, 222, 224, 228,
    236–237
grammar(s)
    generative, 15–16
    and meaning-bearing input,
        94–95, 97, 99, 128, 243
    reducing anxiety about, 93–94,
        101–102

grammar(s), *continued*
    traditional instruction of,
        92–93, 102
    valued over ideas, 67, 147
grammar instruction
    and anxiety, 8, 90–103
    errors, fear of, 92, 101, 241
    explicit, 102
    input processing perspective
        of, 91, 95, 97–102, 147
    lack of, addressed, 93, 102
    too much material, 91, 101,
        243
    typical order of, 97–98
grammar test, 92–93, 101
grammatical sensitivity, 171
group cohesion. *See* community,
    sense of
group/paired activities, 21–22,
    52, 131, 134, 145, 204,
    242–243, 245

habit formation models, 14
"hands-on" preference, 218, 220,
    223, 232
haptic learners, 218, 220, 223, 232
heuristics, 68–76, 81, 84

ideas, learning to express, 67–68,
    147
individual differences, 8–9,
    170–178, 194–207, 245
induced anxiety, 39
inductive language learning,
    171
information gap activities,
    134–135, 245
informing students about
    second-language
    acquisition, 94–97, 102
input
    activities, 98, 245
    link between acquisition and,
        95, 98, 107
Input Anxiety Scale, 251
input processing, 35–36, 50–51,
    95, 97–102, 147, 245
instructional strategies, tailoring,
    227–228
instructor. *See* teacher
integrative motivation, 37
intensive courses, 202

listening comprehension (LC)
and adjustments made for non-native speakers, 110–111
and anxiety, 8, 107–119, 201, 243–244
and fear of failure, 118–119
and gender, 194–207, 244
and instruction in strategy-use, 114–117
and L1 knowledge, 109–110
and structured-input activities, 112, 245
and students' background knowledge, 109–110
and use of schemata, 110
and use of visuals, 108, 117–118, 245
Local Area Network (LAN), 145–148, 153, 158–159
looping, 72, 245
low-anxiety atmosphere in classroom, creation of, 7, 107

male versus female students, and language anxiety, 200, 203, 206
manifest anxiety, 255
Taylor Manifest Anxiety Scale, 255
math anxiety, 30, 193
meaning-bearing input, 94–95, 98, 102, 128, 243
mentalistic approach, 16–17
metacognitive awareness, 58–59
mimicry drills, in ALM method, 14
misconceptions about reading, 51–60, 243–244
modeling, 138–139, 243
Modern Language Aptitude Test (MLAT), 172, 177–178, 185
morphology card sample, 182
motivation, and learner attitudes, 3–6, 19, 127, 172, 255
multiphase reading practices, 52
multisensory learning tasks, 228
multisensory structured language (MSL) approach, 180, 228

narrow reading, 83
native-language coding, 24
native language
and foreign language learning, 171
skills, 8–9, 169–173, 244
Natural Approach (NA), 20, 22, 204
neurolinguistics, 13
non-linear reading, 53–56, 61
novelty anxiety, 30
novice learners, 152–153

open versus closure-oriented learning, 218–219, 222–223, 235
operant conditioning, 21
oral and written input, necessity of, 99
oral testing, 32, 90, 139–140
organizing information, 53, 55
orthography, linked to phonology, 172–173, 175, 180–181, 184
outlining, in writing instruction, 74–75, 245
Output Anxiety Scale, 251–252
output processing, 35–37, 147
overestimation, 32
"overstudying," 34

partner work. *See* group/paired activities
pattern drills, in ALM method, 4
Pavlov, I. P., 14, 21
Pearson Product Moment Correlation (Pearson r), 25
peer evaluations, 67, 245
peer responding, 77–80, 85
Personal Report of Communication Apprehension (PRCA)-College, 254, 259–261
Long Form, College, 254, 259–260
Seven, 254
Short Form, College, 254, 260–261
Ten, 254
personality of the learner, 31–33, 192, 218–219, 222–224, 233
phonemic awareness, 184
phonetic coding, 171

phonology
definition of, 172
linked to orthography, 172–173, 175, 180–181, 184
physiological effects, 39
Pimsleur Language Aptitude Battery (LAB), 171
polylogue versus dialogue, 155
post-reading tasks, 6–7, 55–56
power of reading, 50
pragmatics, in second language acquisition, 13
preconceptions. *See* beliefs about language learning
pre-production activities, 245
pre-reading strategies, 6, 54–56, 61, 109, 245
pretest/posttest format, 54–55
probability level, 41
process approach, 17, 66, 84–85
process, maturational, 15
processing, 35–37, 244–245
input, 35–36, 50–51, 95, 97–102, 147
output, 35–36, 147
units, 108, 112, 114
Processing Anxiety Scale, 251
processing instruction, 90, 7–102
production
with computer-mediated communication, 146–147
of grammatical forms, avoid requiring, 101
pronunciation
fear of errors in, 31, 126, 241
practice in ALM method, 14
social element of, 5
propositional content, 98
PRPSA, 254
psycholinguistics, relevance to second language acquisition, 13
public-speaking anxiety, 31

reading
and anxiety, 8, 49–61, 256
artichoke analogy for, 53, 61
misconceptions about, 7, 51–59, 243–244
multiphase reading practices, 52–59